GEMS & JEWELLERY

A Pictorial History

GEMS & JEWELLERY

Graham Hughes

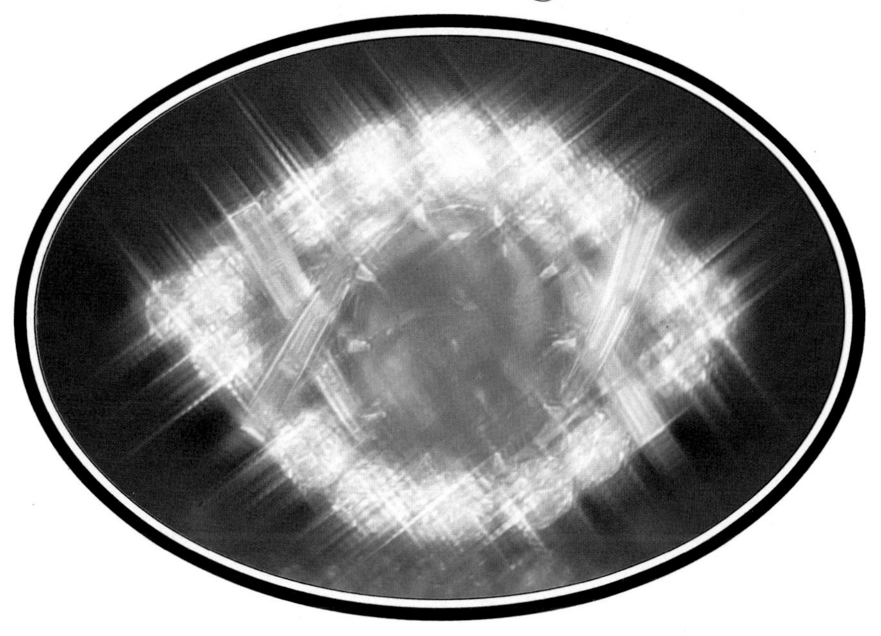

PHAIDON · OXFORD

CONTENTS

Phaidon Press Limited, Littlegate House, St Ebbe's Street, Oxford
First published 1978

Planned and produced by Elsevier International Projects Ltd, Oxford.

ISBN 0 7148 1890 9

Origination by Art Colour Offset, Rome Italy and Colour Workshop, Hertford, Great Britain.
Filmset by Keyspools Limited, Golborne, Lancs., Great Britain.
Printed by Jolly & Barber Ltd, Rugby, Great Britain.

Half-title. Window shopping at Cartier, London.
Title page. Platinum ring set with opal and diamonds.
Right. The Cheapside Hoard, the contents of a London jeweler's shop, discovered under a house near St Paul's Cathedral. The collection probably survived by accident and therefore includes a complete cross-section of the stock of a "high street jeweler" of *c* 1600, modest pieces as well as more ambitious. Unlike cheaper jewelry today everything is well made, even the lightest baubles, presumably because the maker had pride in his work. Most old jewelry dug from underground has been deliberately buried in a grave or to escape invaders, for which purposes the best pieces were usually selected, giving posterity an unfairly favorable impression of what was originally current.

INTRODUCTION

Jewelry is universal. It is spread right round the world and up and down through all social classes and income groups. Few people can own paintings or sculpture, if only because few people have homes big enough to accommodate them. Only some of the world's population can enjoy literature, because so many people cannot read. But jewels are worn and, like music, enjoyed almost everywhere.

Jewelry is a secret art. Jewels have usually been bought and sold in secret, for secret prices, often passing through many hands before reaching the final owner, kept in custody and used as a personal symbol. We do not know who made the majority of jewels, old or new, nor do we know whom they were made for, how much they cost, where they were made, or how they have survived. Jewels have always been intimate and private.

Furthermore, jewelry is often remade; old stones and old metal not only used anew but recarved and realloyed as well, so that the continuity of their history is lost.

Most jewels are, therefore, anonymous. The history of jewelry has no great world figures—no Phidias, no Rembrandt, no Corbusier. It is typical that, even for Cellini, the most famous jeweler, we have no surviving authenticated jewel.

An appreciation of jewels must begin with the enjoyment of their raw materials and this must be mixed with some analysis. Their identification not only satisfies a natural desire for facts, but drastically affects both market value and sentimental appeal. Value is a mixture of love, beauty, history, craftsmanship, and money, and most of these are flavored by hard fact.

The language of jewels is often confusing. For instance, in the middle ages a spinel was often called a ruby, and it was chosen for its size and its dark color, not for purity. Now, words are used more precisely. Ruby has a different physical structure from spinel, just as a deer is different from a dog, although they may look similar from a distance. Again, today we differentiate clearly between silver and gold but, until the metals could be efficiently separated, they were usually unintentionally mixed so the names were not really accurate. The ancient Greeks actually thought that there was a betwixt-and-between metal, electrum, which they found in the rivers of Asia Minor, and they seem to have valued it in that area more highly than either gold or silver.

Each succeeding age has sought for greater purity of stones and of metal. With scientific aids we can at last recognize this purity. Our new-found powers measure not beauty, for this is impossible, but truth, without which beauty is deception.

The old and noble metals—gold and silver, the great stones—diamond, emerald, sapphire and ruby—are all sterile alone. They need clothing with human skill, they need loving treatment by the carver and the cutter, the setter and the mounter and the polisher, most of all they need organizing and assembling by the artist. A jewel may be made up from component parts, each the result of extreme skill, but no one will remember it unless the whole is greater than the parts. It is the task of the artist to perfect this harmony. This book sets out to do the same, to seek out and expose the component parts—the materials, the craftsmanship, the symbolism, the development of styles—and to unite them to reveal the whole; the exotic allure of jewelry.

A group of contemporary jewelry fashioned in lustrous gold.

GOLD

Gold is the aristocrat of metals. Nobody knows whether the earliest jewels used metal at all, or if they were simply lumps of stone, or if, as in some stone age cultures of the South Pacific today, jewels were whatever is rarest—exotic feathers, animal teeth of weird shape, or bits of bright-colored shell. What is certain, is that the earliest surviving metal jewels are made of gold, and that gold has been chosen for the finest jewels ever since. Gold has a longer history, in jewelry, than any other substance. Steatite and slate were popular in Jericho in the tenth millennium BC, and were still popular in the Egypt of the Ptolemies, but are no longer so today. Diamond was known to the Romans, and perhaps to the Greeks two thousand years ago, but probably not before that. Only gold has held its place for at least ten thousand years, more secure today than ever, although we know more about it and there is more of it.

Gold, "the blood of the sun" as the Incas called it, is an element, known by the chemical formula Au. It is not subject to corrosion from any of the usual chemicals, so it does not tarnish when above ground, nor corrode when buried. Pure gold stays bright forever.

But if gold is mixed with silver, as it often is, or, still worse, with copper, it is another story. All these baser metals have a use when used with gold to form an alloy: silver will make gold green, nickel or palladium makes it white, copper tends to a brown or red, and, in different degrees, base metals will make gold harder or less ductile. What base metals cannot do, is to make gold more durable, because these other metals, unlike gold, are subject to chemical change. Probably the least pure gold alloy commonly used in jewelry is tumbago, more than half copper. This was preferred by some of the pre-Columbian South American tribes like the Chibcha and the Chavin, perhaps because they liked very big objects such as life-size funeral masks, and solid gold would have been too rare or too expensive. These tumbago ritual sculptures have survived in some number in the dry sandy strip of Western Peru, yet almost all have deteriorated, often acquiring the bright green patina which one associates with modern copper roofing materials out-of-doors. Pure gold is chemically inert, so survives almost for ever; gold alloys disintegrate with age. Small wonder that, with the birth of modern laboratory science in the 15th century, alchemists tried to turn everything into gold, and were even employed to do so by great renaissance rulers.

One can beat gold extremely thin, from bar to sheet, from sheet to foil, from foil to leaf, so thin that it is transparent, will blow away in the wind and can be carried on a feather. This explains how gilding, on furniture for instance, or even inside shoes or hats, is so common: gold leaf is incredibly thin, and therefore not too expensive. For jewelry, the ductile capacity of gold—the possibility of drawing the metal very fine or very thin—shows chiefly in gold filigree, minute patterns of wire often in spirals, popular in Greek and Etruscan times.

Gold is malleable too—one can bend it almost like paper, and then bend it back again. Hence the mysterious wrinkled textures for instance on modern jewels by Gilbert Albert of Geneva, or by Hiramatsu of Tokyo. Gold is heavy, satisfying to handle and to have. Owing to its mobile surface, it can assume more varied textures than any other metal—bright polished, creased, rough or just glowing. Gold leaf will anneal (soften after hammering) at room temperature and pure gold can be soft as lead, but alloys harden rapidly with working. Hammering will compress them—at least in its hardest alloy, white gold—until they are harder than platinum. So, to gold's range of surfaces can be added the asset of varied consistency.

Gold, although never abundant, is the most widely distributed of all metals. It used to be found on or near the earth's surface. These "alluvial" deposits of "placer" gold were sifted from river waters and from the sand and mud beneath. The origin of the legend of the golden fleece is probably the use of animal skins for washing gold-bearing water so that the gold stuck to the hairs on the skin. Elsewhere the gold would be found in small lumps lying on the earth's surface. The Egyptians had it near the Red Sea, the Irish had it somewhere in Co. Wicklow, the Persians and Indians were rich in it. For the ancient Greeks, it was extremely rare until Alexander the Great chased the coveted yellow metal throughout the near and Middle East. Asia Minor, with its golden river Pactolus and its legendary Kings Midas of Phrygia and Croesus of Lydia, was an especially rich source. The Romans acquired the shallow gold mines of Dacia, and, in Spain, the mines already developed by the Phoenicians. Ancient gold as found in Europe and Asia was usually rather pure, but it almost always contained iridium: modern fakes of ancient work can often be detected by the absence of iridium which modern refiners, unlike the ancients, can, and do, separate and remove from the gold. The South American and Mexican cultures loved gold, and had plenty of it, usually containing a lot of copper. During the renaissance most of Europe's gold came from this "new world," after Europe's own gold-bearing soils, mainly in Saxony and Silesia, were exhausted. In the 16th, 17th and 18th centuries much of it came through Spain, where the resulting profits helped to pay for the Inquisition and the religious wars of conquest, while the Spaniards' desire for gold at home was overwhelming.

Left. Gold is found in hydro-thermal quartz veins, where the minerals dissolved in heated water have penetrated the fractures in rock and crystallized out in a narrow vein, or where sedimentation has created a layer of deposit, as in a river. A ton of ore usually yields only ¼oz. of gold.

Right. Solid gold is too expensive and vulnerable for use in large sculptures and is more frequently used, as in this statue of a Dakini, an Indian goddess, for gilding over the surface, than in solid form. Gilding can appear indistinguishable from solid gold.

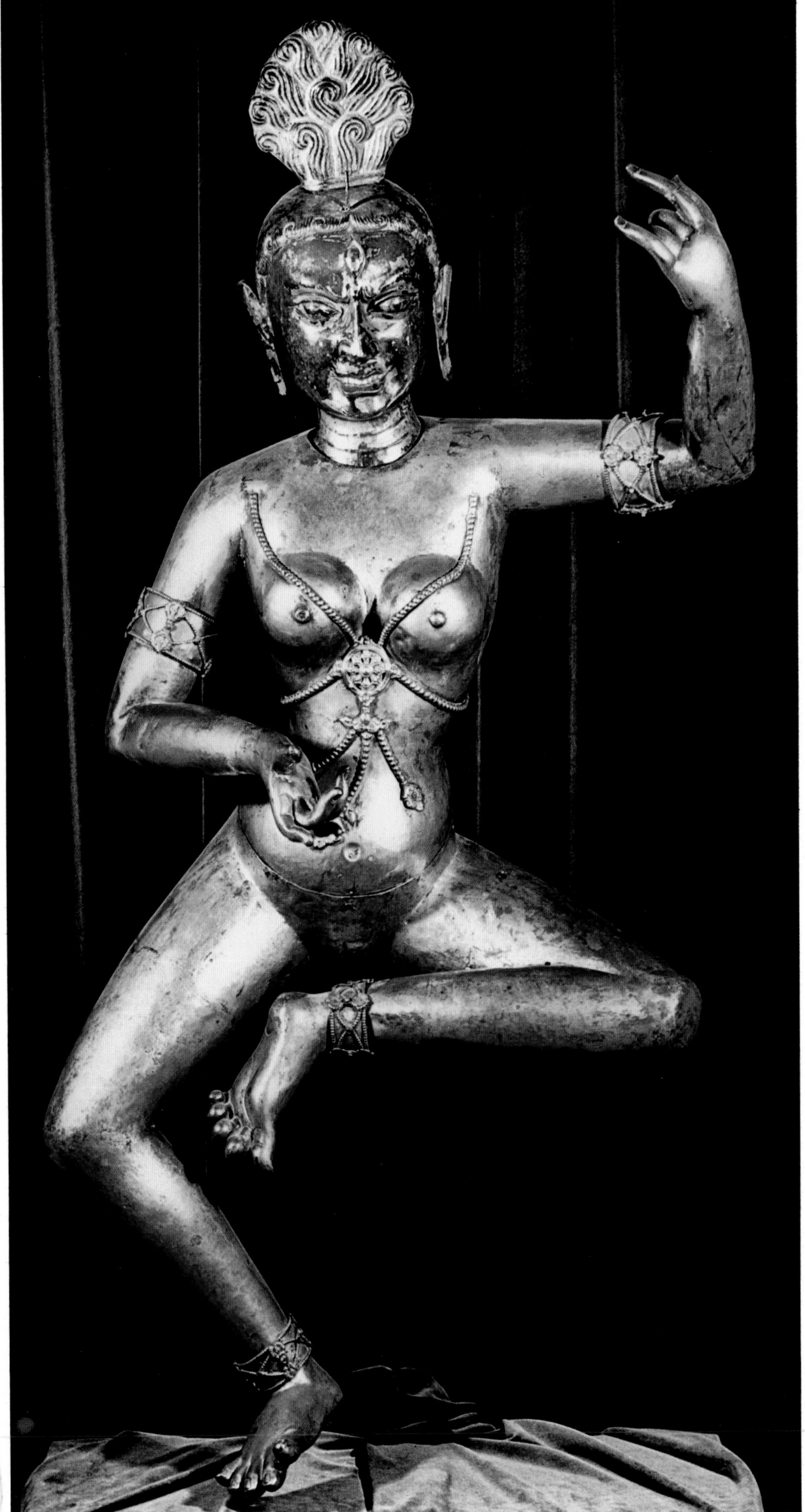

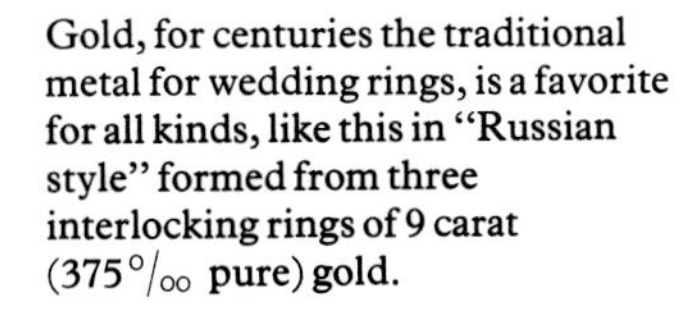

Gold, for centuries the traditional metal for wedding rings, is a favorite for all kinds, like this in "Russian style" formed from three interlocking rings of 9 carat (375‰ pure) gold.

Then came the great Gold Rushes—new discoveries around San Francisco after 1843, culminating in the Gold Rush of 1849, in the North of Alaska on the river Yukon in 1897, in New South Wales, Australia in 1851, round Kalgoorlie from 1893. From 1876 came the huge discoveries in South Africa, which now supplies three-quarters of the world's gold. Soon after, the technology of modern deep mining was born. Russia, Australia and Mexico with South Africa remain as substantial producers.

Lode or reef gold is mined underground and may be about 85% pure; usually about a ton of rock may yield less than an ounce of gold. The deepest mine is Western Deep Levels at Carletonville, South Africa, which goes 2½ miles below the earth's surface. With each 100 yards of descent, the temperature rises by 1°C. One ounce of gold can produce, with modern technology, 50 miles of wire or 100 square feet of foil. In 1970, of the world's total production of 1,638 tons about 1,060 tons was used for jewelry, about 300 tons for other fabrication like dentistry and electronics; in 1976 total world production was 1,378 tons. What nobody can catalog is the amount put aside for hoarding or for bullion investment: that depends on the gold price which over those six years rose from $35 an ounce to nearly $200, then fell back to about $130. During the 20th century, about 74,000 tons of gold have been produced compared with only about 110,000 tons in the whole history of the world. All of it would form a cube of only 17–18 metresides (57ft).

In 1975, South Africa produced about 708 tons, USSR perhaps 407 tons, Canada 50 tons, North and Central Africa 45 tons, Latin America 43 tons—South Africa and USSR accounting for about 81% of the whole. The USA has about 9,000 tons of gold in its reserves, much of it kept with that of other countries in the New York Federal Reserve Bank where there are about 40,000 tons altogether. Measurements are normally by the tonne, that is 1,000 kilograms or 2,200lbs, rather less than the 2,240lbs of the ton.

Often, what is, or was, called gold, is in fact some other metal, gilt. Although an expert may guess at the quality of the metal by the texture and design, judge by the weight and color, whether he is handling solid gold, silver-gilt, vermeil, or even brass gilt as used in French furniture trimmings called ormolu, the various finishes are identical. A layer of gold can be applied on to an underlying base either by fire gilding, sweating the gold on to and into the metal beneath, or by electro-gilding, plating the gold by electro-deposition, often called electroplating. Water gilding, burnishing and damascening, are processes without heat and the golden layer they achieve is seldom robust enough for jewels. Indeed, all types of gilding are unsatisfactory: the gold will soon wear through, and a gilt jewel, if too much worn and loved, will soon look downright tatty. Old gilt can sometimes be distinguished from old gold, simply because the upper metal has worn through, revealing a different color beneath. Worn mercurial or fire gilding will not show a sudden contrast with the metal beneath, whereas worn electrogilding will appear distinct from the foundation upon which it is imposed. So much for identifying gold by instinct and feel—common methods, but commonly misleading.

There are at least three scientific ways of identifying metal alloys. Tiny shavings can be scraped from the edges, and analyzed with some sort of successive test by nitric and sulfuric acid, or by melting in cupels so that the base metal vanishes and only the precious remains. This is satisfactory, except that when a jewel is cast, the alloy may not be stirred into equal proportions everywhere so that unless one takes many scrapings, one may not get a fair representation of the contents.

Another method is by spectrographic analysis, a sort of X-ray which gives only moderate accuracy, and which may entirely fail to detect a thin layer of surface plating. At present, the machine is very costly and therefore available only in large laboratories to specialists and professionals.

Third, and easiest by far, is to look for a hallmark. If there is one, well and good—it is, usually, four or five small punch marks giving the maker's or sponsor's name, the place and date of marking, and the quality of gold, silver and, since 1975 in Britain, of platinum. These tiny, shaped depressions are worth a search because they give so much useful information.

Countries which, like Britain, have a compulsory hallmark, include Sweden (where only a proportion of specimens are actually tested), France, Holland, Belgium and Switzerland. There is no hallmark in Germany (despite the well developed guild system there in renaissance times), Italy or the United States. In some countries like Denmark and Japan the government hallmark is optional. The result has been its simple neglect: makers like the famous Jensen impose their own trade mark but do not bother with the government stamp. Interpreting these diminutive code marks is best done in detail by somebody familiar with them.

For gold, this guarantee of purity is given in carats, a

Top left. The world's richest goldfield is the Witwatersrand in South Africa where the reef is found 1,300 meters underground. The heat this far below the surface is considerable and a detailed knowledge of geology is necessary to follow the narrow seams. All early gold was found on or near the surface, deep mining is a product of advanced modern technology. From the rough ore, hard-won from the rock by the labor of black miners, crushing, milling and separating processes prepare the gold for the refinery.

Bottom left. Molten gold is poured from a crucible into a mold to form an ingot of carefully measured weight. Sieves and sticky surfaces have been used to separate the metal from the rock and many successive smeltings have been necessary to purify the gold before it can reach this state.

Top right. An earring made by Greek goldsmiths *c*300 BC shows how gold can be formed with fantastic delicacy. Filigree or gold wire ornament was used with granulation to define design and to elaborate textures. The Greek colonies, such as Taranto in south Italy where this earring was made, produced especially creative jewelry, probably because they were richer than Greece itself.

Top, far right. Gold can be beaten very thin as in this 4th-century funeral mask from Taman Russia. Such masks were buried with the dead in Syria and the middle east.

Bottom right. A funeral mask of the pre-Inca Chimu culture of Peru, made *c*1200 of tumbago and buried over the face of the dead, tumbago is a naturally-occurring mixture of gold with a high percentage of copper. The copper has corroded leaving a green patina whilst the gold is incorruptible, except by aqua regia which dissolves it.

percentage of purity, not to be confused with the stone-dealer's carat which is a measurement of weight. The figure 22, if you can find it on a piece of gold, means 22 carats pure, out of the maximum of 24. There is no mark for 24 carat, 100% pure gold—and 24 carat is not commonly used today because it is too soft. Since 1975 the purity has been marked in parts per thousand, rather than in carats, so that 916 is 22 carats, 750 is 18 carats and the two other standards, recognized by the British hallmark laws in 1977, are 585 (14 carats) and 375 (9 carats), the last being less than half pure gold and therefore frowned upon by top-class craftsmen. In the US the lowest standard is 10 carats, but in most industrial countries 14 is the minimum.

In London, the hallmark is applied at Goldsmiths' Hall by the only surviving medieval guild of jewelers, goldsmiths and silversmiths, the Worshipful Company of Goldsmiths. This ancient group have executed hallmark laws for the British government since the year 1300, on the same site near St. Paul's Cathedral, and have even given to the process the name of their home: "hallmark" means in origin, the mark of Goldsmiths' Hall London. Tiny scrapings are taken from each piece submitted, one million each month at the end of 1976, and after metallurgical analysis the mark is made with hammer and punch or by a flypress. Other British assay offices are now at Sheffield and Birmingham (both started in 1773) and in Edinburgh, all since 1975 operate under the British Hallmarking Council appointed by the state. Many jewels carry no hallmark but if you see one it not only proves what metal you are buying: it also links you agreeably with history.

Hallmarks are common on silver of many countries since the 16th century, but for jewels it is a different story: all hallmark laws everywhere have always exempted products too small or fragile for marking and, until the past two decades or so, this exemption has been applied to most jewels. In England, the old laws were drafted in a way that modern lawyers find confusing. The crux of the jewelry phraseology was the word "works." These were exempt, and until recently, the authorities took this to mean all bits and pieces of jewelry, hence almost all jewels. So, either because they were deemed too fragile by the assay offices, or because the law was thought so to direct, most old jewels made from the 17th century until about 1950, have escaped the hallmark. The way to evaluate their gold is therefore either by instinct or by consulting an expert.

SILVER

Silver, like gold, is an element—its symbol AG—and it has always been the other principal metal subject to hallmarking. Its relative rarity has been one of its merits for jewels, giving it a comforting stability. The beauty of its surface is marred by one great drawback: silver tarnishes, and in modern industrial conditions, sulfur in the air will give a leaden gloom to a silver jewel in a few short days. Then, the wearer will notice a gray stain on the clothes and skin which makes the background to the jewel as lack-luster as the metal itself. Finally, silver, of course, corrodes, albeit slowly, so it has not survived so well from antiquity; and, because it tarnishes, it has been polished too hard too often by over-zealous butlers and custodians, and consequently has lost its original detail which is so often beautifully retained in gold.

Silver may have been as popular as gold with the early-6th- and 5th-century BC Greeks: they had shallow mines at Cape Sunion, on Thasos and Siphnos. Later, in Hellenistic times new silver mines helped to build the power of Macedon. The early Greek coins were normally of silver (in contrast to the Romans' later bronze) which suggests that the metal was not impossibly rare. The Greeks made gold coins only in times of acute crisis, to inspire confidence. But surviving Greek jewels, like jewels from every other period and place until the past century or two, are mostly gold, because of that metal's incorruptibility.

Silver was the standard metal for Chinese jewels, those web-like constructions which dangled and swayed above the world's most fantastic coifs. Gold would have been much too heavy, and anyway there was very little of it. In Japan, too, silver was popular for hair pins, often topped since the 19th century by a small but elaborately-carved silver flower. But gold was the preferred metal in Japan, although extremely rare, and there was enough to make gold thread embroidery for kimonos, gold damascened inlay for sword ornaments and, most prized, gold lacquer for combs.

Silver had a big vogue in European jewelry in the 18th and 19th centuries when diamonds were being scientifically polished for the first time. Silver, being white, was then thought more brilliant than gold. It endorsed the diamond's own color on the smartest pieces, as well as on paste, the soft and beautiful substitute for diamonds.

Today, silver has a new vogue partly because, with the social revolution we are living through, more people can afford jewels than ever before, but many of them cannot afford gold. Partly, too, young people mistakenly associate gold with comfortable, wealthy old age. The new boutique and open-air pavement trade, in the sophisticated capitals of Europe, is more for silver than for gold. And there is one part of the world where silver has always been a very strong second to gold, even under the gold-loving Vikings. This is Scandinavia. Perhaps it is the cold light, perhaps the socialist politics; perhaps the enormous respect given to the giant silversmiths, such as old Georg Jensen, who almost never used gold. Probably, for all these reasons, more silver jewelry is seen in Stockholm, Copenhagen and Oslo than in Paris, London or Rome. In New York, gold is a fetish, silver hardly worn at all—Americans are proud of their wealth, and like to wear it, always a reason for sporting gold. In Japan people do not show off their riches, preferring to live an unostentatious private life. What is more, the pearl has become the national stone. Silver and pearls are considered the ideal partners, white goes with white in that discreet country. In Thailand too, silver is especially coveted and used, for similar reasons, this time because it is the ideal foil for the steely-gray color of local niello inlay work. Another traditional local product, the result of local natural resources, is the bright cut silver jewelry of Mogadishu in Somalia, East Africa, where it has captured the public fancy. Silver is not just a poor man's gold; its rich, soft color has made it loved through the centuries, and so it will continue.

Silver has great artistic virtues, even more appreciated on the table in the form of cups and pots, than in the hair or on the lapel. But it has technical problems, too. The principal worry is tarnish. Another snag is a similar, but deeper, coating of black, called fire-stain. This oxide forms when silver is heated (or annealed) in order to soften it periodically during the work-hardening. It may be that an alloy will soon be invented to make silver as free from tarnish, for instance, as is stainless steel. There is already a method of avoiding fire-stain: by annealing silver in a vacuum, so that the impurities in the air cannot form oxides on the silver's skin. But only the bigger factories can afford to buy a vacuum.

One cheap and common modern treatment for silver, which overcomes both these unsightly outbreaks of blotchiness, is rhodium plating—the silver is electro-plated all over with a hard layer of rhodium. No more tarnish, no marks on clothes or skin, no black fire-stain clouds lurking behind the lovely white of silver. Rhodium plate is certainly an effective remedy, but drastic too: it completely hides the silver, and there is no practical method of removing it. Instead of the marvellous muted colors of silver, you see the garish blue-white of an automobile bumper: rhodium is first cousin to chromium. Nevertheless, in Japan the convenience of rhodium plating is considered to be all, and it is practically universal in the huge industry for pearl jewels. In Europe and especially in the US, rhodium is popular too as a trouble-saver. But where silver is truly loved, particularly in Denmark, rhodium plating is hated as a prostitution.

Although tarnishing must remain, fire-stain can be neutralized either by grinding and stoning it off, as is normal today in Scandinavia: with the stain the surface hammer marks are also lost; or the stain may be deliberately deepened by several annealings in quick succession. This retains the hammer marks, but the silver does not achieve its full subtlety of color, and eventually, as with much antique table silver finished in this way, the fire-stain will rub through in places, revealing an unpleasant patchy effect. There is no ideal answer.

But lovely, cool-colored silver, called by the Incas "tears of the moon," does have a clear advantage over all other metals and that is the hallmark. Since about 1900 a much larger proportion of silver jewels than gold have been marked. This is probably because silver, being less precious, tends to attract robust craftsmanship, so that silver jewelers cannot easily claim their works to be too delicate for marking, as so often with gold. Silver is the hallmark material par excellence—the marks, especially the British marks, are well-known and much used by dealers and wearers throughout the world. As with gold, the hallmark story is usually contained in four punch marks. For silver, there are two recognized standards of purity: Britannia 95.8% pure, and sterling 92.5% pure. On the European continent and in the US, the lower standard of 80% purity is popular, normally marked 800 (for 800 parts pure silver in 1,000). But this rather base mixture is illegal in Britain.

Silver mining is less romantic than gold: the metal is less valuable, the deposits are larger and less widespread. Perhaps the most memorable source was Mount Potosi, the "silver mountain" in Bolivia. After Pizarro's conquest of the Incas in 1530–33 the miner's life, a hard one everywhere, became especially punitive there.

Opposite. Kabyle silver. Made and worn by this nomadic Algerian Berber tribe these pieces were made for women to wear at weddings and other ceremonial occasions and then passed down as an heirloom and form of wealth. Jewelry of this kind is still made at Bemiyeni, although now largely for sale to tourists.

Top. Danish silver jewelry by Georg Jensen. The matching bracelet and pendant date from before 1920, the other bracelet from 1955–60, and the brooch from *c*1950. Jensen were the world's first silver factory to publicise their designer names.

Above. A Victorian dragonfly brooch, *c*1870, shows the way in which silver (used for the wings) and gold (used for the legs and to mount the eyes) differ in the way they set off the diamonds, emeralds, Burmese rubies and pearl.

Another source was Zacatecas, discovered in Mexico in 1548, the two places establishing silver as the basis of the economy of Spanish America: much silver was refabricated locally by the colonists, making church ornaments and jewels. Nevertheless, between 1500 and 1650, legitimate traders alone carried back to Spain perhaps 16,000 tons of silver. There may be as many as 2,000 Spanish treasure galleons now on the sea bed, wrecked off the coast of Florida in hurricanes, testimony to this vast trade in bullion. In the late 19th century Canada joined Mexico and Peru as a leading producer.

OTHER METALS

Bronze has been the most popular jewel metal, after gold and silver. It is an alloy—usually made up of about 97% copper, 3% tin, with sometimes some lead too, especially in ancient China. It does not last as well as gold, it is not so hard as iron. The millennia of the Bronze Age followed the Stone Age after a short transitional age of copper. From about 6000 BC until iron became common under the Romans, bronze was the standard metal successively in most of the ancient Mesopotamian, Persian, Cretan and Greek cultures, for men's shields, spears and helmets, for leg and chest armor, and for agricultural implements.

Because copper corrodes quickly, relatively little bronze jewelry has survived. What there is has a massive, rather masculine quality, due no doubt to the metal's special suitability for casting and its rather unrewarding behavior when worked by hand. Bronze is the ideal of every sculptor, because it flows well when cast, with chemical surface treatment it has more beautiful patinas than any other metal and, once formed, it has the strength to maintain its shape better than gold, silver or lead.

The Persians loved it: their most characteristic jewelry *c* 800 BC is in bronze, different from all other contemporary work, from Amlash and Marlik in the North and Luristan in the West; it manages to be superb sculpture and just about wearable too, although some of the bigger bangles and covenant rings would need a crane to support them, if worn at a Manhattan cocktail party.

Platinum, like gold and silver a metallic element, was originally a by-product of the gold mines of Darien, but is now found in Russia, the US, Canada and South Africa; its gray granules, as mined, usually contain gold, copper or iron, and some of the similar metals like osmium (the heaviest substance of all), rhodium and iridium. At first the Incas and the Russians thought it just a nuisance, intruding on other more useful substances. But slowly it was recognized as the most versatile of all the metals. It is unaffected by the atmosphere, resists any single acid, is ductile, malleable and very tenacious. It is popular in scientific laboratories and may prove indispensable in the manufacture of motor exhaust clean air devices.

In jewelry, its cold blue/gray/white luster, its hardness and the fact that it was then by far the most precious suitable metal, gave it a vogue in this century until 1939, especially in the art deco period, for setting big rectangular diamonds with a minimum of metal surround. Perhaps its most useful jewelry characteristic is the rapidity with which it work-hardens. Hence part of its popularity for stone settings. More recently, platinum has lost the snob appeal of its price tag. Further inroads on the jewelry function of platinum have been made by the new gold alloys, which have created a white gold harder, more beautiful and more practical than platinum. The Platinum Guild was set up in 1975 in London as an international marketing organization to bring platinum into the crafts, in the same way as Intergold is increasing the use of gold. But platinum is the most masculine of jewelry materials; as jewelry becomes more imaginative and playful, so platinum will probably fade from the scene. In 1976, Japan used some 38 tonnes of the metal for jewelry, compared with only two tonnes for the whole of the rest of the world.

Other metals: iron and steel in Japan, brass, nickel for the Bedouin tribes, these are less than universal to jewels, but each in its own area is considered wonderful. Brass is copper and zinc, often known as gilding metal. Nickel silver ("German" silver) is brass with the addition of 8%–30% of nickel; a hard white alloy which contains no silver. Both brass and nickel silver are used as a base for cheaply produced plated jewels.

Several metals which were unknown, difficult to find, or impossible to use until the past decade have now become popular because of improved technology. Newcomers to the jewelry scene are the very hard metals which change color under heat—tantalum, osmium, zirconium and titanium. Iridium is another, although since it costs twice as much as gold, its appeal is limited. Titanium in particular has caught the fancy of the younger generation of artists, despite its extreme hardness and the impossibility of soldering it. It is used in turbine engine blades, in surgery as a replacement for human bone, it is tough and tensile, anti-corrosive and a slow conductor of heat. It has a wonderful sheen, and changes color under heat like a chameleon. Local heat—which can be applied direct, or by electric current—will give it dramatic ranges of local color. It is possible to crowd many bright patches of red, blue or green into one small jewel; here is a radiant new opportunity for craftsmen.

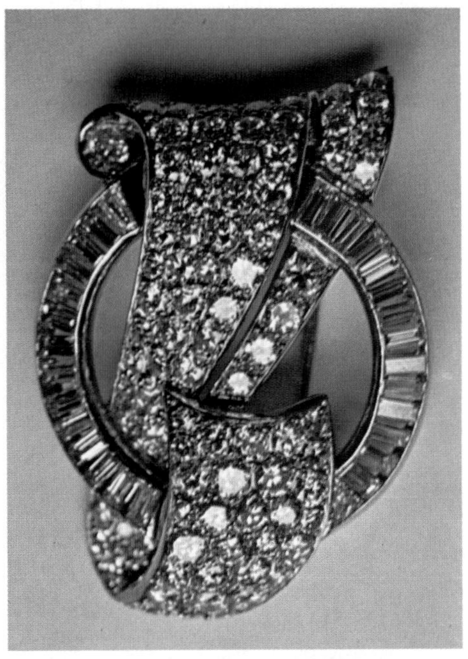

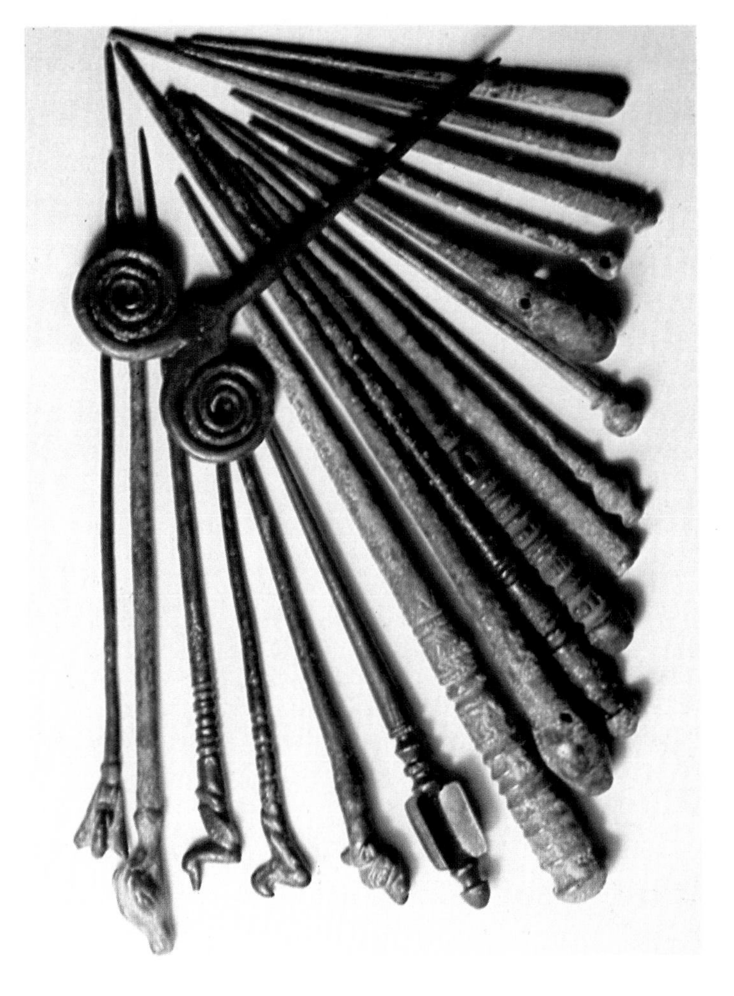

Far left. Jewelry in black steel, gold and diamonds by Annabel Jones, London, 1977. Jewelers often achieve novelty by using unfamiliar materials and unusual techniques such as setting precious diamond straight into base metal.

Above left. Platinum and diamond brooch *c* 1930. Platinum became popular for jewelry *c* 1925.

Left. Pendants in titanium, gold and other metals by Kevin Coates, London, 1977.

A group of bronze pins from Luristan. About 800 BC this culture of western Iran produced very imaginative casting in bronze, often incorporating spirals and animal forms, as jewelry, horse harness and parts of armor. The metal is heavy to wear but achieves a beautiful patina. Luristan work is much collected today and fakes abound, but they are usually easy to recognize because they lack the imaginative line of the originals and, if copy casting, have too artificial a patina.

PEARLS, GLASS & IVORY

There are two luminous visions, neither metal nor stone, which have intoxicated us all—pearl and glass. Glass is a chemically produced jewel created by the fusion of substances at high temperatures. Pearls are produced by the oyster to counteract an irritant within its shell, an organic jewel formed of the nacre with which the mollusc lines the inner surface of its shell.

Complete shells of other molluscs, or pieces cut from them, ivory from the elephant, coral and the fossil resin amber are other softly gleaming animal jewels.

Pearls

In ancient times pearls were probably the most precious and beautiful objects known: the Romans valued pearls as we do diamonds, and paid high prices for them. Good tides, warmth, a shallow bottom, and clean salt water all help to make the oyster fructify, and pearls have been found in many parts of the world. Since earliest time pearls have been recovered from the seas around China and Japan. In the 1890s the industry became concentrated into the bays along Japan's east coast between Tokyo and Osaka, around Toba, and turned from natural to cultured pearls. Since 1894 the world's pearl market has expanded dramatically, largely owing to the persistence of Mikimoto who, beginning as a humble noodle salesman, became obsessed by the pearl, and determined to find a means to produce more pearls. He transformed first Japan's, then the world's, pearl industries, during the 80 years after the development of his "cultured" pearls, almost extinguishing the old natural pearl industries of Sri Lanka and the Persian Gulf. Toba today is his shrine, with several splendid museums demonstrating the techniques he developed, and with a flourishing local industry as a tribute to their success.

From the straits between Sri Lanka and India, another big industry formed its central depot at Mannar Island, on the north coast of Sri Lanka. This is a region settled by Moslem arabs; the pearl fishing trade was probably introduced by the arabs from Malabar where they themselves probably invented it. Here pollution has not diminished the incidence of natural pearls, as it has done in industrial Japan, with all the poisonous effluents of factories. But the demand for the Mannar natural pearls has shrunk steadily in the face of competition from Japanese cultured pearls. Pearls are no longer a big export from Sri Lanka, attention in that island now being concentrated on the expanding gem-stone industry round Ratnapura. Natural pearls are similarly now only occasionally fished in the ancient manner in the Persian Gulf and the Red Sea. Oil has displaced pearls as the principal industry. Bahrein and Dubai, the two main pearling centers, used to send out nearly a thousand ships each for the two or three months of the season, to anchor and live on the pearl

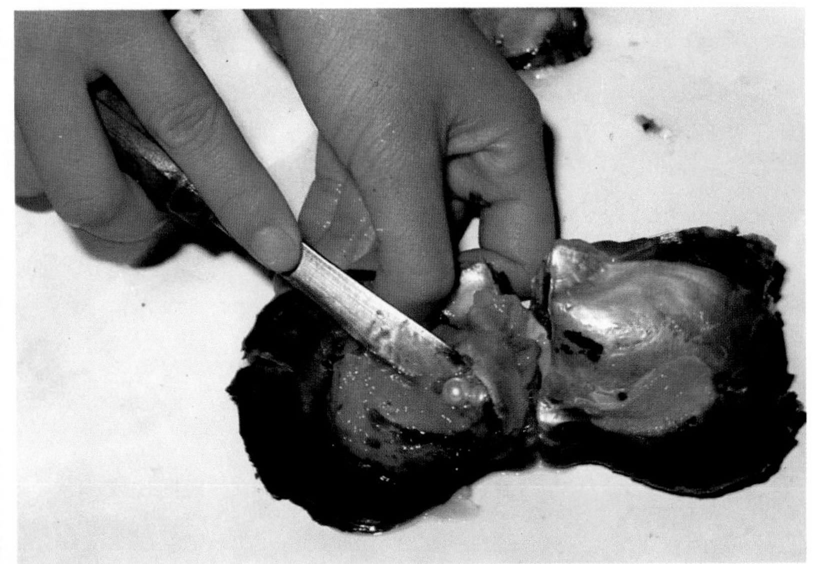

The world's chief pearl oyster beds were in the Persian Gulf but the islands of the South Pacific and off northern Australia are now more active sources. Pearl diving has little commercial importance today but women divers can still be seen at work at Toba, Japan (*left and top center*). When the oyster is opened and any pearl carefully removed (*top right*) its value will depend upon quality (being judged, *above*, by a merchant in Bahrain, once a major pearl diving center, where divers and crews were all men). Pearls have a unique glow and subtlety of color. A group of jewels by Charles de Temple, London, 1976 (*bottom right*) flatters the different shades, from black to white, by amusing compositions and by the warmth of gold. Modern jewelers sometimes delight in an irregular shape as in the ring by Andrew Grima (*below*).

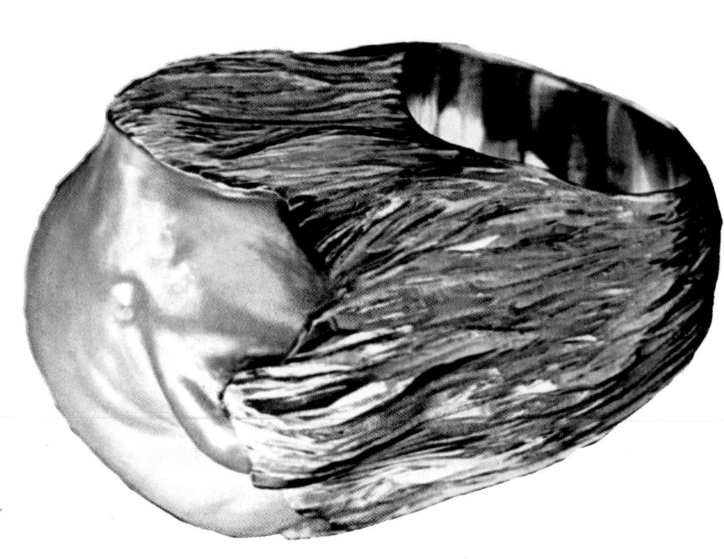

shoals. Now, there may be only half a dozen. Fresh-water pearls of exotic color and shape are found in the Mississippi, popular with American collectors, in Scotland's River Tay, by Chittagong in Bangladesh and in Japan's Lake Biwa. But probably most pearls in Western jewelry shops today, come from the new fields off Cape York in Northern Australia, developed in the past 30 years; and from the still newer, more experimental areas of the South Pacific, like Tahiti for instance, recently exploited on French government initiative.

Near Davao in Mindanao Island in the Philippines, is the Aguinaldo Pearl Farm, comparable to Toba in Japan but much smaller and newer; there, tourists may see racks of oysters hanging from a pier, adjoining the operating "theater" where the unfortunate molluscs are hygienically persuaded to accept the foreign nucleus around which a pearl will eventually form.

Pearl fishing is one of the many ancient craft industries frowned on by modern medicine, but apparently enjoyed by its practitioners. Doctors say that to stay under water in conditions of pressure and physical exertion is a dangerous risk. In Japan nevertheless there were still some 6,000 women pearl fishers in 1975. It is considered to be women's work—women, so local legend says, have an extra layer of fat beneath their skin, to protect them from the cold. Often, the work is done by a husband/wife team: the husband, in a boat on the surface, lowers his wife over the side with a heavy weight to help her sink quickly, then hoists her up again when she pulls her signal cord. Girls start their apprenticeship around the age of 14, and there is no more charming sight than their white heads—they wear a white cap and hip-length skirt costume to frighten off the sharks—bobbing in the waves, pushing before them their big round floating tubs, ready to receive the coveted oysters or shell fish when brought up. Modern metal racks and bamboo cages suspended in rows beneath the water, marked with buoys and flags, are serviced by these girls and have diminished, not yet destroyed, the pearl fisher's life.

Good natural and cultured pearls are indistinguishable to the wearer and to the eye. They are formed over the same period, about seven years, by the same mollusc, often even in the same stretch of water. Real and cultured pearls are both made by the oyster to shield its soft body from an irritant; often, in the case of a real pearl, this is a tiny worm or organic invader, sometimes it is a minute particle of sand. The cultured pearl has a larger, inorganic fragment placed at its center by human beings and the surrounding pearl growth, being the result of a desperate reaction to a surgical operation, often has a flat linear, not a spherical, grain. Thus the difference is partly the grain, partly the size of the speck of grit. This is inserted into the soft flesh of the oyster after the two half shells have been levered open with a wooden wedge. A surgical scalpel makes the hole, carefully antisepticized, and the two halves are clipped together again with a sort of clothes peg. The operation may last three or four weeks, and the casualty rate is high—only about one-eighth of the pearls cultivated by Mikimoto at Toba, for instance, survive and make sufficiently fine shapes and colors eventually to be sold for jewels.

Until a pearl is drilled—a quick and simple job with a revolving needle on a lathe—almost nobody can tell if it is cultured or natural. After drilling, a special microscope can usually spot the dark fragment of shell, which caused the pearl to grow around it. When cultured pearls reached world markets about 1921, the price of the real pearl initially collapsed, but it stabilized and now remains many times that of the cultured.

Artificial pearls are the lowest of the pearl order, a clever use of the scales of freshwater fish. Digested in ammonia, the nacreous material is injected into thin glass balls until a film forms on the inner surface of the balls. Wax or gum is then injected into the middles for stability, and the glass shell removed with hydrofluoric acid. By another method, the nacreous substance is deposited outside, not inside, the glass ball, thus forming a lighter, thinner, substitute for real pearl. The factory processes differ, but there is no mystery about the end product: it is symmetrical, not very translucent, not very soft in texture. But price counts, and these imitations are produced and bought by the million world-wide.

Glass

Glass is another substance which has always brought glory to jewels. Recently it may have become associated, as paste, with cheap imitation, but its grand cousin, enamel, still enjoys respect as a special craft in its own right. Glass seemed a miracle when invented in Syria and the Levant 6,000 years ago, and it was still considered full of wonder when, as late as the first century AD, Pliny wrote of it in his Natural History. He records a good fable—that some Phoenician (Syrian) sailors accidentally discovered glass when lighting a fire on a beach, the heat causing the sand to fuse. Like many legends, it could be true, and it serves to introduce us to the composition of glass—mostly silica (sand and quartz) with a little alkali (usually soda or potash obtained from wood or seaweed) and calcium carbonate (lime). Syria and Egypt were ancient glass-making centers partly because they were areas rich in these necessary minerals.

It seems that as early as 4000 BC the Egyptians were already able to use glass as a coating for such simple jewels as steatite

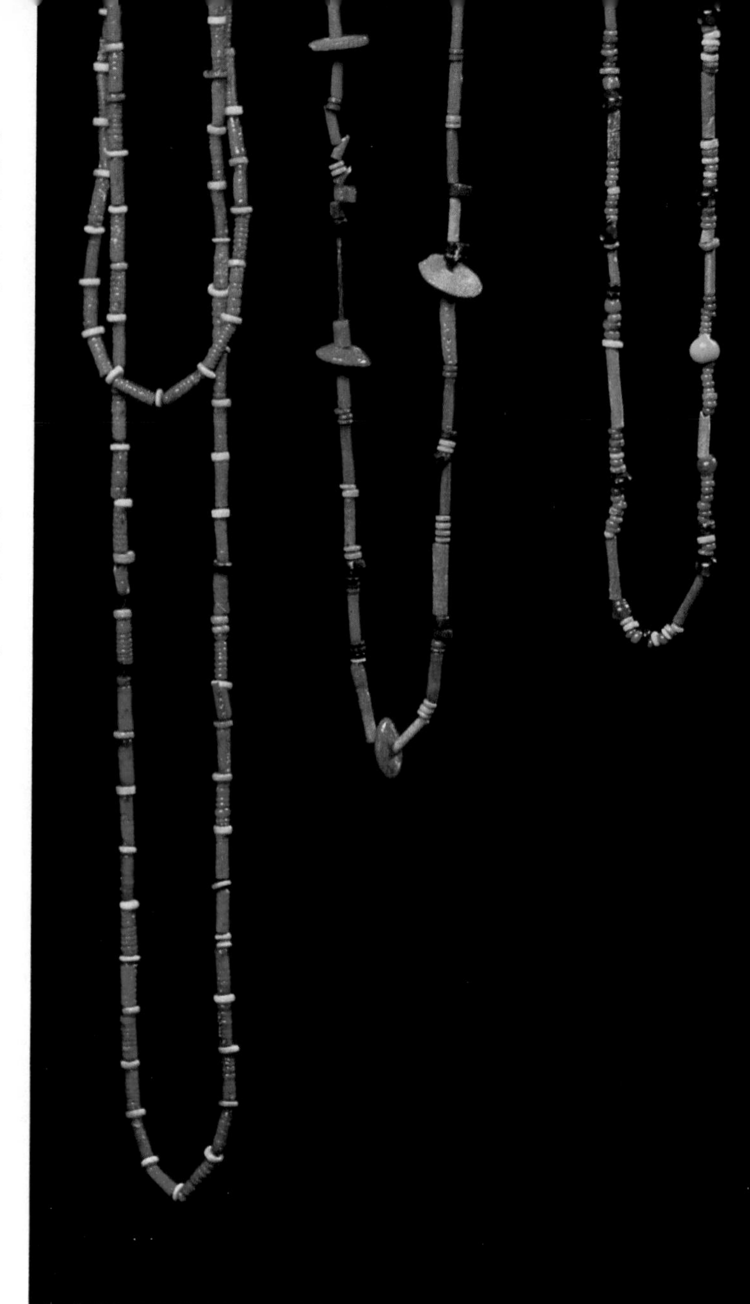

beads and amulets, possibly to enhance their glitter, possibly to imitate semi-precious stones. Deep colors resembling those of stones, were obtained by using metal oxides. These lovely colors also served to hide the normal green or brown resulting from impurities of iron oxide from the sand. One early piece of interest to jewelers, is an Assyrian magnifying glass from Nineveh of about 800 BC in the British Museum. Our forebears were more clever than we sometimes think!

Until perhaps the 1st century BC, glass was moulded by wrapping round a core, or perhaps cast by the lost wax process, being poured between inner core and outer mold. Alexandria became famous for its glass. When Octavian, later the Emperor Augustus, conquered the great Egyptian city, some of his tribute was paid in glass. No doubt many of the later Egyptian faience greenish cylindrical beads, often made into complex and marvellous checkerboard corsage ornaments and necklets, came from Alexandria. So, too, did the early Roman massive round beads and later intricately cut and layered cups and bowls. By the 1st century AD, the Romans had evolved a way of blowing glass much as we do today: their glass-makers' guild originated in Rome in 14 AD. Pompeii became a sophisticated center, with elaborate cutting and polishing, followed by Cologne and other great cities.

Enamel is simply powdered glass with carefully organized color and a good chemical mix to make it stick to its metal background. This sticking must have been a problem for

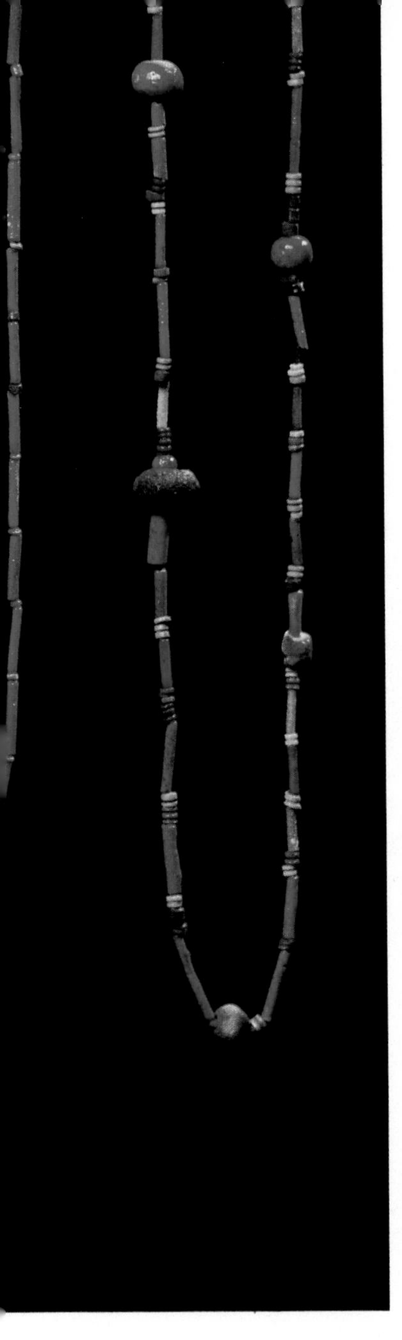

Far left. Egyptian and Phoenician glass and faience beads. The Syrians were apparently the first masters of glass, but Egyptians used it more, no doubt because their women were more important, especially in Ptolemaic times. Their blue-green faience was very widespread, being coated on to small ceramic amulets, ushabti figures (which toiled for the dead in the underworld) and pendants as well as to form beads. Faience is still made today: old beads can be distinguished by their more even and pleasing texture and a more subtle variety of tones of color, mostly in the blue and cream-yellow range.

Above left. Early glass jewels were often made of tiny size for children, or for the grave. In either case durability did not matter, so stones were not necessary. The transparent Roman bracelets and finger rings, *right* and *center*, *c* AD 300 are from Syria, where glass remained popular, perhaps because of the ready availability of its raw materials. The Roman gold bracelet shows how closely glass followed its metal prototype, except that glass could not emulate the efficient "slip-knot" for adjusting size. The opaque glass, *left*, comes from Egypt, *c* 500 BC. The Roman playing counters show how glass becomes pitted with age—unlike the adjoining carnelian set into a gold ring *c* AD 100. The harder gemstone does not easily chip and finer dimensions are possible in gold than in glass.

Below left. A group of English jewels carved from ivory *c* 1860.

enamels were used sparingly in ancient jewels. The Byzantines, however, seem to have been intoxicated by their glass technology—some of it makes a fine show today at St Mark's treasury in Venice.

The Egyptians were the first great jewelers in enamel, with their faience, and the Byzantines the second with their cloisonné outline drawing of saints and crosses. Byzantine jewels used enamels usually applied into cavities in the metal, and decorated within the cavity with wire cages or cloisons forming enclosed compartments for the enamel. The design was usually pictorial, different from the patterning of stones, no longer imitation but a true expansion of artistic vocabulary. The Goths, the Franks and other "barbarian" peoples on their great migrations, used enamels in abstract patterns very much as they used stones and shells, so much so that it is often difficult to tell the difference. The Sutton Hoo Treasure in the British Museum for instance, the greatest surviving group, is often today wrongly described by scholars: the predominating rich red color is solid garnet, not enamel. Another great piece, the Towneley brooch, uses stones and enamel apparently indiscriminately, the enamel perhaps providing color for which stones could not be found.

The next big development was paste. This was a feature of the late 18th century, when it became a language of its own, not just a cheap imitation of diamond.

Glass made two more specific appearances in jewelry. First, Venice developed, probably from the 18th century, an exotic many-colored striped bead for the African market, eventually becoming so popular that it was used for money throughout the north and west coasts. Second, and not so local as might be imagined, were the pressed-glass cameo portraits, usually of famous men like the Duke of Wellington. They were mass-produced in the 19th century and after, satisfying the human yearning for hero worship which hand-carved cameos could no longer keep up with in an ever-expanding market. Glass gave a peculiar glow to art nouveau. Lalique molded it for his jewels and eventually glass seduced him away from jewels entirely. In modern times Jaroslav Kodes of Czechoslovakia has used the gleaming transparency of glass effectively, but most jewelers prefer the deep luster of real stones, now easily available to an ever more wealthy world.

Ivory

Ivory's tendency to discolor and to crack along its strong grain has limited its use in jewelry. Its appeal lay not only in its beautiful color but, before the African elephant massacres began a century ago, in its rarity. Indian ivory was never popular for Indian jewels: the Indians liked luster and glow. Ivory may regain some exclusive appeal as elephants are now scarce, but most artists and designers now shun it because of the imminent threat of the elephant's extinction. Instead jewelers sometimes work in bone or horn.

PRECIOUS & SEMI-PRECIOUS STONES

The stones used by the jeweler range from the very rare and valuable, like diamonds, which may be mined from deep in the earth, to an ordinary pebble chosen for its interesting appearance, or polished to reveal hidden beauty. Some are transparent allowing light to shine right through, others have crystalline structures which bend and reflect the beam and some permit no light to pass at all. Those which have been most highly valued for their beauty come from many places but stone deposits, like all the world's riches, are exhaustible. Persia was the source of most of the hardstones used for seals throughout early Mesopotamia—the Sumerians, Babylonians and Assyrians all seem to have imported their semi-precious stones from their neighbors across the border. Yet today, Persia is known only for her turquoise: the other colored stones have become rare; hematite and lapis lazuli, jasper and cornelian, bloodstone and chalcedony, even the commonest of them all, agate, to whose family they mostly belong. Cornelian, so popular in Ancient Egypt, is no longer found in the old, shallow deposits by the Red Sea and along the edge of Nubia. The Aztecs, and their Mexican predecessors 2,000 years ago, tended to work in black stones, perhaps as a symbol of death—obsidian and granite, with transparent rock crystal, perhaps for eternity. Jade seems to have meant life; inlaid turquoise and coral enhanced the color given by local feathers. Yet today, Mexico is no longer one of the world's leading stone sources.

South of Dresden, in the Erzgebirge Mountains and in nearby Mount Kozakov, at the northern tip of Bohemia, a great range of colored stones was found. From the dark ages right up until the 18th century, the wealth of Central Europe came from these stones, and from the neighboring coalfields, the foundation of the power of Saxony and Poland. Today uranium has been found, but the wonderful store of colorful jewels is almost exhausted, replaced by Bohemian glass for costume jewelry.

More constant are the ancient and still prosperous sources of Thailand, famous for its sapphires, Burma and Sri Lanka. In Burma, Mandalay is a big jade center and the surface ruby mines at Mogok and Mogol are still operating, though on a diminished scale, their products smuggled overland by radio-controlled convoys through the forests to Bangkok. In the fields around Ratnapura in Sri Lanka, one can still see holes in the mud and wooden gantries—the deceptively simple apparatus which still supplies much of the world's colored stone, as it has done for thousands of years past.

More recently discovered stone deposits are those of Brazil, developed by the Portuguese in the 18th century, and now famous for their tourmalines. In Russia malachite, a hydrous copper carbonate, was produced from 1702 from the Gumishev mines, and the bigger Mednorudiansk mine owned by Prince Demidoff came into production as late as 1835. North America has fine jade from Wyoming, pale sapphire from Montana, and turquoise from California, all developed in the past century or so. Iran is an old and continuing source of turquoise; Afghanistan is famous for its lapis lazuli, Australia for opals, China for jade, and India for everything.

The cycle of diamond supplies is dramatic. Until the 18th century, most diamonds came from central India, from the surface deposits in Hyderabad. They were sold in the huge market at Golconda and, as late as the 17th century, European travelers, like Tavernier who supplied Louis XIV of France, marveled at their splendor. By the 18th century Indian diamonds had become scarce. Brazil supplied diamonds to the world throughout the age of elegance until the Brazilian supplies, too, were exhausted about a hundred years ago. Providentially, the De Beers brothers, humble Boer farmers, found diamonds near Kimberley in 1869 and South Africa quickly became the focal point for the world's hardest substance. In 1932 this domination was emphasized when Sir Ernest Oppenheimer set up the Central Selling Organization which now handles some 85% of world diamond output.

Rough diamonds and cut diamonds set in platinum, photographed with a sieve used for sorting diamonds by size.

Russia, with mines in the Urals and a polishing industry at Smolensk may cause the next big diamond upheaval.

The fascination which stones have exercised has not been limited to their appearance. They have been linked with the zodiac and attributed with occult properties by many different cultures. They have been thought to confer fortune or to bring bad luck. The idea of birthstones appears in the Book of Revelation in the Bible, Pliny wrote a treatise linking stones to birth signs. Since then they have been interpreted in a variety of ways, the idea being especially popular in Germany and Poland in the 16th century. The different interpretations form an intriguing historical muddle.

The *Natural History* of Pliny the Elder, published in AD 77, is the source of much amusing, and possibly accurate, lore about stones. For instance, he ascribes to ruby the power of giving light in darkness, perhaps an idea evolving from the ancient Zoroastrian "fire" temples in Persia and elsewhere which show little or no trace of fire today. The fire may have been real and have been contained, as it is for modern Parsees, in urns, or it may conceivably, according to modern theories, not have been live fire at all, but lumps of ruby or sapphire caused to give off "laser beams" of light by the gamma rays from adjacent uranium-bearing rock: all these minerals were found in Persia. Old legends may often be more true than modern cynics realize.

Pliny records that the Ethiopians increased the splendor of their rubies by immersing them in vinegar for 14 days, thus increasing their color temporarily but also making them weaker and more easily shattered.

Great thinkers of other times have written extensively about them, especially in the middle ages and early renaissance in Europe. Rubies, for example, were considered by various authorities to be powerful amulets against poison, plague, sadness, evil thoughts and wicked spirits. Pliny claims that the Romans knew a source for rock crystal in the Alps and Roman physicians used crystals as lenses to burn out sores and as spheres for gazing into for divination. In later times rock crystal goblets were thought to shatter if used to contain poison.

Such qualities owe more to poetic fantasy than scientific fact but science has a valid poetry of its own: refractive index, dichroism and doubling, double refraction and color zoning. What do these strange terms mean? Clear language is a necessary prelude to accuracy.

Synthetic means a man-made stone possessing all the physical and optical qualities of the natural stone, sometimes made by heat, sometimes by chemical growth processes. These synthetics, especially sapphire, ruby and emerald, are becoming increasingly common.

Imitation means artificial—a more or less similar appearance to nature but a different physical structure, the most common being glass.

Luster means reflection—the degree to which light is thrown back into your eyes from the front or back surface of a stone. It is the quality of a mirror.

Brilliance is refraction, the amount by which light passing from one substance to another is bent.

Fire is the degree of dispersion—the amount by which the different component colors in a ray of light are separated and distinguished when the light comes back from a gemstone. It is fire that makes a white diamond flash in many colors.

In luster, brilliance and fire the diamond is supreme: other stones may rate higher in one of the three areas but only the diamond has them all. That is why you usually cannot see through a diamond. Hold one diagonally, for instance, and try to look through it: you will see almost nothing coming from behind, only sparkles of different colors from the front.

Another guiding characteristic is hardness. Again the diamond is supreme. Scrape a diamond with a tempered steel blade and you will leave no mark, only blunt the blade. The normal jeweler's measure of hardness goes from 1–10, although not in equal stages—the gap between 9 and 10 is much bigger than that between 1 and 2. Diamond is alone on the pinnacle of 10, sapphire and ruby considerably softer at 9, whilst glass is about 5 and organic ivory and amber near the bottom at about 2½. Most of the less precious stones are comparatively soft. This standard scale of hardness is known as the Mohs scale after its inventor.

An old-fashioned analyst may successfully diagnose glass compared with diamond by trying to mark it with a needle. He will only spoil paste, leaving genuine diamond unscathed. Another test for diamonds, popular in the 19th-century diamond rushes at Kimberley, was misleading. You banged the stone with a hammer. If your hammer bruised you probably had a real diamond—but if the stone shattered, nothing was proved. It was not then realized that diamond is quite brittle—hence the modern method of shaping it by "cleaving," or shearing off a section by a blow with a sharp edge along the grain. Diamond is so hard that it can be cut only with another diamond: but, given a skilful cutter or a lucky direction, diamond can be divided.

Gemstones are colorful and fascinating, and much of their value lies in their color and shape, obvious and appealing to everyone. But scientific analysis today requires sophisticated gadgets. One technical aspect of crystal structure, visible through a magnifying glass or microscope, though not always to the naked eye, is known as double refraction. Looking into the center of a stone you can often see all the cut edges and triangular facets in it, not once but twice. This double refraction occurs in most hardstones in measurable quantity, related to the amount of refraction of the stone (the refractive index), so one may speak of DR (double refraction) in natural ruby, for instance, as 0.008, whilst ruby's RI (refractive index) is 1.76–1.77. Very precise, if you have the right measuring equipment. Without specialized devices, it is more useful to remember where there is no double refraction: single refraction is seen in diamond, spinel, garnet, fire opal and glass.

There are two further simple aids to recognition: air and water. Breathe on a real diamond and it may not cloud over, whereas most of its imitators will: they have lower specific heat. Immerse a stone in a tumbler of water, and you may see a previously invisible join. One form of economy in stone is to stick a cheap bottom on to a real top, forming what is called a doublet. The join is usually at the stone's girdle, or fattest edge, and may be difficult to spot with the naked eye. But underwater, the evidence is often devastating. What seemed to be one stone of uniform color, is transformed dramatically by the change in direction of light under water: refraction of the light beams, instead of "joining" the two (or sometimes three) portions of the stone, causes the parts to separate, and with the separation the true color of each stone appears.

The gemologist's first tool is the naked eye. If the stone is held close to the eyelash, you can spot some quite technical phenomena. Look at an electric lamp filament reflected on the surface, and you can assess the intensity of luster or reflection; you can evaluate, by the intensity of the rainbow of different colors, the fire or dispersion; and you may establish double refraction, seeing double edges on the stone's far side, and double filaments in an electric light bulb seen in the distance through the close-up stone. By holding the stone at arm's length from the eye and looking through it first horizontally, then gradually tilting it to a more diagonal position, you can see the degree of refraction: high refraction, as with diamond, means that the stone never empties of its brilliance, and you can never see through it.

To amplify the evidence of his eyes a jeweler will want a magnifying glass. Enlargement by ten times is often preferred by jewelers: by using the same magnification, there is a

Left. Diamonds are a girl's best friend—if they are real ones.

Right. Silver button set with brilliant-cut paste, Birmingham, 1790. The paste "stones" can be distinguished from diamond by their chipped edges, curved corners and lack of brilliance.

Far right. Diamond pendant *c.* 1810, silver front, gold back, typical of the rather cold, precise composition of Georgian England, when jewelers tried to set stones using as little metal as possible. The central diamond is a brilliant cut with a large flat 8-sided table on top. The brilliant cut became popular in the 17th century, increasingly accurate in the 18th, and precise and perhaps, therefore, monotonous in the late 19th and 20th century. Here the asymmetry of the table edges can be seen, an indication of early date. The corners and facets of diamonds are always sharp, the reflections and refractions, brilliant and confusing. When breathed upon diamonds will not cloud over as glass does but this alone is not sufficient test to authenticate the stone.

Lower right. Detail from silver flower brooch set with paste, English, 1770. The "stones" are rose-cut faceted all over, a style popular from the 16th to the 18th century passing out of fashion about 1780. The setting is inspired by the new fashion for claw settings, but not thoroughly executed—the stones are actually held in place by colets not claws.

possibility of speaking a common professional language. The merit of a magnifying glass is that the gem can be moved so that the light may fall from every side, allowing an examination of facets round the stone, and of flaws inside it. You can make the light reflect from the surface of the stone, perhaps showing up tear marks which may mean a synthetic rather than a real emerald; or you can search for bubbles in the stone which may mean that it is glass or synthetic, or inclusions which suggest real stones. You can follow the facets: if these lines and angles are sharp, you may have a diamond; if rough, it is probably one of the soft substitutes—strontium titanate or "yag" for instance.

A further enlargement under a microscope will show the structure of the stone, the curved bands of color and bubbles which may mean synthetic, the straight geometric rhythms and lines crossing at 60° which may mean a real sapphire or ruby crystalline inclusions.

The refractometer, a small metal box containing lens and viewfinder, and platform upon which one lays the stone to be analysed, throws a shadow onto a numbered grid. From this, if recognized correctly, the refractive index number can be read. If the shadow has not one edge, but two, each with a different intensity, then that means double refraction. Another way of detecting double refraction is through what is grandly called a polaroscope—at its simplest, two sheets of polaroid glass, through which a doubly refractive stone will penetrate clearly.

A spectroscope directs light from a stone through a prism, not only separating the different colors, but giving to each color a prescribed proportion of the whole area. Just as refractive index, and double refraction, once established, can be located on an appropriate list of the qualities of specific stones, so also the spectrum gives another clue, rather more difficult to recognize.

The ultra-violet light box has replaced an older apparatus called the Chelsea Filter. Stones react differently to an ultra-violet ray, some becoming invisible, others luminous. This may prove a decisive test between stones which are otherwise confusingly similar.

The last piece of equipment is in some ways the most dramatic of all: a row of bottles, each containing a different liquid. In methylene dioxide, for instance, a diamond remains itself, whereas a synthetic spinel, in some ways similar to diamond, becomes quite invisible. If a gemstone is not set in a metal frame its specific gravity can be gauged with ease and accuracy by measuring the amount of a fluid of known density that it displaces: the Archimedes principle. But unset stones are normal merchandise only for professional jewelers and gem collectors. Identifying stones is becoming increasingly difficult as the geographical variety increases and the methods of scientific imitation and of analysis improve. An expert may spend hours on a single stone with equipment worth hundreds of pounds.

The very great majority of old jewels, and of good quality new ones, are exactly what they seem to be, but cheaper modern jewels need very careful attention. If a gemstone is not set in a metal frame, its specific gravity can be gauged with ease and accuracy simply by measuring the amount of fluid of a known density that it displaces: the Archimedes principle. But unset stones are normal merchandise only for professional jewelers and gem collectors. So much for the basis of detection, usually more ingenuity than enjoyment.

Gemstones were first—and sometimes still are—used in their beautiful natural crystalline state where the emphasis is on the outside. Skilled cutting and polishing will show the internal qualities.

The principal gemstones and their substitutes

Diamond chemically pure carbon which occurs colorless and in all colors. It keeps its brilliance whatever the angle of sight (unlike some of its imitators, such as spinel or yag), so that you can never see through it: precise facet junctions but often unsymmetrical: high surface luster so that you can be dazzled by the reflection of the filament of a light bulb if you hold the stone close to your eye: many inclusions, usually visible near the girdle: does not mist over if you breathe on it. Wide range of pale colors. H (hardness) 10 (on Mohs scale); RI (refractive index) 2.41; DR (double refraction) nil.

Strontium Titanate (often used as a substitute for diamond). Because the stone is very soft, facet edges are rounded, not sharp. Very brilliant, but not uniformly so. Transparent at certain angles. RI 2.41 (same as diamond); DR nil; hardness $5\frac{1}{2}$ (so soft it can be pricked with a needle, but the owner might not be pleased).

Yttrium Aluminate (Yag) very brilliant, but only moderate fire. White. Will not bite against synthetic corundum crystal, which is often useful for tests; bright specks in stones seen through lens. RI 1.83; DR nil.

Emerald green variety of beryl, recognized by its rich color. Principally mined in Columbia and in the Ural mountains emeralds of gemstone quality are rare and often have flaws. A pure stone is more valuable than a good diamond, but impure (as normally used in antique jewelry) costs little. They are fragile and therefore often "emerald-cut": rectangular with bevelled corners which are difficult to chip. A Chelsea filter produces pinkish colors. Many inclusions, always green, show as ladder-like rods, long slender needle-like crystals, jagged cavities orientated the same way, silvery films, etc. Round bubbles are encountered as inclusions within inclusions. H 7.5; RI 1.76–1.58, slightly variable; DR 0.006.

Although most diamonds are mined they can be found by panning in Borneo. The pan is filled with water and loose material from the riverbed, larger lumps removed and then a rotary motion used to create settlement of heavier minerals at the bottom of the pan. It is a simple but laborious process.

Synthetic emerald colors often not quite right. Some "Chathams" too bluish and hard. Gilsons are often yellowish emerald green. Suspiciously clean gems lacking in characteristic inclusions. Normally produces pink or dull red fluorescence under ultraviolet light. Chelsea filter and spectroscope produce very marked results—generally lower RI than natural observed on refractometer or in liquid. Typical flawing seen as swirling veils. H 7.5; RI 1.56–1.565; DR 0.003.

Sapphire form of corundum, usually colored blue by titanium, although yellow, green, purple, pink and colorless stones are also known, sometimes with a beautiful 6-rayed star when cut into a rounded cabochon shape. Less fragile than emerald they can be cut in many ways. Color is bright and hard and crystal inclusions are usually visible under a lens. Found in Thailand, Kashmir, Burma and, most common, in Sri Lanka. They are frequent in antique western and modern eastern jewels. H 9; RI 1.76–.77; DR 0.008.

Ruby red variety of corundum, found in Burma, where the fullest red color is called pigeon's blood, Thailand, where rubies are often browner, Sri Lanka where they are paler and Tanzania, where they are always red. They are second in value only to emeralds and diamonds. Rubies were believed to darken when evil was encountered and to lighten when it passed. Eastern superstition gave the wearer the power to predict calamity. Birthstone for December. H 9; RI 1.76; DR 0.008.

Synthetic ruby fine bubble clouds, often following curved path visible in lens; brilliance empties, stone becomes transparent on tilting. Rich red color often small crystal inclusions. Red glow under Chelsea filter and ultraviolet light produces exaggerated reds in synthetic ruby, whereas glass and garnet inert RI 1.76–.77; DR 0.008.

Other gemstones

Agate variety of chalcedony with a banded structure of different colored layers which is found in various forms. Moss agate, usually whitish, has a moss-like, dark gray-brown pattern in the stone, known technically as dendritic inclusions; other forms produce patterns like plant forms and landscape views as though organic life was trapped in the stone. The porous white layers of agate can be artificially dyed to form a wider range of colors. Onyx, which is frequently artificially colored, is agate with black or grayish and whitish bands, very clearly divided from each other, and was often used by the Romans to accentuate portrait cameos. Sardonyx is banded in brownish red and white. Other agates include sard, normally beige, also used for Roman cameos, and bloodstone, a red-speckled green sard. H 7;RI 1.53.

Amethyst its distinctive purple color has made this stone popular throughout history. Found widely in Brazil, Sri Lanka, Russia and Madagascar it is a member of the quartz family. Often used for bishop's rings it is linked with constancy in love, vocation and friendship. Relatively cheap and soft, it yields more color for cash value than other stones. Birthstone for February. H 7; RI 0.544; DR 0.009.

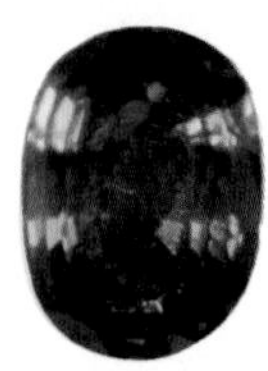

Andalusite unusual transparent stone, green or red-green in color. H 5;RI 1.64.

Apatite uncommon stone found in many colours, including purple from Maine (US) and the yellow-green "asparagus stone" from Durango, Mexico. H 5; RI 1.658.

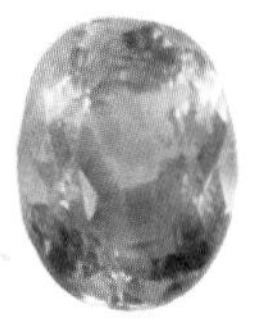

Aquamarine light blue to greenish variety of beryl. H 7.5; RI 1.575.

Benitoite rare stone of sapphire blue. H 6.5; RI 1.78.

Beryl group of stones which include the emerald and the aquamarine; color can also range from clear and colorless to intense pink. During the middle ages beryl seems to have been used to indicate any clear, crystal-like stone which could be used as a transparent cover in monstrances and reliquaries. It was believed that it could also form a mirror in which to see the future. H 7.5; RI 1.75–.59.

Brazilianite unusual yellowish-green stone. H 5.5; RI 1.612.

Carnelian, also known as Cornelian, a form of chalcedony ranging from flesh red to brown which was especially popular in ancient times as a stone for carved seals. H 7; RI 1.53.

Chalcedony part of a group of crystalline quartzes which include agate, carnelian and chrysoprase, it is a pale and creamy bluish-greenish white, ranging from translucent to opaque, and was especially popular for renaissance and art nouveau cameos. H 7; RI 1.53.

Chrysoberyl valuable and important gemstone which takes three forms: chryso-beryl, cat's-eye and alexandrite. The first ranges from yellow, through tobacco tones, to lime green; cat's eye is characterized by a band of light which looks like the narrowed slit of a cat's eye, moving across the surface at right-angles to the alignment of the stone's particles; alexandrite appears a soft moss green in daylight but changes to red or purple in artificial light. H 7;RI 1.53.

Chrysoprase apple green form of chalcedony, used for cameos during the renaissance and in art nouveau. H 7; RI 1.53.

Citrine yellow to brown-colored crystalline quartz. (Also produced by heating amethyst.) Often confused with topaz, which is more expensive, often smaller in size and of quite different composition. H 7; RI 1.548.

Cordierite uncommon blue, pale brown or gray-blue stone. Iolite, the violet-blue form the usual gem color. H 7, RI 1.535.

Corundum all corundums, except red ruby, are called sapphire with appropriate color prefix.

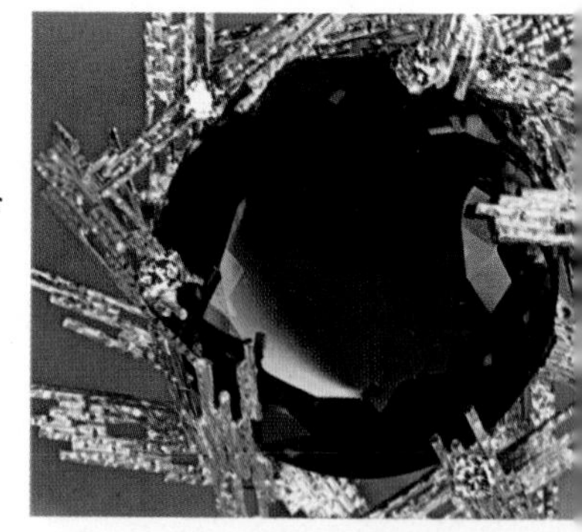

Dioptase a copper silicate, emerald green. Its vivid color makes it popular with modern artist jewelers. H 5; RI 1.65.

Feldspar group of quartzes, includes amazonite, labradorite, moonstone and orthoclase.

Garnet group of stones and especially the name form which is dark red, with a good luster, which was the most popular in the 18th century, when Bohemian deposits were exploited. It is now used chiefly in doublets as facing for another stone. Other forms include the glowing red pyrope, brown to violet-red alamandine, rose-red rhodolite, orange spessarite and green demantoid.

Hematite iron oxide of cold, steely gray. Popular for seals in Old Babylon, and with modern artists. H 5.5–6.5; RI 2.94–3.22.

Idocrase, calcium aluminium silicate. Its exciting blue-green color and craggy crystal form appeal to modern artist jewelers.

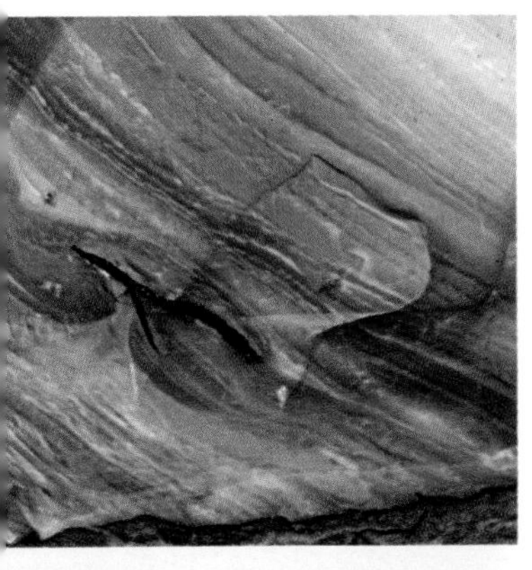

Jadeite green, white, yellow, brown, pink or violet stone, the green most highly prized by the Chinese. It is rarer than nephrite, the other form of jade. H 7, RI 1.66.

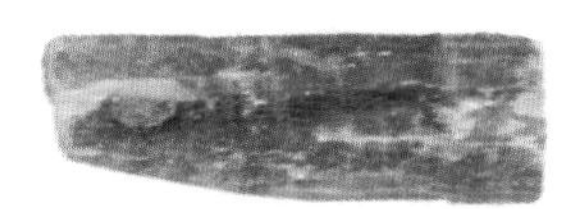

Kyanite transparent patchy blue stone chemically identical with andalusite and sillimanite. Can be scratched along the crystal but very hard across it.

Lapis Lazuli dark blue rock of mixed minerals, recognized by minute inclusions of pyrite or flecked with white in Andean forms. Much used in ancient Egypt, and now found mainly in Afghanistan. H 5.5, RI 1.5.

Malachite Banded green stone, once believed to make the speech of animals audible. H 4, RI 1.78.

Marcasite and **Pyrites** non disulfide of metallic luster, popular in late 18th-century buckles, sometimes confused with cut steel.

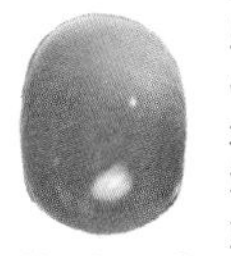

Moonstone soft, creamy colored and transparent member of the feldspar family which gives a pearly opalescent display of colors. Found in Sri Lanka, where it is much used in local jewels, it has been popular since the 18th century, and especially recently when its subtelty appeals to artists and in cabochon form it contrasts well with bright-colored facetted stones. It will not cut into rock crystal. It is a birthstone for June. H 6, RI 1.53.

Nephrite One of the forms of jade, may be dark green, brown, yellow, gray or white. H 6.5; RI 1.62.

Opal colorless, white, orange, varicolored or black it produces brilliant flashing colors from minute spheres of crustobalite. Fire opals, often Mexican, are usually hazy orange and of constant color. Prized in the orient as a symbol of purity and a health talisman it has a reputation for bad luck in the west, but this superstition does not harm the wearer with a clear conscience. H6; RI 1.45.

Peridot olive to pistachio-green olivine known to the Egyptians, who prized it highly, as topazion. Mounted in gold and worn on the left hand it is said to dispel melancholy and put ghosts and demons to flight. Birtstone for August. H 6.5; RI 1.6.

Quartz consisting of crystallized pure silica, quartz takes many forms from rock crystal, amethyst and citrine, all used as gemstones, to the ornamental stones of the agate and chalcedony group. H 7; RI 1.53–1.548.

Rock crystal colorless quartz which was popular throughout history and often a substitute for diamond, from which it is distinguished by its softness and lack of brilliance. Seldom used today except with the dark-colored rod-like inclusions (rutiles) which modern designers find exciting. Bites on knife blade, harder than glass and feels cold against the cheek. H 7; RI 1.544, DR 0.009.

Far left. Turquoise.
Centre, top left. Amethyst; *top right.* Opal; *bottom left,* Tourmaline; *bottom right,* Rock crystal. *Right.* Tourmaline.
The jewelry on this and the preceding pages is by Andrew Grima, except for the small ring, *left,* by Nevin Holmes.

Scapolite unusual white or grayish-blue stone, or a transparent yellow form from Brazil and Madagascar more frequent as a gem, a pink variety occurs as cat's eyes. H 6; RI 1.545–1.57.

Scheelite very rare gemstone of yellowish, golden, brown color with adamantine luster. H 4.5; RI 1.925.

Sillimanite Transparent pale blue stone.

Sinhalite uncommon gemstone from Sri Lanka, yellowish to deep brown and transparent. H 6.5; RI 1.685.

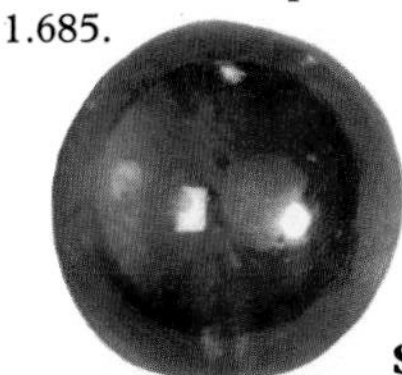

Sphalerite uncommon gemstone; transparent yellow, orange or green with a metallic luster. H 5.5; RI 2.37.

Sphene uncommon but much prized transparent stone of yellow, green and brown. Colorless crystals from St Gothard district of Switzerland have a brilliance and "fire" greater than that of diamonds. H 5.5; RI 1.96.

Spinel Fairly common stone of the corundum family, its large crystals occurring in all colors except yellow, green and brown. Inclusions are like grains of sugar. Many ancient "rubies" are actually spinels, including the Timur Ruby in the British crown jewels, and the Black Prince's ruby. Found mainly in Sri Lanka today. H 8; RI 1.717–1.78.

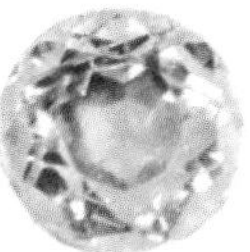

Spodumene rare stone related to jadeite. Kunzite is a pink-lilac form and hiddenite a green variety. H 7; RI 1.67.

Staurolite a metamorphic mineral whose large brown crystals are often found intergrown in the form of a cross and worn as a pendant in some Christian countries.

Topaz the normal stone of yellow color in old jewels, now increasingly replaced by citrine; occasionally occurs in blue, green and pink. Striking in clarity and transparency it is found in Brazil, Siberia and Sri Lanka. H 8; RI 1.6–1.64.

Tourmaline popular stone which may be colorless or shades of almost any color or black, most frequently a soft blue-green. Produced mainly in Brazil, where tourmaline jewelry is a national industry, but also comes from Siberia, Madagascar and Sri Lanka. It is common but was little used before the 20th century for it was too cheap to be popular in precious jewels. It is the muses' stone, aiding inspiration, and a birthstone for October. H 7; RI 1.63.

Turquoise opaque pale to deep blue and greenish blue stone, sometimes veined in brown, found mainly in Iran. In the east it was considered the protector of riders and of the innocent and it is a birthstone for December. Fakes, which are common, have uniform texture. H 6; RI 1.61.

Zircon transparent, colorless stone, known in India as jargoon, or in dull pastel shades of pale yellow, green, blue or red, much used in cheaper new jewels for its high optical qualities. Found widely, including Sri Lanka, Thailand, Brazil. Normal and low types have different qualities. H 6.5–7.6; RI 1.79–1.98.

IN THE WORKSHOP

A jeweler's workshop equipment is simple: good light; good ventilation to get rid of acid fumes; a bench normally with a large semi-circular hole in the front and a sheepskin or other hide hung beneath to catch the filings and precious scraps called "lemel;" a low stool (too much height will cause stooping and back strain)—the seat is often the wood segment cut from the table; a gas torch with a blowpipe (either operated by mouth or by tap) to control, direct and intensify the flame; a container for diluted sulfuric acid, usually a fire-resistant glass to enable the acid to be heated over a flame, thus speeding its action; and water, preferably running water, to wash jewels after they have been cleaned in acid or "pickled."

Metal can often be bought ready prepared in the form of "findings" from a bullion dealer, but there may be a rolling mill for sheet, and another for wire—they look like small clothes' mangles (and it is just as painful inadvertently to flatten a finger in them). A draw-bench is for making wire thinner—the thin end of a wire is fitted through a hole of the required size and section, pierced in a steel plate, the same thin end is attached by a simple clamp to a leather belt which in turn is wound round a spindle with huge wood spokes. The process has not changed for centuries—a choice renaissance example, ornamental and 500 years old, but with the same engineering as today's, is at the Musée Carnavalet in Paris. A drill may be the old "Archimedes" drill, in which the vertical rotating metal rod is harnessed to a horizontal wooden driving bar by leather thongs wound spirally round it. When this bar is pulled up and down between finger and thumb, a limited, accurate and easily controllable boring process results. Power drills, like those used by dentists are very common nowadays, but in inexperienced hands they may go too far too fast. Last, there may be a polishing lathe, fitted with all sorts of mops and pads and polishing abrasives and rouge—but, once again, hand-rubbing and burnishing are safer, for the inexpert.

Beneath or on the work bench would be found saws for cutting out and for saw-piercing, like a carpenter's fret-saw; files, known as "needles," "rifflers" or "joint-files;" metal vices, wood clamps, parallel pliers and a wire mat or "wig" as a bed for holding the piece when soldering or annealing; charcoal for the same process; plasticine or wax in which the parts can be assembled; plaster of Paris in which the side not in plasticine can be embedded, the plasticine then being removed to reveal one side for soldering; flux to make the solder flow; a 10% solution of sulfuric acid for cleaning off the flux and indeed the whole surface after soldering; a chasing hammer and a set of different shaped punches which can reach round any corner and tap any selected shape into the metal's surface; a lump of pitch to hold the metal being chased; a simple brass float cut with spherical depressions into which a sheet of metal can be embossed or domed; another cube with grooves for forming ridges, or "swaging;" a set of round-bottomed hammers for embossing, and flat-bottomed hammers for flat-hammering a surface, and, if big pieces are made, steel anvils or "stakes" for "raising" a flat sheet of metal to a cup shape, and a further variety of convex-ended raising hammers. With this equipment there are several ways in which the surface of the metal can be decorated, all known since very early times.

Chasing is punching ornament on to the outer surface with hammer and shaped tool: a process much used in jewelry to clean up the finish, after the piece has been modelled and cast roughly to shape. Repoussé is the same thing done from the back. Engraving is cutting a design into the metal. Planishing is hammering the metal smooth with repeated stroking movements of a special flat-ended hammer.

Soldering

The most important jewelry process is the soldering of one piece of metal to another. Any technical manual will describe solder, few will reveal the essence of jewelry soldering, which is temperature control. If a delicate, part-finished piece is heated above the melting point of existing solder, the piece will of course disintegrate. The correct method is either to solder everything simultaneously, which is not always practical, especially if enamels are involved, or to use solder of successively lower melting point, on each succeeding joint. Metals change color as they change temperature and, to the skilled, this is an invaluable guide. Modern research into antique jewelry has probed into the fascinating technique of solder. How did the early civilizations achieve such amazing delicacy and precision when they had no gas pressure to obtain localized heat, no thermometers to guide them as to what was happening, no metallurgy to gauge the quality of alloys? One answer is that we always underrate our ancestors: in fact, patience is a primary prerequisite for any jeweler, and it is quite possible that we are the least patient people ever. Furthermore, ancient peoples did not try to make every

jewel different and original, as we do now, so a detailed technique, once mastered, would continue in use for ages.

More specifically, the miracle of ancient soldering which almost passes our comprehension, and which quite outclasses our 20th-century manual ability, is granulation. Metals tend to become treacly when almost molten, solder to be untidy, spheres to become pear shaped tiny balls to roll on a flat surface, still more so on a curve. Yet many Mediterranean people decorated their gold jewels with myriads of almost microscopic balls of gold arranged in precise geometrical patterns, both as patches and as lines. The balls are still round now, after heating and fixing, not pear shaped, and the solder marks beneath are invisible. Was there a secret? Research in Britain, Germany and America has yielded similar answers without exactly discovering how the minuteness of old work was obtained. At London's British Museum, H. A. P. Littledale used a paste of vegetable or fish glue with copper carbonate or copper hydrate, to stick the parts together. At 100° Celsius the copper hydrate oxidizes; at 600° the glue becomes carbon; at 850° the carbon absorbs the oxygen from the oxide, leaving a thin layer of copper, which lowers the melting point between the pieces to be soldered; at 890° the mixed copper and gold melt where they are touching, and are joined. Fine silver will not melt until 900°; gold until 1,000° and most alloys until still higher temperatures. So there is some margin of error between the moment when the copper-based solder melts, and the whole jewel falls apart! Littledale formed minute granulation patterns by first engraving the pattern into soft metal; then rolling gold balls into the grooves; then laying over the balls a stretched piece of paper coated with tacky varnish; then lifting up the balls on the paper and painting them with glue and copper hydrate; then laying the balls on to their final placing, which he dampened to dissolve the glue; then sticking the balls to the metal beneath; then soaking off the paper with varnish solvent. Some such transfer process certainly seems easy and practical and may well have been generally used by the Etruscans, the granulators-in-chief of antiquity, the Greeks, Persians and Scythians. Granulation may have been coarse gold filings mixed with powdered charcoal and heated in an iron vessel.

But these processes do not explain the result; how were the gold balls made? Were magnifying glasses used to obtain the wonderfully accurate small scale work? There is the Nineveh example, but there is probably only one mention of magnifying in an ancient text, and that is by means of looking through the curved mass of water in a bottle. Only very few prisms, which might have been used for magnifying, have survived—in the Heraklion Museum. The naked eye seems more likely.

Early Techniques

A fresco in the British Museum of an Egyptian bead and necklace workshop and a carving of a Roman workshop at Pompeii, manned by cupids, in the Naples National Museum, are clues to ancient jewelers' methods: they are far from being a scientific analysis such as Diderot gave of 18th-century techniques in his Encyclopédie. Two or three ancient Greek coin dies have survived, of the thousands that must have existed, but they do not explain the balance between modeling to achieve the sculptural effect, and carving into the die. In the same way, the exact procedure for old jewels is still a mystery.

Except for the development of new ways of cutting stone in the 17th and 18th centuries the technique of jewelry manufacture by hand has changed very little for 2,000 years. It is still a matter of tiny scraps of metal, thin wires drawn to a consistency almost of hair, the whole soldered together with meticulous care and burnished. Sometimes the mountings for the stones are made separately from the main frame or gallery

Opposite, top. A typical modern jewelry workshop in London's Hatton Garden, for centuries a center of the jewelry trade. Each craftsman has his own set of tools and workplace.

Opposite, bottom. Rough stones and partly polished stones held on the ends of dop sticks. The jeweler's wax on the end is softened by heat, the stone pressed into it and then held firm when it hardens. The stone can then be held against an abrasive, wheel or rubbed with abrasive powder to form its basic shape.

Top. Granulation: the decoration of surfaces with tiny balls of metal is difficult because the balls tend to merge under heat. The Etruscans loved it and it is a particular feature of their work, as in the ring center foreground. The Greeks used it less richly, as shown in the gold and garnet ring, *c* 300 BC, right foreground. Later variations of this lovely decorative technique shown here are a Roman earring incorporating lapis lazuli, *c* AD 250, *left foreground*, a Byzantine cross, *c* 650, an English fob seal, *c* 1850, *center*, a cufflink by Andrew Grima, London, 1964, *top right* and part of a necklace by Gerda Flockinger, London, 1968.

Above left. Soldering: temperature control is critical in this process. Too much heat will melt the jewel and any previously soldered joints. Color changes in the metal will guide the craftsman in knowing when the temperature is right and with modern sophisticated tools control is easier. For safety jewels are often soldered on an asbestos surface as seen here.

Above right. Polishing: revolving mechanical mops and scratch brushes are normally used for silver, the piece being moved against the wheel. With jewels a smaller hand-held polisher is often safer, the jewel being held in one hand, the polisher in the other. Precious filings or scrap are carefully kept for melting and reuse.

of a brooch, by a specialist mounter. Then comes the setting, often done by another specialist; the skill of both mounters and setters being concentrated mostly into diamond jewelry because the stones are so valuable that they need extra care. Once the jewel is assembled, often before the stone is set, it receives a final polish with some form of revolving wheel or mop, again a slow and responsible craft where one slip could mean ruin.

A watchful eye can often date a piece by spotting machined components. Sharp edges, straight lines, smooth surfaces all suggest a recent date, probably after mass-produced jewelry became common a century ago, certainly after the arrival of machinery in Birmingham, England, a hundred years before that. Steel guillotines for cutting, steel edges for straightening and power-driven mops for polishing all leave their traces on a jewel, all give a different polish, a harsher, more rhythmical effect than rubbing and burnishing by hand. Sometimes this can be seen by the naked eye, sometimes only through a microscope, which often reveals a machined surface. So power has transformed the jewel through its raw materials.

Casting

Casting is different. It is a rapidly developing technology, it may change the face of jewels more than anything since the brilliant-cut diamond in the 17th century. Casting has enormous potential for bad or good. Used as a means of cheap imitation it is horrible; as a calculated way of lowering prices, of bringing the pleasure of jewelry to poorer people, of making possible more adventurous designs, it is a marvel. Sand casting is pouring molten metal into a cavity formed in damp sand by a wood or metal pattern, the sand sometimes placed in two open boxes which, fitted together, provide a mold all round the cavity. It is impractical to have a core, so the resulting cast will be heavy and solid, more useful for silversmiths, medallists and sculptors than for jewelers. Even the finest special sand being porous, a sand casting will be rough, like the thumb piece on a 17th-century silver tankard. Undercut designs are difficult—the pattern cannot be extracted from the sand, if there are overhangs, so sand casting is cheap, easy and rough.

The lost-wax process is nowadays more common than sand casting, used for 5,000 years all over the world. A wax model is surrounded with plaster investment, the wax burnt out, metal poured in, and the investment broken away. This is more accurate but more expensive than sand casting.

Easy access to pressure and to rubber molds has facilitated a technical revolution through a new casting technique, not developed until 1939. A refinement of the lost-wax method, it involves the use of pressure either by a centrifugal machine, or by vacuum, to make sure that the molten metal fills the whole cavity and make possible a new degree of accuracy in reproduction. Many identical replicas can now be made from one pattern, and, often, molds are now made of rubber or synthetic soft materials, which, unlike hard plaster of Paris, can be peeled away from the object cast, and used again, instead of being broken or dissolved and destroyed. Casting, however, still has two inescapable characteristics: the metal, not having been hardened by hammering, is rather soft and weak so that a cast jewel may not be as robust as one made by hand; secondly, casting always involves shrinkage because metal is more bulky when molten than when cold. Cast copies can often be distinguished from the original only because they are softer and smaller. But dental equipment has now made same-size copies possible—useful to honest and dishonest jewelers alike!

Making a ring

With simple designs, batch production workshops usually model a ring in metal. But initial preparation in wax is becoming increasingly common. When making a prototype ring in metal, the carving techniques are those of a craftsman, carving out the metal to remove it, and soldering other pieces of metal on to it to make a raised or attached portion. Working in wax is quicker and rather different: designing a new ring, a piece of wax of appropriate size is set on a hollow metal former, and carved out from the hardened cold wax, using special cutting tools. For additions, for instance, when small raised portions or small projecting bits of metal are required on the finished piece, hot wax is provided by medical cauterising equipment. Particularly when a complicated design is prepared, pieces are made individually and mounted together later. A designer sometimes starts with a rough

Left. Casting: ancient peoples achieved amazing subtlety with wax and a ceramic mold. The ring is the oldest piece in this group and is Roman, *c*250. The animal form was made in Panama *c*1500, the large disk on the necklace is Ashanti work *c*1800, from Kumasi, Ghana, and the silver flower is by Georges Delrue, Montreal, Canada, 1969, the petals being cast paper-thin by his own wax pressure casting technique using a plaster mold or investment.

Opposite, top. Detail of champlevé enamel on a brooch once owned by Shah Jehan, *c*1620, made in Delhi or Jaipur. The picture and pattern were carved from the metal background and the cavities filled with enamel. The method allowed a more subtle treatment than cloisonné and was popular in medieval Europe.

Opposite, bottom. Painted enamel on the back of a baroque brooch, probably Spanish, *c*1700. The color was painted on the surface after the glass had been fired, not mixed with the crystals, and then fired in. This allowed more delicate shading but gave less vivid colors than the colored enamel techniques.

sketch of an idea, but this is seldom more than a simple record on the back of an envelope. It bears only a superficial likeness to the finished article.

A wax master is mounted on a "tree," which is a wax tube that can be melted. The tree is mounted on a base, and a steel cylinder is placed over it, completely surrounding it. A plaster slurry or "investment" is then poured into the cylinder so that all the space is filled and it is then "vacated"—that is to say, the air and moisture are taken out by placing the cylinder in a vacuum container. The wax is itself then "vacated" by putting the cylinder in a very hot furnace so that the wax evaporates and leaves the impression of the rings in plaster. The mold that is created in this way is then placed in a specially designed machine in which it is rotated at high speed and molten gold is thrown into it from a crucible by centrifugal force. The cylinder is then plunged into a tank of water which dissolves out the plaster, and what remains is a tree of gold rings.

Sometimes a piece is created by stages. If more work is needed on the gold master, it is molded into a block of rubber and the rubber mold is then cut apart. The mold is cut by a special technique so that the two halves of the mold are keyed, enabling them accurately to be put together. Then the wax is pressed into the mold under pressure. Another version of the original is thus created and can be used to work on as before, the decoration on the wax being modified until ultimately the metal master is exactly right—sometimes the wax may go to and fro in this way two or three times. From the initial idea to the production of a master ring may well take over two weeks in a small-sized factory, if the ring is a large or complicated one. More often, it takes seven to ten days.

For commercial mass production, as opposed to small scale batch work, a rubber mold is prepared from the master, which is carefully kept. The rubber mold can then be used a great many times before it wears out. In use, the wax is inserted into the mold under pressure and allowed to set, the mold is then opened and the wax taken out and mounted on a tree. This process can be done many times so that for economy a tree can be built up containing fifty, or hundreds of rings which will be cast simultaneously when the molten metal is poured.

These may all be the same pattern or of different patterns: the rough rings are then sent to be hallmarked and when they are returned they are cleaned up and polished. Stones may then be put in by craftsmen. An ordinary small manufacturer may produce two or three ranges of new jewelry every year, each range consisting of 12–18 rings. Machines have increased productivity, but made production less personal.

Enamels

As with most other jewelry techniques the principles and methods of creating enamels are the same today as centuries ago, except that to create the high temperatures required gas and electric kilns (which jewelers call "muffles") with accurate controls are now used instead of charcoal braziers. Enamel is formed from high quality flint glass, colored by metal oxides or salts, today it is usually bought in powder form, otherwise, if it is in a lump or cake, it has to be ground to the consistency of sand with a pestle and mortar. The powder is washed first in nitric acid, then in several changes of water. It is applied as a paste while still damp and completely dried in the warmth near the muffle. Slowly it is put into the muffle which is already at full working temperature. Most enamels melt at about 700° Celsius; and 900° to 950° or 1,000° for hard enamel, are normal settings for a muffle. As soon as the enamel melts into a mass the object is removed quickly, and cooled gradually, lying on or by the muffle. Its surface can be finally smoothed by rubbing with a fine carborundum stone and water, or a charcoal block and water, or with mops coated with

"tripoli" or putty powder. The enamel can be refired and, to avoid cracking, it may be applied on the back as well as the front of the object, so that there is an equal tension on both sides when they cool—called counter-enameling.

All crafts are the fruit of long experience, but none more so than enameling. There are many snags for which the only remedy is experiment. On impure metal, the enamel color will be dramatically affected, for instance, by copper oxide released on the firing. All enamels change color when heated and, if over-heated, they may get bubbly or streaky. Any impurity may cause unexpected chemical reactions, the most frustrating being a failure of the enamel to adhere. If the metal beneath is soft or has an uneven surface, for instance because it is cast, the enamel may not take. Metal expands and contracts under heat and cold more quickly than enamel, a permanent cause of disequilibrium.

Champlevé enamel is applied into a carved recess or, as literally translated, "raised field," and reached its climax in European medieval work in the 14th century. Basse taille is transparent champlevé with the field beneath the enamel of varying depth, and sometimes patterned too, especially refined in the 15th century. En ronde bosse is simply the coloring of modeled figures. It was the courts of Burgundy and of Paris which brought into being the beautiful technique of "enamels in the round:" a modeled piece of metal was dipped into enamel, the details were enameled separately, the whole achieved astonishing pictorial vividness in tiny pendant

Center of a Burgundian brooch, *c* 1420, in *en ronde bosse* enamel. The central figure is about 250mm (1in) high. This sophisticated technique was popular in France and Burgundy in the 14th–16th centuries, and hardly used at any other period. As each color requires a separate firing, and enamel when liquid tends to flow off a curved surface, the difficulties are extreme.

jewels often with religious scenes. Enameled pictures became ever more sophisticated—the French renaissance idea "émail en résille sur verre" was the ultimate. Renaissance enamels sometimes looked almost like paintings with a special glow. Plique à jour is transparent, the enamel appearing between the strands of a sort of metal cobweb. Painted enamel is like a picture, with many colors brushed and shaded, barely separated from each other, popular in 16th-century Limoges. The Verdun school and the Mosan school and early Limoges pieces, all of the early middle ages, concentrated on boxes and tableware, and hardly impinged on jewels.

Niello

Niello is a sulfide of silver (two parts) copper (one part) and lead (three parts) giving a metallic gray color, used rather like enamel. The three metals are melted into flowers of sulfur, cooled on a cold steel slab, ground like enamel, mixed with thin borax or sal-ammoniac, laid into or on to the prepared area, heated over a blow pipe or bunsen burner (not overheated or they eat into the back-ground) then cooled and polished.

Being metallic, the surface can be burnished and pinholes in it closed, a convenience which is impossible with enamel, and which explains the fine smooth finish of so much niello. Thailand is the world's great source of niello; every jeweler in Bangkok knows its secret, every tourist there finds it the ideal souvenir.

Lapidary work

Another craft skill is that of stone cutting and polishing, or lapidary work. This still presents a surprisingly ancient appearance, although now mechanized. The truth is, that the minute scale of jewelry detaches it from the normal clamor and regimentation of factory life. The main European colored stone center, Idar-Oberstein, south of Frankfurt, is the home of hundreds of stone cutting and dealing firms, many of them hundreds of years old. Idar has been famous for its agates since the dark ages, and one can still see huge water wheels with gears, to cause a small polishing wheel to spin with the

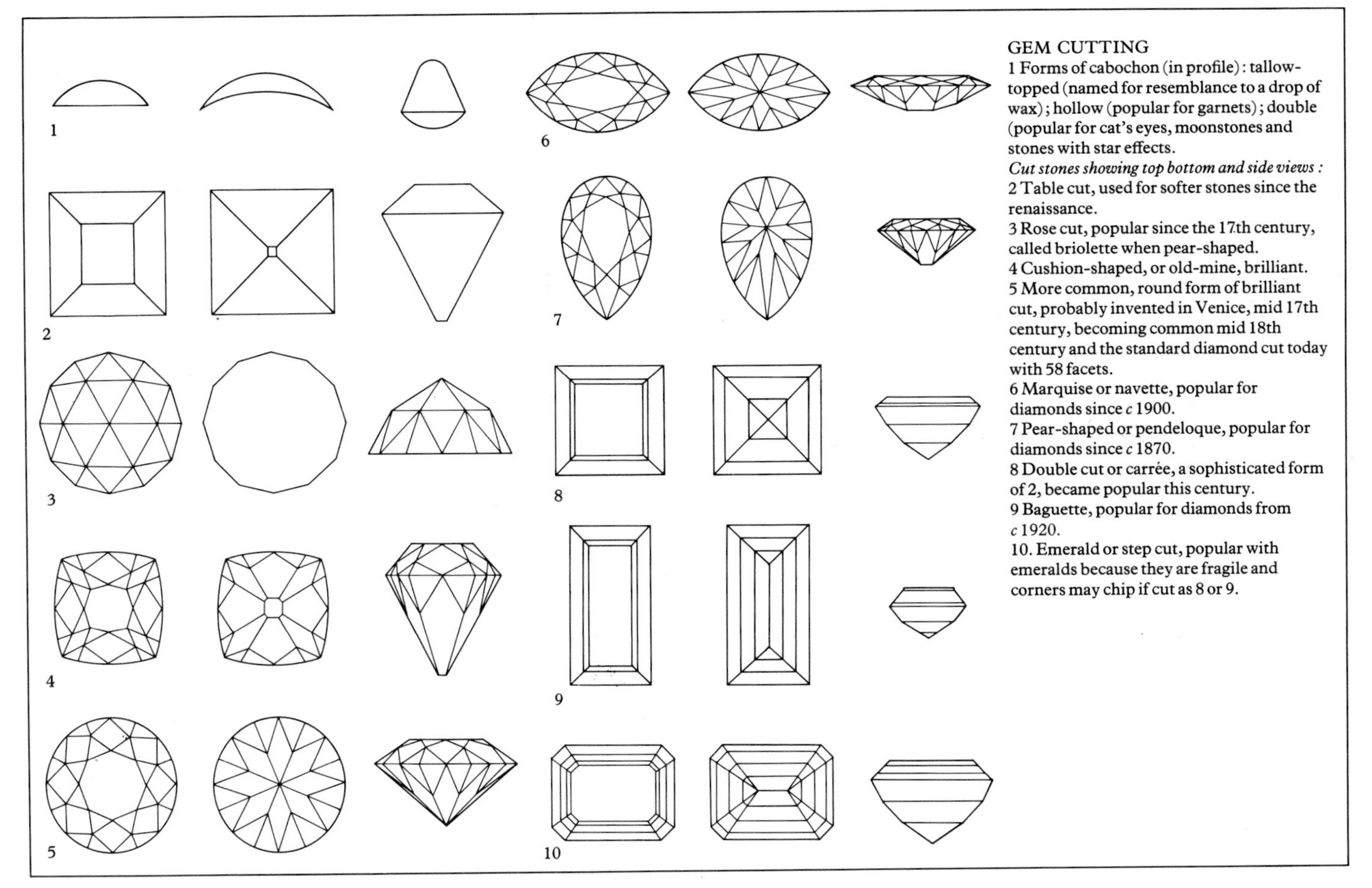

GEM CUTTING
1 Forms of cabochon (in profile): tallow-topped (named for resemblance to a drop of wax); hollow (popular for garnets); double (popular for cat's eyes, moonstones and stones with star effects.
Cut stones showing top bottom and side views:
2 Table cut, used for softer stones since the renaissance.
3 Rose cut, popular since the 17th century, called briolette when pear-shaped.
4 Cushion-shaped, or old-mine, brilliant.
5 More common, round form of brilliant cut, probably invented in Venice, mid 17th century, becoming common mid 18th century and the standard diamond cut today with 58 facets.
6 Marquise or navette, popular for diamonds since *c* 1900.
7 Pear-shaped or pendeloque, popular for diamonds since *c* 1870.
8 Double cut or carrée, a sophisticated form of 2, became popular this century.
9 Baguette, popular for diamonds from *c* 1920.
10. Emerald or step cut, popular with emeralds because they are fragile and corners may chip if cut as 8 or 9.

necessary force and speed. But nobody walking through Idar today would imagine it to be a factory center. It has the air of a small country town, with small, three- or four-story office blocks. Only inside do you realize that each one is like a human ant-heap, with six or eight people in each room sorting or polishing or buying or selling stones.

Stones are split down the grain of the crystal with a cleaver, a sort of axe, like a wood chopper, and cut by rotating disks edged with diamond dust. To hold a stone for polishing it is fixed upon the dop, the craft word for a wad of sticky lacquer on the end of a stick, or the arm of a mechanical device somewhat reminiscent of a gramophone; this holds the stone while it is pressed against the polishing wheel.

Diamonds are so hard that they require extreme skill if they are to be cleaved and many jewelers now prefer to use extremely thin disks for cutting all except very large stones.

The parts of the cut stone and its setting all have their technical names. The girdle is the outside rim of the stone, the table, the flat upper surface which, when held close to the eye, will show the stone's luster, by the vividness with which it will reflect on its surface the filament of a distant light bulb. The crown is the upper portion of the stone above the girdle, the pavilion the lower part, the culot is the bottom point. The bezel is the central upper part of a ring, in contrast to the shank or handle which goes round the finger. The collet is the rim of metal by which stones were held in position before the invention of claw settings. Bort is bad quality diamond. A carat is a measure of quality in metal, 24 carat meaning 100% pure; whereas for stones carat is a simple unit of weight.

Stone cutting and mounting

Dating and placing jewels by their stones, is not easy. For instance, in the 17th century, most of Europe's gold and emeralds came from the Spanish conquests in Mexico and South America. But this does not mean that all jewels made of emerald and gold, were made in Spain, for the simple reason that the Spaniards exported these valuable materials everywhere. Big emeralds and heavy gold do however suggest 17th- and early 18th-century origin, because that was the period when this form of bullion from the New World was most common. Throughout the span of the 18th century and most of the 19th, the cult of the precious stone continued unabated and the variety of available stones increased. Stones gradually replaced enamel as a source of color. Cutting became ever more precise and a glimpse through a loupe will often differentiate the irregular 17th-century art from the classical symmetry of a hundred years later. Better cutting and polishing made the stones more rivetting to the eye, so settings became more sparse as the 18th century progressed. In the 17th century silver settings had become increasingly popular, probably because, being lighter in color, they made a more delicate impression. But silver backs leave a black mark on the skin or on the clothes of the wearer, so, a few generations after the rise of silver, a further refinement was introduced: gold backs fixed to silver fronts. The backs were always solid, often with a layer of colored or silver foil between the back of the stone and the metal, to give a mirror-bright effect. Today, water or damp have often penetrated on to this reflective surface, darkening or streaking it so that the jewel no longer gives its original effect. Diamonds, when the foil is dirty behind them, appear to be an exciting black color.

Then about 1780, came another milestone in the march towards more brilliance: the backs, whilst still made of gold, began to be open instead of closed. Thus the stone could pick up light from behind as well as from the front, and the use of colored foil became unnecessary: all the color now came from the stone itself. About 1840 came the ultimate in nakedness: the claw setting. Not much used since Ottonian times 1,000 years before, and rare since the big bishops' rings of the 14th century, this means of letting as much light as possible reach all facets of the stone again became customary and has remained so ever since.

ANCIENT JEWELS

Left. Duck pendants, amulets and weights, showing different degrees of stylization. The more lifelike the sculpture the later the piece. Used as jewels and to weigh valuables (probably gold) they usually measure only 10–20mm ($\frac{3}{8}$ to $\frac{3}{4}$in) and are common finds from the 2nd and 3rd millenia BC throughout Mesopotamia. *Center:* Sumerian, steatite, *c*2500 BC; *bottom:* Sumerian, red and white striped agate *c*2500 BC: *left:* Old Babylonian, hematite (a metallic, heavy stone favored by Babylonians) *c*1000 BC; *top and right:* Assyrian, chalcedony *c*800 BC.

Right. A group of Assyrian stamp seals in chalcedony and one in red jasper showing kings and altars and made about 700 BC. Although similar in style, each was nevertheless unique and functioned as a signature, a security key, a talisman, a beautiful pendant jewel, a personal token or even as money.

The earliest jewels were probably seals, lumps of colored stone engraved with more or less personal symbols. Sometimes they showed a scene of devotion: a king bringing a tribute to a priest, for instance, with an altar between them—there are many thousands of survivals of this theme—and they often have signs, such as a tiny fish or bird, to show who the owner was. There are more primitive seals carved with simple zig-zag or geometric devices which are also very common and must have been difficult to distinguish one from another. Gradually, however, the character of the seal became clearer and designs became more varied with engravings, for instance, of recognizable animals and people, often with their names as well. Seals were the signature of the owner, before the invention of writing, a function that has lasted to the present. The earliest seals were rolled or stamped on to clay to confirm authenticity or to secure property against opening. Because they were used by kings and governors they became associated with the glory of their owners and later became tokens of exchange, precursors of the first coins, and they acquired a magic value as amulets. Perhaps their most modern use of all was to impress a trade-mark, as on pottery before firing. Many early pots with marks rolled into them have survived.

How were these tiny miracles of sculpture fabricated? Metal was used to carve them from the 4th millennium BC and must have provided the main cutting edge, supplemented by hard stone powder as abrasives. From the old Babylonian period, circles began to appear which indicate instruments with a circular cutting edge. The basis of design on many seals is simply a series of drilled holes, subsequently joined by shallower lines. There is scant surviving evidence about technique: probably the tools were rudimentary.

It is often difficult to tell where and when seals were made, as they are the easiest of all archaeological objects to excavate illegally, and many are in private collections with no provenance. The earliest seals were probably made in Anatolia in the shape of a conical stamp with a hole through the shortest section of the top. In Mesopotamia, before the invention of writing (*c* 3300 BC) the cylinder form was preferred, perhaps because, when rolled over clay, it could cover more area than a stamp. The image on a cylinder was engraved round the side whereas the identity of a stamp is underneath.

Cylinders soon achieved their standard form, being bored not through the short upper section but down the middle. They could then easily be rolled over soft clay surfaces to close storage jars or to authenticate letters and lists. Both stamps and cylinders were popular together throughout the Near and Middle East. In Egypt, probably because documents were written on papyrus not on clay, stamps were preferred to cylinders (which are difficult to roll on paper); in Greece and Crete also, stamps were preferred, a taste which shows in their love of medallic art, and, later, of coin design. Cylinder seals rolled over large areas of clay more effectively than stamps. But as clay was slowly displaced by the more modern writing materials leather or papyrus, so the stamp was again introduced, eventually and finally displacing the cylinder.

Often there is no clear distinction between seals of succeeding empires. But script is sometimes an obvious clue: cuneiform for the Sumerians, Aramaic for later Assyria and new Babylon, starting about 1000 BC. The 5th-century royal seal of the Persian king Darius in the British Museum has the king's name and title in cuneiform with, exceptionally, three languages—Old Persian, Babylonian and Elamite, the three official languages of the Persian Empire, as on the rock face at Behistun where they made possible the decipherment of cuneiform after 1837.

Such seals are charged with feeling. Holding one in the hand, you know that it has been of extreme importance to someone, probably to several generations of people, thousands of years ago. Artistically, seals represent some of the first and finest gropings of the human race towards systematic representational art, but little is known about them.

To recognize an old seal is mostly common-sense. The stones preferred were nearly always hard. Holes nearly always go right through, so that the seal could be worn as a pendant, and the holes are nearly always crooked—it must have been almost impossible to drill right through a hard stone with primitive equipment, and quite impossible to drill it with geometric precision. The engraving has a lively, spirited quality. Fakes can be spotted because they are usually too perfect, their designs are usually meaningless when rolled or stamped on to clay or plasticine, and, if they have a meaning, they are usually badly spaced. And most fakes are in soft stone. Cut a seal with a penknife: if you scratch the stone, it may be new. Good fakes are rare: the price of antique seals does not yet provide a sufficient incentive, but it is rising and fakes will improve, although few people have the skill and patience to make a fake seal: any jeweler who has tried to carve agate, even with modern equipment, will tell you that the job is almost beyond human endurance—hardly an attraction for a slipshod faker who is trying to make easy money.

Although the most easily obtainable today, stones were not the only jewels of these early times. Metal may have been more popular than stone. The few untouched prehistoric finds in Mesopotamia have been rich in gold. At Ur, Sir Leonard Woolley found enormously sophisticated jewels, including all sorts of gold rings, necklaces, ribbons and earrings dating from about 2450 BC. Two thousand years later, Greek writers were amazed by the wealth of the Persian empire and when Alexander the Great captured the royal treasure of King Darius 7,000 pack animals were needed to carry it. Some of this gold and silver was probably inherited from prehistoric times: certainly the taste for bullion would not have sprung into being spontaneously with recorded history. The fact that more stone than precious metal has survived may reflect, not the balance of prehistoric jewelry, but the diligence of robbers in their search for gold.

Even more misleading may be the remains of the Indus Valley civilization, discovered only in the past half century. Sir Mortimer Wheeler led teams to Mohenjo Daro and Harappa in Pakistan, amongst the world's earliest brick-built cities, but he recovered tantalisingly few jewels from them.

Above. The simple shapes and natural forms of ancient agate stones have aesthetic as well as antiquarian appeal.

Right. Cylinder seals, Persian Achaemenid dynasty *c* 600 BC. Persian seals were more naturalistic and more deeply and accurately carved than earlier ones; they often pictured rural scenes rather than the earlier religious rituals. *Back :* Agate steatite and jasper; *front :* carnelian, favorite stones in Mesopotamia at this time.

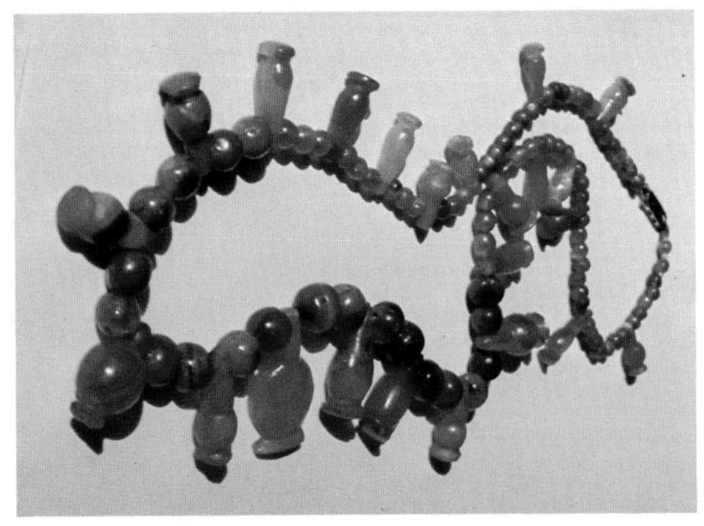

Above. A carnelian necklace in the form of seed pods, made during the Egyptian eighteenth dynasty. Later Egyptian jewels were less gorgeous than the early gold and enamels, but more wearable. They were possibly made more for the living than the funeral goods familiar from tombs like that of Tutenkhamun (*c* 1350 BC) which consumed so great a part of the craftsmen's finest skill and effort.

Top. An Egyptian fresco of 1400 BC, found at Thebes, shows gold from Nubia being presented in tribute.

The beads and dice and clay pots stand beside only a few particles of gold. It is the same at Ban Cheng, the newest "oldest" culture, unearthed during the past decade in northern Thailand: beautiful beads, almost no metal. Thieves, like jewelers, love gold and silver and find it easy to sell, often, tragically, after melting it down. Carved seals and beads conversely are difficult to recognize, and appeal only to a small and specialized market where stolen goods are immediately suspect.

Prehistoric Ireland is unique: no prehistoric buildings, no records, no seals or stones, no surviving mines, only gold. It is almost the opposite of Mesopotamia. It seems that this Irish gold must have been relatively common and popular, because pieces of the same alloy as that found in Ireland, and of similar design, have been found as far away as the river Rhine, and even the island of Cyprus. The earliest types of piece (*c* 2000 BC) were the twisted torcs, and the lunulae—flat crescent moon shapes elongated almost to a circle. A thousand years later, these two ideas merged into the gorget—again an incomplete circle, but now with parallel sides as for a torc, and hammered into a relief pattern of parallel grooves, and decorated with a spiral motif clearly descended from the torcs.

Throughout prehistoric jewelry, there is a startling resemblance between one area and another sometimes hundreds, sometimes thousands, of miles away. Jewelry must from the very beginning have been a useful means of barter and probably therefore traveled more widely than the kings and priests whom it so nobly adorned.

As prehistory merges into recorded fact, surviving jewels become rare. Those that have been found are of staggering modernity and technical perfection. These early jewelers' creations were full of wonder, like the great granulated diadem from Abdera in Thrace of *c* 200 BC in Berlin, the masks from Mycenae of *c* 1250 BC now in Athens, or the contemporary ornaments of Tutenkhamun's tomb, now in Cairo. In each culture, early work is semi-abstract, the later, almost fleshy and naturalistic.

The Egyptians were masters of color and in particular of the green-blue glass called faience. Their most characteristic product is the scarab, so well liked that Greeks and Etruscans (who admired the Egyptians) later used it too. They probably forgot the Egyptians' almost sacred attitude to the beetle, gained by his seemingly magic ability to blow his ball of excrement in front of him and to create new life from another ball—his egg—behind him.

Genuine Egyptian beads and scarabs, both of colored stone and faience, are still common today, but much outnumbered by modern fakes. The fakes can sometimes be detected because their glaze has a hard, uniform color—the product of modern temperature control—instead of the old soft patinas. Modern carving tends to be crude and insensitive whereas the original would be precise and delicate. An expert can often detect that modern hieroglyphs are meaningless. Modern work is usually in suspiciously good condition. The best indicator, as with all old jewels, is the general look and feel, an instinctive response which can be nurtured only by experience.

The Greeks' achievement in jewelry was less impressive than in the other arts. Their specialities were thinness and delicacy, probably because of their shortage of precious

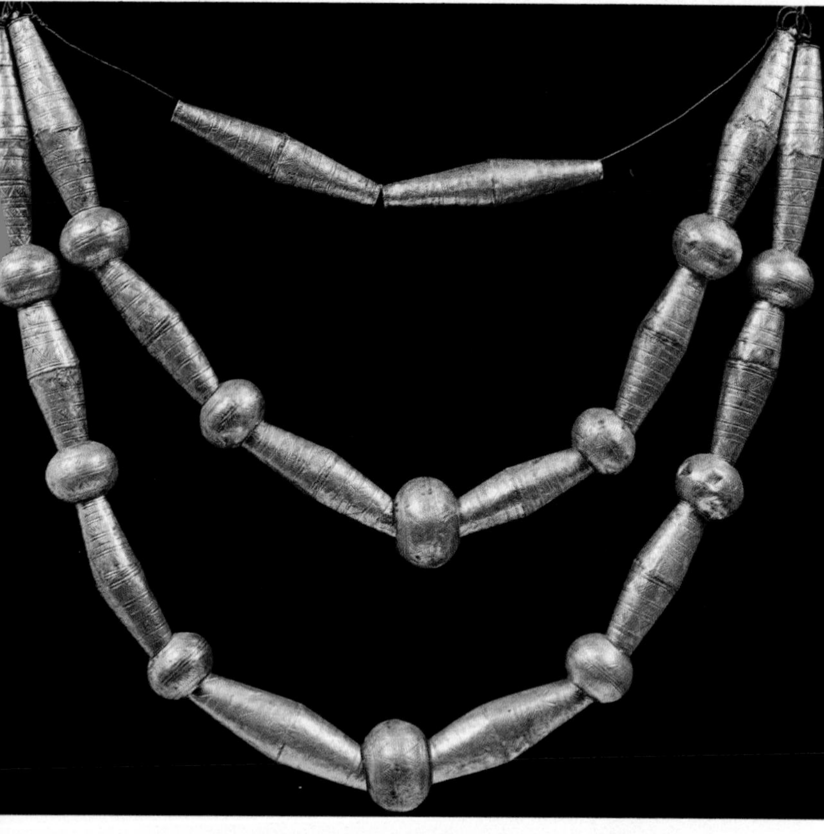

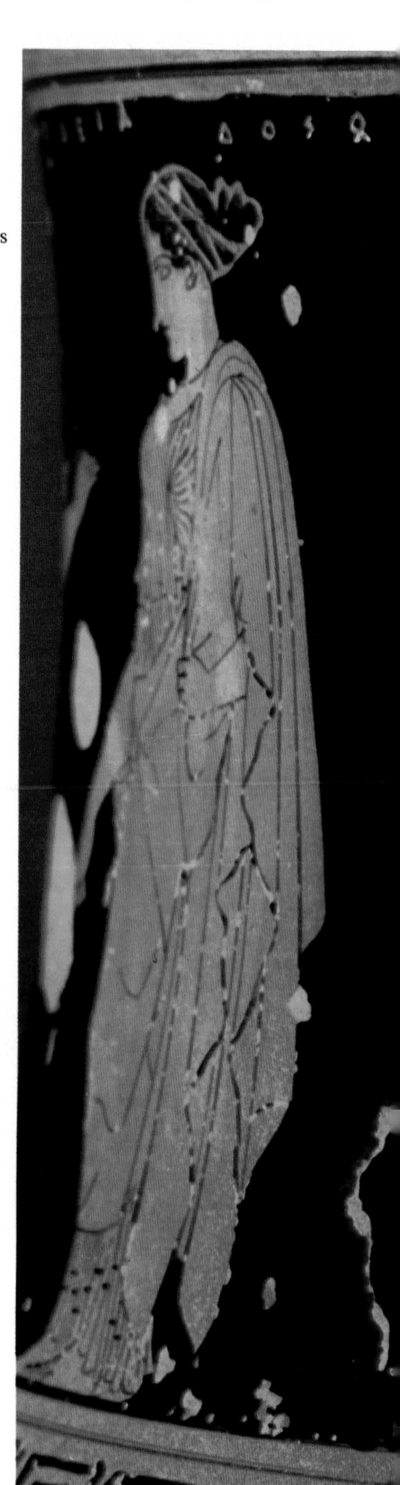

Left. Conical and spherical gold beads found at Larthia, decorated with incised designs. Early Etruscan jewels were normally much more imaginative, the abstract patterning here shows the approach of Roman logic, *c* 600 BC.

Bottom left. Classical Greek work was flimsy, almost fussy, perhaps because of shortage of gold. These earrings are all Hellenistic, *c* 300 BC, by which time the conquests of Alexander the Great had made more bullion available and the stable colonies he formed indulged in the luxury of jewels. The Greeks, unlike the Romans, liked hoop earrings with animal heads, often worn, surprisingly, upside-down. Here, with a solid Roman finger ring to indicate size, are Persian lion-head earrings with turquoise, another pair with ibis and emerald, a Greek pair from Macedonia with carved amethysts (*bottom*) and one from Anatolia with goats and enamel. Filigree spiral ornament especially suits the circular form.

Right. A woman at her toilet is dressed by her slave who is about to put her necklace on. Scene on a red-figure vase, *c* 400 BC. Early Greek women had scarcely more status than slaves themselves and consequently not much personal wealth. Large personal jewels became possible only with the decline of the ideal of the male hero. Since Greece was a comparatively poor country and her important dead of later times were burned not buried very few Greek jewels survive. More are known from the Greek colonies of South Italy where the people were more pleasure loving.

metals, and they loved diadems of all sorts, their form derived from the olive-leaf wreath. Greek athletes, gymnasts and victors of every kind were, at first, crowned with a wreath made of real olive leaves. Later came gold wreaths, later still, for example in Syracuse, prizes tended to be big gold coins. Gold funeral diadems, by a natural association of ideas, often resembled olive garlands, like the superb example of *c* 200 BC in Berlin's Antike Sammlung where olives are represented by emeralds, and where a bee, the coinage badge for Ephesus, forms the central glory. The Etruscans and, closely linked to them, the later Hellenistic Greeks, mastered filigree and granulation with a mature balance of form and ornament which is the wonder of all who see it. There were three innovations in style, about the time of Alexander the Great *c* 300 BC: tiny dangling cupid figures, the knot of Herakles and the cameo engraved in relief as opposed to the older recessed intaglio. In a cameo, the background is cut away; in the older intaglio process, which always remained more common, the design itself is engraved into the surround. Museums are well stocked with such pieces, but the collector will find scant reward so early, and will do best to look to the great riches of the Roman Empire.

Rome

The Romans may have been the first people in the history of the world to make precious jewels for the living, rather than the dead. Nobody can be sure. It is a fact that the finest jewels from ancient Egypt and Sumeria, from the Myceneans, the Greeks and the Etruscans, have all been found in tombs. But Roman jewelry has been found scattered everywhere, and most of it in private dwellings.

Roman jewels were for wearing and they are consequently

Left. A portrait of Augustus' sister Octavia as Artemis, carved in sardonyx. The Romans were the first great portraitists: the Greeks and earlier peoples made their rulers on coins and medals look like gods.

Right. Earrings form some of the most enterprising Roman designs: impressive geometrical rhythms are punctuated by colored stones from all over the empire. Today the most fruitful excavations for collectors are along the Mediterranean's east coast, especially in Syria and along the Golan heights, near the old centers of colored glass making—but academic archaeology is the loser because the finds are mostly unrecorded. This group made c AD 300 is set with lapis lazuli (*top right*) glass (*below*) and emerald (*left*). A solid finger ring is included for size.

hard and practical, big and tough. Earlier cultures may have produced jewels that were more delicate, more elaborate, more sophisticated, more inventive or more fine but Roman jewels are modern in the sense that they are nearly always fit for wear. Rome represented power and order, a direct and open attitude of mind, Roman jewels were the same. Heavy and simple, they appeal today in the same way as a Roman bridge or road.

Perhaps it was a shortage of the raw materials which caused the jewels of earlier empires to be light and fragile—in Rome there were no such inhibitions. Spanish silver and gold mines, Romanian, Thracian and Egyptian gold, even silver and tin from Britain, formed a huge and previously unobtainable mineral wealth. The piety of the Greeks—temple offerings at the great shrines like Dodona and Delphi—was usurped. Roman jewelers used thicker and heavier gold than anyone before, and a bigger variety of stones. The whole civilized world was theirs to draw upon and their jewels show the fruits of Roman material greed.

There was some Roman memorial jewelry—for instance, face masks were specially made for the dead in the eastern Mediterranean—but most surviving jewels were made for use and enjoyment. They have been preserved for us because they were accidentally dropped, trapped in the volcanic ash and mud which overwhelmed Pompeii and Herculaneum or, perhaps, were buried to save them from pillage by invading barbarians in the latter days of Empire. Most of them look worn, if not exhausted, and must have undergone a lifetime of service. But actual examples are not the only source of information about old jewels; we can learn a great deal from pictures and carved monuments. Here Roman evidence is clear and convincing—in Rome it is feminine jewels which come to the fore. Frescoes at Pompeii and in the Naples Museum, frescoes and mosaics at Catullus' villa at Sirmione, at Piazza Armerina in Sicily and in Tunis all show finely built women wearing noble armbands and bracelets, anklets and coronets—sometimes with very few clothes to distract.

Literature tells the same story. Petronius' crude *Satyricon* describes a dinner party: "Soon Fortunata took the bracelets from her great fat arms and showed them to the admiring Scintilla. Then she even undid her anklets and her gold hairnet, which she said was pure gold. Trimalchio had it all brought to him and said, 'A woman's chains, you see. This is the way us poor fools get robbed. She must have six and a half pounds on her. Still, I've got a bracelet myself, made up from the one-tenth per cent offered to Mercury—and it weighs not an ounce less than ten pounds.'"

Roman designs are easy to recognize because of their simplicity. Gone the intricacy of the Etruscans, the flimsiness of the Greeks, gone also the mystical animal carvings from Mesopotamian seals. Instead, each piece usually expresses only one idea, and surrounds that idea with space, much as a modern picture frame will contain a complex painting within a plain card surround, to concentrate attention on the incident inside, to rest the eye outside.

On a Roman snake bracelet, for example, and it is one of the commonest Roman types, the serpent heads at either end are separated not by an exotic, textured, twisting body, but by a simple flat band wound twice or thrice round the wrist, for ease of taking on and off. A similar clever device is the modern sailor's double sheet bend, resembling the immobile reef knot or knot of Herakles, but now tied so that it becomes a slip knot. These bracelets, like the snakes, must often have been removed. Society was so stable that temporarily changing for dinner became normal. Jewelry became fun for women, instead of what it had been—a ritual attempt by men to please a hostile deity.

There are almost no rings worn in Greek vase paintings before the 4th–3rd century BC; even after that they always remain a rarity in Greek painting. Etruscans and Sabines, unlike the Greeks, used rings as a badge of rank. So did the Romans, but the privilege of wearing a gold ring became steadily more general. Augustus granted it to physicians and, in AD 197, Septimius Severus granted it to all soldiers. Verres gave it to his private secretary. Until about the time of Christ, gold rings were a rare symbol of grandness: they became common only after the end of the Republic. This is why most surviving Roman gold rings can be dated to the 2nd or 3rd century AD. Before then stone seals were already in use, but were usually contained in iron rings. The iron has now perished, which explains why so many early Roman seal stones are unmounted today.

Finger rings, worn by men as much as by women and children, usually have a smooth shank and bezel, often framing an engraved stone, perhaps by now a picture of a real person instead of the earlier mythical animal or god. The favorite color for the stone seems to have been red—the translucent carnelian or, rarer, the opaque jasper—and, whenever stones were used, the metalworking seems to have been impeccable. When solid the rings are especially impressive; when filled with plaster stuffing the hollow gold or silver sheath is sometimes poorly rounded at the edges. Martial mentions a man who wore six rings on each finger, night and day, because he had no case for them; Lucian, a man in a dream wearing sixteen rings. Pliny records the Roman

Below. Roman finger rings were big, heavy and simple. The engraved stone seals are cut intaglio (recessed). Cameo (when the subject stands out in relief) was invented about 300 BC but did not become really popular until the 16th century. Stones were most frequently of the agate family. The rings *right* and *lowest center* are forged hollow and feel much lighter in weight; the more satisfying rings were cast in solid metal.

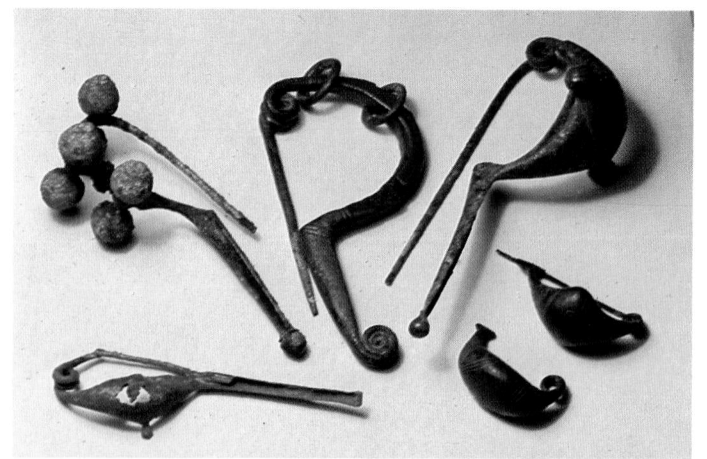

Left. A Roman belt buckle found at Homs, in Libya, made of bronze and inlaid with colored glass, *c* AD 200. Later Roman jewels have, as here, a very modern aspect.

Above. The most common ancient jewel is the fibula or safety pin, used in Greece, Etruria and Rome to clasp the cloak or other garments. The biggest of these is 152mm/6in long and they are all of *c* 650 BC. Etruscan bronze was as original as their gold. The design is practical, but the purpose of the two small rings on the bow (*center top*) is not known: nor is it easy to wear such heavy bows so that the ornament stays uppermost, rather than hanging down.

custom of using a plain iron ring without a gem, to signify betrothal.

One romantic conception of the later Romans was however the engagement or betrothal ring. There is no evidence of the Greeks using them, and Pliny in his *Natural History* (AD 77) mentions only iron for the purpose. Gold rings used in some sort of promissory way, succeeded iron in the 2nd and 3rd century AD. Isidorus of Seville writing as late as the 7th century AD says that women only used rings sent by their lover at betrothal, and seldom wore more than two rings. Sometimes portraits of a man and woman appeared on one ring, sometimes there was a pithy inscription such as "PARUM TE AMO" "I love thee too little" (British Museum). Before the Romans, rings were used mostly for seals.

Earrings are the most inventive Roman creations. They are built round a myriad of variations on the basic Roman vocabulary of cones and tubes, balls and pods and shields and hearts, and they seldom repeat themselves. By modern European standards they are heavy, because they always leave room for a balanced proportion between the decorative device and its frame. But the loop to go through the ear is thinner than with Greek or earlier pieces: perhaps Roman ladies, like their modern counterparts, liked to change their earrings, not to wear the same pair all their lives.

Another speciality, was the safety pin. This evolved from the big ornamental fibula of earlier times. A pair of bronze fibulae from Boeotia, of *c* 700 BC, now in Berlin, measures no less than 216mm (8½in) across. By Roman times, the safety pin, whether of the crossbow type or of the more modern design with parallel wires and a nub at either end, seldom measured more than 64mm (2½in) overall. It evolved into the pierced ring or penannular brooch, then the round brooch of the barbarian migrating tribes. For the Romans, however, pins seem to have been more for joining than for decorating. Hinges (possibly a Roman invention) replace the earlier springs, and the silhouette becomes a steady, graceful curve instead of the huge rectangles and circles of the earlier Greeks, Villanovans and Etruscans. It is down the spine of this curve that Romans showed the discipline of their ornamental sense: herring-bone patterns, rhythms of squares and dots, or perhaps a continuous torque. In such ways, both in bronze and in gold, was fantasy married to form.

There was an evolution through the 600 years of the Roman period: a gradual softening of the sharp details of previous cultures until, by the time of Augustus, there was sometimes no ornament at all; the intricacies of Greece, Egypt and Etruria, were eliminated in favor of Roman efficiency. But, as the empire expanded, so the influence of the surrounding tribes became more felt. The animal-centered cultures of the barbarian nomads to the north and the Celts, who were squeezed ever further west, liked organic curves. Then there was the wild life from North Africa, source of the Romans' favorite sports in arena, amphitheatre and hippodrome. Birds and beasts began to appear on Roman jewels, as well as in their mosaics, influenced no doubt by travelers from the imperial outposts. Christian crosses, fishes and haloes move westwards from the land of Christ, becoming common in Syria and through the Byzantine empire from the 4th century AD. Enamel and colored stones became commoner too. East again, the Egyptians under the Ptolemies made their rulers look like rather fleshy saints, and the fetish jewels of such semi-Christian sects as the Gnostics fitted human features on to a semi-animal form. The plain vision of the Romans was ready for an organic injection.

BARBARIAN MYSTERIES

The Romans disliked and feared the "barbarians" outside their empire. These tribes were a direct military threat to Rome's security and, equally dangerous, a philosophical question mark hanging over the Roman ideals of law and order. So the Romans probably tried to blacken their adversaries' reputation but, as the tribes lived almost entirely by word of mouth, the Roman records are our main surviving explanation of the sense of wonder and awe, of passionate vitality, which suddenly transforms European jewels. The Spanish Christian Orosius, for instance, described why so many iron-age weapon and jewel finds in Denmark are badly damaged: "After a Germanic victory over the Romans, clothes were rent asunder, gold and silver thrown into the river, the armor of the warriors broken up, harness torn to bits, the horses themselves thrown into pits, the captives hanged by the neck from trees; there was no more booty for the victors than there was mercy for the vanquished." Posidonius wrote of Celtic head-hunting in 2nd-century-BC Gaul: "When they depart from the battle they hang the heads of their enemies from the necks of their horses, and when they have brought them home, nail the spectacle to the entrance of their houses." Livy, Strabo and Diodorus Siculus refer to the Celts embalming their chief enemies' heads in cedar oil, covering skulls with gold and using them to drink from.

This is the time of myths and mysteries, of human union with the elements, with earth and nature, with the Great Spirit. Imaginary leprechauns and fairies unite with powerful gods like Odin and Thor, the shape of whose hammer is

Above. Viking rings, silver, dating from the 9th century.

Right. The powerful vision of the barbarian tribes "loosened" the heavy Roman style within the Roman empire and helped to form Byzantine work although the latter was Christian and the tribes were inspired by nature. The greatest of all the barbarian hoards of buried treasure to have been discovered is now in the Bucharest Museum. Found by peasants at Petrossa in 1837, it had been buried during the fourth century AD. The finders stole many of the stones, including some from this pair of large brooches (240mm/9½in long) in the form of magic birds.

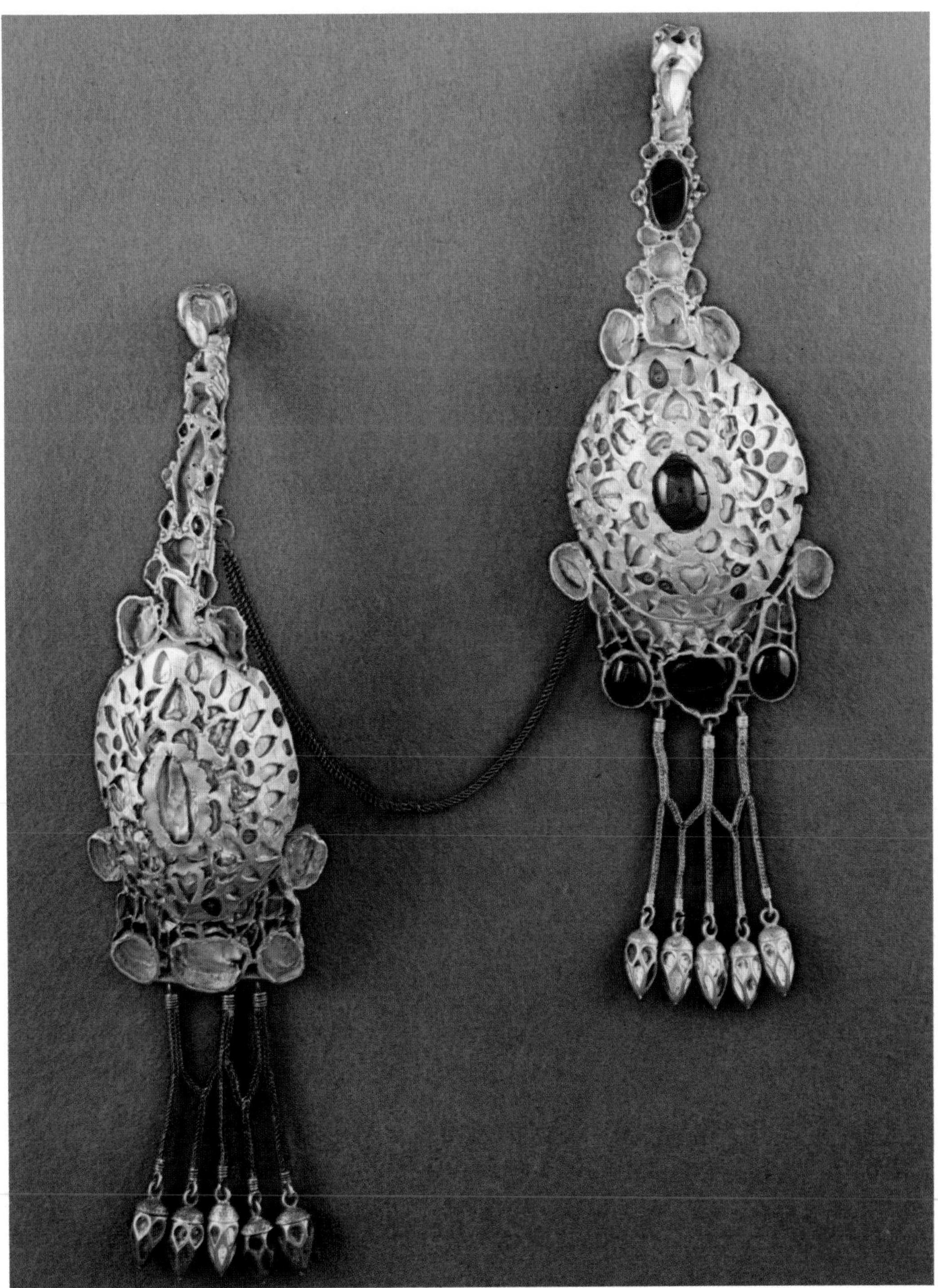

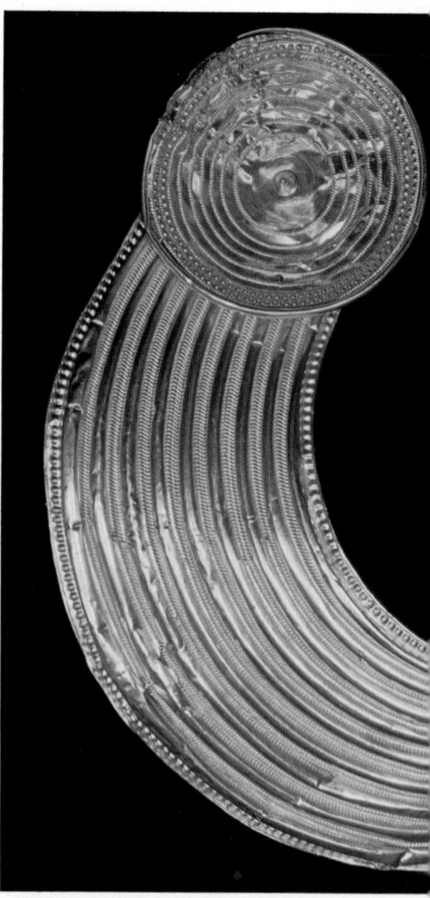

Above. The Tara brooch, made in Ireland in the 8th century. The outer ring is gold, the spandrel silver perforated on copper, resembling niello (which did not reach Ireland until about the 12th century). The remotest people achieved the most astonishing results. Ireland produced wonderful gold from prehistoric times (*c*2500 BC) until the triumphs of Christian times such as the Ardagh chalice made about AD 1100. This brooch represents the imagination of the Celtic people undisciplined by the Romans, who never conquered Ireland. The fibula, or safety pin, of the Romans became first a penannular brooch with an aperture for the pin, then, as here, a ring brooch, with a continuous ring and a sliding pin, then, in the middle ages, a round brooch with solid front and back.

Right. A late 6th-century bow brooch with an oval foot and radiate head. Probably Lombardic, it was discovered at Cividale, on the border of northern Italy, and is one of a distinctive group of brooches found in southern Germany and Italy.

supposed to have inspired much Scandinavian jewelry. Myth turns into reality with the discovery of grave treasure: such as Europe's greatest find at Sutton Hoo in England (now in the British Museum), or the most imaginative of all the hoards, from Petrossa in Rumania now in the Bucharest Museum. Jewels are the chief surviving testimony to a nomadic age, and they are fabulous in every sense.

We tend to underrate our forebears. From the 4th to the 12th century, trade was much more widespread than we imagine. For instance one style of Scandinavian jewelry, the so-called "gripping beast" from Bøorre, has been found in the Gnezdevo cemetery near Smolensk in Russia, and in barrows to the south of Lake Ladoga, as well as in Ireland, the Isle of Man and England. Arab coins from the East, raw material ready for melting and use, were in the 10th century AD silver hoard found at Bjorko in Sweden. Gold jewels of the same alloy as that common in Ireland went as far afield as the Rhine basin and Cyprus in the eastern Mediterranean. The Kingston brooch in Liverpool and St Cuthbert's cross in Durham are both inlaid with oriental white shell.

People went with trade. One can summarize the whole thousand-year period as the spread of the Celtic culture which had survived round the edge of the Roman Empire; its flowering all over Europe; and then its decay in the face of Christianity, which itself had survived in the west of Ireland, in Iona and in Northumbria. The Celts were a group of tribes first known in central Europe and the Rhineland about 1000 BC. They wandered from South Germany and Bohemia as far as Spain perhaps as early as 450 BC. Another tribe crossed the Alps to the Po valley, reaching Rome and even Sicily. Others went east to Macedonia, Thrace and Thessaly, plundering the temples at Delphi. They were prominent as mercenary soldiers in the 3rd-century-BC Greek wars. They reached Asia Minor and settled there in Galatia. The Belgae moved northwards and westwards. The earliest Celtic survivals can be traced between about 800 and 400 BC at Hallstatt in Austria, the salt

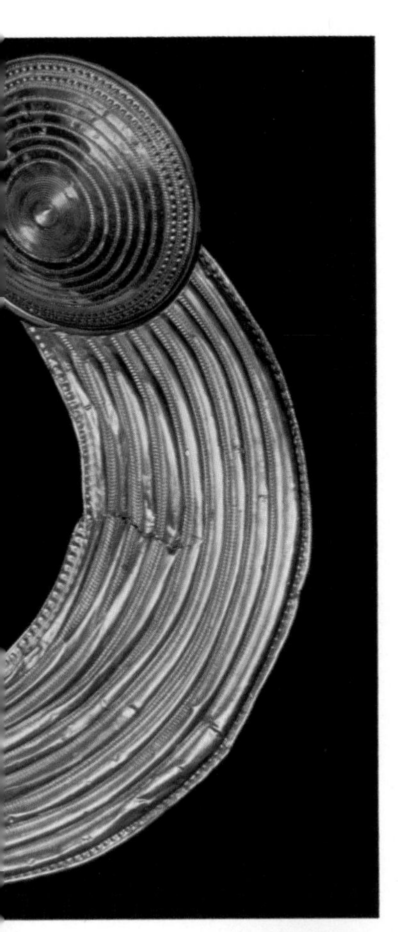

Left. A gold torc, boldly decorated with repoussé work, made in Ireland in the 7th century BC.

Below, center. A gold collar from Alleberg, Västergotland, *c*800, decorated with twisted gold wire which has been shaped into back-turned and couchant animals. This is one of a series of fine collars from central and southern Sweden, many of them found on the rich merchant island of Gotland.

Below. A 6th century Visigoth eagle brooch of gilded bronze and garnet, believed to come from Calatayud near Saragossa, Spain. Similar brooches, attributed to the Ostrogoths, have been found in Italy. Each of the great migrating tribes, such as the Franks or the Alemanni, had their own favored style, most of them seemingly intended to placate animals or natural forces.

and iron mining center where some of the best iron pins were found. The next Celtic outburst is known as La Tène from a village in Switzerland, and it is the style of metalwork there which pervaded Europe, and especially Britain and Ireland, for the next thousand years. The animal style, whose greatest expression was its first, by the Scythian tribes of Southwest Russia in the 5th century BC, spread everywhere with the Celts.

But that is only part of the story. Other tribes came westwards from the Russian plains, pushed perhaps by Huns' agitations around the Gobi desert, and each tribe settled in its own huge area, creating there a specific local jewelry flavor.

Frankish jewels feature wonderful bird brooches, all similar but each with its own favorite details; Burgundian and Alemannic iron buckles have silver inlay of endlessly intricate lines; Merovingian treasures, more dynastic than tribal, lovely T-shaped brooches with fleshy, embossed lozenges all over and strange fan-shaped tops surmounted by a radiating row of balusters; while the Visigoths produced colored geometric inlay work, close to Roman glass, and the jewelry of the Ostrogoths, the Angles, Saxons and Jutes all have elements which mark them from their neighbors.

Gold—often treated in a Byzantine manner, with wire cloisons enclosing areas of different color, either stone or enamel, becomes less common, gilt brass more so, usually decorated in the champlevé manner, as in the Romanesque enamels from Limoges and the Meuse valley (perhaps surface gold supplies and gold coinage were becoming scarcer as society became more nomadic), until the modern nations of Europe began to take shape around AD 1000. Bronze may have become commoner in the north for another reason: it was wanted less in the south. The iron age had arrived in Italy about 800 BC, and weapons thenceforth were made increasingly of iron, releasing bronze for export: the age of iron did not arrive in Scandinavia until perhaps 400 BC and, during the few centuries before, bronze Scandinavian jewels for women achieved unprecedented size and weight. But analytical and geographical evidence are still very spasmodic and erratic. This is the period of the senses, not the intellect: its jewelry is numinous and instinctive.

Viking jewels were one of the most long-lasting groups, and the Vikings seem to have absorbed little art from their subject peoples until Christianity reached them. With the new religion came the new romanesque imagery, coupled with the Christian church's prohibition of the burial of treasure and jewels with the dead. It is possible to trace a sequence of Viking styles with finds at Børre (a single animal hugging itself, perhaps AD 850–1000), then Jelling (a long thin animal with double body covered by interlacing), then Mammen (vegetable tendrils, contorting and endlessly entwining, reminiscent of contemporary Winchester England and Ottonian Germany, 980–1060), Ringerike (long, thin tendrils and snakes, no animals) and Urnes (unrecognizable organic abstractions 1040–1130). There is a great collection of them at Visby Museum in Gotland. But categories are helpful only for cataloguing, not for understanding.

The real message is the power and urgency of nature. Animals devour each other, chase and entwine themselves. Slowly over the centuries, animals give way to plants; perhaps as the travelers became farmers they wanted their jewels to express the joy of growth more than the glory of the hunt. The excitement of war and movement yields to peace.

The accompanying evolution in metal is from the fibula or large safety pin, popular up till about the 9th century, through the pennanular or ring brooch, which lasted until perhaps 1050, to the circular button-shaped brooch: all were, of course, used together, but there is a suggestion of a groping towards a sense of fashion—the fundamental human preference for change.

BYZANTINE COLOR

The whole period of the great migrations can be interpreted as the triumph of the curve: Celts and other tribes liked curves and disorder, whereas Romans preferred regularity. Taste in the Byzantine Empire, the eastern half of the Roman world, which survived the fall of Rome and lasted from the 5th century AD through to 1453, was betwixt and between.

Byzantine jewels have a glowing richness of color and a mystery which was hardly to be found under Rome. Their jewels, like their churches, consist of endless pierced arcades and interweavings with glowing, often irregular, stones, and often with a shape only hazily defined. The Byzantines liked hanging chains and—their great achievement—inlaid cloisonné enamels. But the really big change was brought by the Christian religion: Byzantine jewelry abounds in beautiful crosses, enameled saints, pictures of Christ, and all sorts of imagery, as impressive as it is familiar to our still Christian eyes. Whereas the Roman characteristics were mass and form, the Byzantines preferred their own kind of mystical intricacy: pierced surfaces (their spatial mosaic, called *opus interrasile*, was always cut by chisel not, as with modern fakes, by piercing fret saw), many-colored enamels, clusters of uncut, rounded stones, long dangling pendants both for earrings and pendants—all these suggest the slow-moving, hieratic quality of Byzantine city and court life.

Modern attempts to recreate the Byzantine style fail rather like American Camembert cheese: they are too clean, and therefore miss the essential flavor. No symmetry, no hard edges, no bright polish, no matching stones are some of the negatives overlooked by the copyists of the Plaka, Athens' antique quarter in the shadow of the Acropolis. Byzantine influence lives on today in the buildings and life of Russia and Greece. Byzantine art, like oriental, is almost ageless but, as Christians did not bury much jewelry with their dead, we know Byzantine styles not so much from their rare surviving gold as from their superb church mosaics. The great 6th-century emperor Justinian and his wife Theodora, gazing from the wall of San Vitale in Ravenna, are loaded down with jewels.

Far left. Christian crosses were very popular in Byzantine art. Here the uncut emerald is reminiscent of Roman work but the perforated, almost gothic, flowers for the pearls indicate a late date *c* 1000.

Left. A group of earrings, a brooch and a ring found in Syria. They are Byzantine work of the 5th–6th century. Chains, crosses and perforations and the enamel work all contribute to the richness of the style, contrasting with the simpler forms of Rome.

Below. Gold earring, delicately fretted with a design of birds and trees, Byzantine, 7th century.

Far left. A gold pendant inlaid with enamel, made 10th–11th century. Gold cloisons, or wires, separating the colours of the enamel (cloisonné) were a Byzantine speciality. Here the formality of Byzantium is already yielding to the human type of imagery of the middle ages.

Left. The Empress Theodora, who with her husband Justinian dominated the history of the Eastern Empire in the 6th century, depicted in a contemporary mosaic in the church of San Vitale, Ravenna.

PRECOLUMBIAN GOLD

Pre-Columbian gold has a history as spectacular as its appearance. Garcilaso de la Vega, writing 70 years after the event, describes how in Peru in 1532 "The Spaniards marched to Cajamarca and there in the Great Plaza first encountered the Inca and his nobles. The Inca [Atahualpa] was brought to the meeting place on a gold litter carried on the shoulders of his men. He was accompanied by members of the royal court, and was preceded by a military escort made up of four regiments of 8,000 men. The Inca's camp was three miles from the Plaza of Cajamarca where the Spaniards awaited him, but with all imperial pomp, the glittering procession took more than four hours to reach the square."

Captured by the Spaniards, the Inca promised a ransom of a room full of gold and, although the conquistadores failed to keep their part of the bargain, and Atahualpa was murdered, the ransom was collected. Its value has long intrigued investigators. It has been estimated at anywhere from a conservative $8 million to an exaggerated 19 million, flavored by legend, misrepresentation and fraud. Most of the gold was immediately melted down and divided. The portion sent intact to Spain as part of the fifth share which by law belonged to the King of Spain was melted there, the fate of almost all indigenous American goldwork until the 20th century. The Incas and Aztecs thought of gold not as money but as power. The Spaniards proved that it was both.

The oldest pre-Columbian American gold objects were made in the southern highlands of Peru from about 2000 BC; but a continuous artistic development can be traced only from the Chavin period, *c* 800 BC. The second area to go in for gold metallurgy was Colombia and the Isthmus states around Panama and Costa Rica; apparently, gold was used for making jewelry there from the early centuries AD.

In Panama and Costa Rica casting and embossing were more popular than sheet metal work. The main gold-making sites which have been identified were Cocle, about 800, and Veraguas, slightly later. In Colombia, the main sites are Quimbaya, Sinu, Tairona, Chibcha (Muisca). In Equador most of the gold came from the coast, the oldest sites apparently being at La Tolita. There the situation is typical: more treasure than knowledge, more variety than consistency. The few gold pieces have been outnumbered by thousands of ceramics. The gold was small, except for one spectacular find in 1912, when large gold discs, pectorals and head ornaments were discovered in a small clay chest containing the skeleton of a child. One could say that the history and legend of early American gold certainly exists: most of the hardware, however, still has to be found.

In Peru, casting was less popular than fashioning from annealed sheet gold—Peruvian pieces are rather flat-surfaced and linear, very stylized and often difficult to relate to a

Above. A masterpiece of Aztec jewelry—a pectoral in the form of a two-headed snake, made of wood encrusted with a delicate mosaic of turquoise with red coral and ivory. Such work is now extremely rare, probably because the wooden base would often have disintegrated and the stones have been reused.

Left. A Mochica gold cult mask in the form of a puma with two condors, perched upside-down on either side, symbolizing strength. This thin gold sheet was cold-hammered *c* 200–400 in the northern coastal area of Peru.

Right. Gold earrings in the form of a skull from which tiny bells are hung, Mixtec work from Monte Alban, *c* 1350. The Mixtecs were ancient Mexico's most skilful craftsmen. A big hoard of their work from Monte Alban (now in the museum at Oaxaca) has allowed detailed study of their technique, probably the most varied of precolumbian America.

Far right. A head carved in jade (*center*) made by the Olmec people of Mexico, *c* 300 BC, and two in granite from the Aztec culture at Vera Cruz, *c* AD 1200. Each is pierced so that it can be worn as a pendant. Despite their undoubted power as stylized sculpture, Mexican stone heads of all periods show a sinister preoccupation with death.

prototype in nature. Gold was used with silver, and with inlays of mussel shell, turquoise and sodalite, more in Peru than elsewhere. In the north only the Mochica culture seems to have mastered the casting traditions of Central America.

Almost all gold jewelry from Mexico, the area conquered by Cortes, was melted locally or marketed and dispersed when it arrived at Seville. Probably only half a dozen pieces survived and they cannot be identified. Jade and obsidian, in contrast, were of little interest to the European invaders, were often hidden underground, and are now being recovered. As so often, our knowledge of these jewels depends not upon what was worn by the living but upon what was buried with the dead, which may have been special ceremonial regalia, never intended for everyday wear. The Aztecs and their predecessors seem to have attached more importance to death than to everlasting life—their funerals were probably more gorgeous than the burials, furthermore their cities were often on swampy or rocky ground (Mexico City itself was constructed in the center of a lake) which made tomb construction difficult. Very little metal jewelry has been found since the booty removed by the Spaniards in the 16th and 17th centuries. The great exception is the gold treasure from the Monte Alban temples, now in the Oaxaca museum nearby, which suggests the savage fantasy which so thrilled the painter Dürer when he saw Mexican treasure being assembled in

Brussels for the Holy Roman Emperor Charles V.

Records and carvings on temples tell us of the Mexican love of decoration made from feathers, inherently fragile and perishable. Similar, but more durable, brightly colored work in turquoise, crystal and coral is powerfully represented by inlaid masks and decorations. However, frightening carved human heads in dark-toned stone, known from the Olmecs onwards, are much more common. They clearly show the sinister Mexican preoccupation with death, so different from South American jewelry's joyful representation of life, of animals and of useful objects. Massive, simple stone beads, often as much as 40mm (1½in) across, are common too: but we do not know how they were used. We cannot really know the ancient jewelry of this part of the New World because the greed of the Old World destroyed it.

The fate of South American gold was equally drastic at the time, but there personal treasure was buried in graves. Excavation has revealed wonderful deposits so that we have a clearer idea of what it was that intoxicated Pizarro in Peru than we have about the riches which were found by Cortes in Mexico, but it may be that the best South American pieces also perished.

Both the chronology and the quantity of the work found are mysterious, partly because much of the excavation is illegal, so that the gold treasures are removed without any proper record of their provenance. Because much of the work was cast it is

ideally suited for faking by modern casting. Prices for genuine pre-Columbian gold are very high, giving a great incentive for fraudulent copying. It is sensible to be suspicious of anything in really good condition, unless its source can be proved.

Even research into ancient metallurgy has been inconclusive. Gold seems often to have contained a platinum alloy of irregular proportion—about 2–30% with gold of about 50–80%. The metal seems to have been fabricated by sintering—fitting the alloys together till they are only partly fused. The Indians could not achieve temperatures high enough to melt platinum, so they must have mixed the grains with the gold, especially in Equador.

Below. The chronology of pre-Columbian work is still obscure but the style of the different areas, especially Peru, Columbia, Panama and Costa Rica, is clear, as is the preference for casting in Panama and Columbia and for forging sheet in Peru. This cast pair of frogs from Columbia were links in a necklace of *c*1400, the dog pendant was made in Panama *c*1200. Modern demand and interest in the history of the New World has caused prices to rise, giving fakers a strong incentive, and the accuracy of modern casting has made detection difficult, especially when the original was cast, not beaten.

Far left. Beaten gold from the Tolima area of Columbia, probably 14th-century work. These stylized human forms, which display the character of beaten gold, are related in shape to ceremonial knives. The central figure is horned and has flowers in its mouth. Solder was hardly ever used by this culture, probably because it was difficult to create sufficient heat in a small controlled flame, even though big kilns made expert castings.

Left. A gold disc from Ecuador. The stylized central figure combines the figure of a woman, whose breasts are indicated by raised dots, with that of a lizard, frog or a tree. It was probably a fertility amulet and made *c*13th–14th century.

ORIENTAL JEWELS

Probably the one thing that all Oriental jewels have in common is their unchanging nature. It takes a very keen eye indeed to know the difference between sacred jade discs of the Han and Chou dynasties, made in China at least 2,000 years ago, although there may be hundreds of years between them. A carved Chinese jade bracelet made in the T'ang dynasty about AD 600 can easily be confused with a similar elaborate roundel of the 17th-century Ming period. Wonderful dragons pursue their ferocious way across Chinese jewels, representing a sacred, stable order, trying to be the same as what went before. Only the foolhardy would claim to date Chinese jade jewels accurately.

In the great imperial treasury taken from Peking to Taipeh in Taiwan by Chiang Kai Shek, and now beautifully shown there, is a huge "first-rank concubine's winter crown" of the Ching dynasty (1644–1912), a light web-like fantasy of silver wire and bright blue kingfisher feather inlay. Nothing could be more different, in purpose or shape, from European taste. Hair ornaments like this were worn by men as well as women, and the kingfisher's flashing color gave them a unique panache. But jade (the word means "beautiful stone" in

Chinese) is commoner, better preserved (it is one of the toughest stones) and more typical of the Chinese; nobody else has ever had the patience to use it so much.

Dragons were associated with the emperor, the phoenix with the empress: hence perhaps their popularity. Round beads meant heaven, square the earth. A servant could not touch the emperor's hand, so the Pi, or sacred circle, made the connection. This beautiful symbol of fortune was often placed on dead bodies, sometimes together with rice, to secure their future.

Many of the Chinese habits were very practical: funeral pots had holes in the bottom to stop living people from using them. Special paper (*washi*) sheets were made to separate the embroidered layers of the dresses (*kimono*) whose fabric would otherwise stain from the metal thread. Purses were made specifically to hold Buddhist beads: there were jade knot-untiers, belt hooks and brush washers, as well as the more normal jewels—beads and pendants and archers' rings. One of the purposes of the exquisite, fragile ornaments which dangled from their girdles was to stop people moving about too quickly. Ancient Confucians would have been amazed at the unaesthetic, harrowing stampede of the rush hour crowds today in Paris or New York, London or Tokyo. The beauty of Chinese jade "created a standard of conduct to be followed by the ideal man."

Below left. A Chinese jade pi, or sacred disc, and an axe head, both Han dynasty, *c* AD 200; a sword guard, Sung dynasty, *c* 900 and two archer's rings, Ming dynasty *c* 1500. Chinese art is especially timeless and dignified. The larger pieces were buried with the dead, the pi sometimes under the back to help the body to fly to heaven.

Below. Japanese men did not wear jewelry as we know it but the inro (medicine container), netsuke (toggle by which the inro or other things could be suspended from the sash at the waist) and ojime (bead running on the cord which holds the inro secure when closed) were valued highly, exquisite to the touch as well as to the eye. The inro here has a black laquer ground which has faded slightly to a dark brown, decorated with gold, silver and red lacquer in low relief and with inlays of mother of pearl. It depicts Moso, the Chinese paragon of filial piety, who went out in the depth of winter to dig bamboo shoots for which his aged mother had expressed a strong desire.

The netsuke, carved in the form of a bamboo shoot, is of ivory inlaid with semi-transparent horn, *c* 1800. Netsuke were frequently in the shape of men, animals, and other natural objects.

The ojima is a piece of mother-of-pearl, drilled to take the cord.

Right. Traditional Japanese combs in horn and tortoiseshell, lacquered and inlaid with mother-of-pearl. Rich embroidery was used on kimonos instead of women wearing jewels but in their elaborately dressed hair they wore combs and pins. All 19th century.

Left. Enameled gold bracelets, one from Benares with pink enamel and one from Hyderabad of a rather coarser green and red, both *c* 1800. Each Indian center within the Moghul empire had its own enamel style but Jaipur's was the most delicate and is the only center active still. The diamond chips used here are so small that they have little value: indeed, jargoons, white sapphire or crystal were considered almost equally good for erratic scattering like this.

Right. Indian Moghul enamels from *c* 1600–1850 were probably the most emphatic the world has ever produced. This detail comes from a necklace, probably made in Lucknow. Vivid with color it shows the wonderful sense of pattern which also gives such pleasure in the inlaid floors and walls of the great palaces and tombs. India today is still the world's leading user of gold in jewels, although, in theory, it is illegal to import the metal. Indian men and women use gold as their bank balance. Those who are poor, with no home or bank have to wear everything, thus setting an exotic standard of metallic display.

Chinese history is continually expanding backwards. In 1974, peasants digging an irrigation ditch in NW Shensi province unearthed some 10,000 relics, warrior figures and weapons from the time over 2,000 years ago when Chin Shih Huang first united the country.

In Japan, the situation is a little clearer simply because there are no old jewels. The country was poorer than China, and women had, and still have, a very low status. Their decoration was confined to beautiful embroidery on their kimonos, often with gold thread, and to combs and pins for the hair, often in tortoiseshell, bone or lacquer. Metalwork was, and is, a rare luxury, mostly confined to men. As St Francis Xavier wrote on introducing the Jesuits in the 16th century, "The Japanese have a high opinion of themselves because they think that no other nation can compare with them as regards weapons and valor, and so they look down on all foreigners. They greatly prize and value their arms, and prefer to have good weapons decorated with gold and silver, more than anything else in the world. They carry a sword and dagger both inside and outside the house and lay them at their pillows when they sleep. Never in my life have I met people who rely so much on their arms. . . ."

The marvellously detailed, and today much collected, metalwork elements of Japanese armor include the Skagashida, for the top and bottom of the sword handle, the Menoki, decorative animals on the scabbard; the Kinai, decorations based on lotus leaves; and the Tsuba, hand guards or shields, between handle and blade. Kozuka are dagger grips. Zogan is the Japanese name for damascening gold and silver on to iron, with lacquer burnt in as a protection against rust; Shakudo is copper with some 5% gold, usually used with a form of damascened pattern. One of the glories of Japan is its lacquer, loosely called japanning. A most evocative symbol of all this craft achievement is a golden lacquered treasure chest in a remote shrine at the old capital city Kyoto, called Hokoku Jinjya shrine. This belonged to the greatest of all the Japanese warriors, builders and art patrons, the 16th-century emperor Hideyoshi. What glories it must have contained, what memories it suggests!

Francis Xavier, almost contemporary with Hideyoshi, continued his revealing diary: "Tea ceremonies for the Japanese are very important occasions, the utensils used for drinking 'cha' are always displayed with pride to an honored guest."

"The caddy in which they place the cha leaves, the spoon with which they scoop them, the ladle with which they take the water from the kettle, and the stove—all these utensils form the jewelry of Japan, in the same way as rings, necklaces and ornaments of magnificent rubies and diamonds do with

Shah Jehan, who built the Taj Mahal, painted *c* 1640. Indian Moghul princes wore wonderful and varied jewels and so did their women, an unusual example of both sexes being equally colorful. Whilst marble, alabaster and jade were favored, it is enameled gold for which this civilization is chiefly famous. Miniature painters have left a detailed and fascinating record of Indian court jewels.

Left. Indian Moghul archers' rings, *c* 1650. The one in steel was once the property of Shah Jehan, the others are of jade set with stones. The ring protected the wearer's thumb from chafing by the bow string and made possible a more sudden release of the arrow with consequently improved speed and accuracy.

Below left. Oval steel Japanese scabbard ornament, 37mm (1½in) at widest, called a *menoke*, showing a noble in leisure clothes with pouch and fan. The steel is burred to make a surface to which the thin sheets of gold and silver will adhere. This kind of thick damascening is still common in Japan.

Below. A jade bangle carved with a dragon, representing eternal life. This theme is constant in Chinese art making it difficult to date accurately but it is probably *c* 1200. Jade, imported from Tibet, was popular in Chinese jewelry despite its extreme hardness. 80mm (3¼in) diameter.

us. And they have experts who appraise these utensils and who act as brokers in selling or buying them. Thus they give parties to drink this herb (of which the best sort costs nine or ten ducats a pound) and to display these utensils, each one as best as his wealth and rank will allow. . . ."

Perhaps the Japanese craft which corresponds most closely to western jewelry—beautiful, playful and individual—is that of the netsuke. From the 17th to the 19th century, traditional Japanese men's dress had no pockets. The purses (*sagemono*) and, later, medicine boxes (*inro*), and writing cases hung by a cord from the waist sash (*obi*); the netsuke was the toggle at the top of the cord, useful, agreeable to toy with in the hand, and now valuable too. The makers' names are often known from their signatures, but their lives remain obscure. All they have left us are these exquisite, tiny animals and natural pictures in wood and ivory, a monument to patience and perfectionism.

In India, gold was the great romance, and still is today. Huge, swollen bangles of the early Buddhist cultures, from about the time of Christ, can be seen today in the Buddhist shrine of Taxila, and in the Karachi Museum. The wonderful champlevé enamels introduced to Jaipur by the Moghul conquerors in the 18th century, are probably the most exciting jewels of the East.

Indian precious gold jewels of the later Moghul period, 18th and 19th century, are still quite common. Like the architecture of the period, they show an obsession with pattern, an intoxicating geometrical ingenuity never rivalled by any other culture. And this creative imagination was fed by rich local supplies of diamonds and colored stones especially from the South, with famous sapphires from Kashmir, pale yellow sapphires from Pukhraj, emeralds from Panna. The centers of enameling were Jaipur with its delicate linear interlacings, where thousands of craftsmen may still be seen at work; Lucknow, with its broader slabs of color; Benares, whose special delight was an exotic faded pink; Hyderabad with richer coarser colors, and Delhi for technical virtuosity almost a second Jaipur.

Specialized processes, all of which are used in jewels, if only humble peasant brass bangles, have become localized. In Moradabad in Uttar Pradesh, 60,000 craftsmen make sand-cast brass of all sorts—often with engraving, chasing, and coloring from infills of low-melting-point colored metal. At Varanasi (Benares) repoussé and lacquer work are the favorites, not only for jewels but mainly for lotas and suharis, bowls for carrying the sacred Ganges river water all over India. In the museum there are India's two most illustrious jewels—the ruby and the black jade ring of the great emperor Akbar, the first of which was later owned by Shah Jehan, builder of the Taj Mahal. Jagadhari (Haryana) is a center for cooking utensils, Patna (Bihar) and Pareao near Patna for hand-beaten bell metal utensils. Nadavaramba, near Trichur in Kerala in the South, for casting of temple lamps of amazing thinness, Tanjore near Bombay for silver and copper repoussé work on brass. Karimnagar produces silver filigree, Patubkar a sophisticated gold tracery on green glass, popular on jewels as well as on dagger and sword handles and on scabbards, Makrana near Agra the carved marble which is one of the glories of Indian jewels. Jaipur is also famous for its inlaid jade. Kuttack filigree and painted enamels from Kutch are much in demand today. Even in such a vast country as India the skilled jewelry crafts were, and are, a matter of strictly local, often even of family, pride.

The orient is almost timeless. Old blends into new, so that it is the art, not the date, which matters. Jewels from the east are therefore shunned by smart dealers and can easily be bought in any market in Hong Kong or Tokyo, Bangkok or Singapore, in Delhi or Kandy or Lahore. These superb pieces can give the buyer more pleasure for less cost, than any Western work.

THE MIDDLE AGES

An early 14th-century German bishop's mitre. Gold filigree diaper work contrasts big, plain stones which are erratically placed and shaped, showing Byzantine influence.

European jewelry in the middle ages was, like all the arts, Christian. Its subject matter was to describe God, and its purpose was to help the worshipper to feel close to God. Jewels were often in the form of pictures showing scenes from the New Testament, such as the Crucifixion or the Annunciation; or they might be part of the apparatus of worship—a reliquary to hold some part of a saint's anatomy, an object associated with a saint, or a portion of Christ's Crown of Thorns or His True Cross. Such reliquaries and shrines, both large and small, were a necessary focus for worship and were often not only portable, but wearable too. From the making of humble rosary beads to the decoration of great gold and silver altars goldsmiths worked for the church. Production was large, the imagery, from the Apocrypha as well as the Old and New Testaments, was wide ranging and stimulating; yet medieval jewels are extremely rare. To the normal loss, theft and deliberate melting or remaking, has to be added destruction caused by religious strife.

Some of the most impressive wearable pieces have been recovered from tombs. Although the Christian church forbade the burial of treasures with the dead, the source of so many antique pagan jewels today, it was the custom for bishops' and saints' graves to contain a specially made chalice, therefore rather thin and poorly executed, and the actual episcopal ring.

The period begins with the elaborate late Ottonian style: a thick type of filigree ornament, punctuated by dots of enamel and by blobs of gold, a sort of articulated vermicelli which twines all over the surface in a rather clumsy arabesque pattern. This pre-romanesque jewelry, like architecture of the time, seems designed to avoid precise definition: just as, with buildings, endless arcades pierce the walls to give a feeling of mystery and space, so the jewels tend to be patterned all over the gold surface, with big patches of colored enamels and stones, an echo of Byzantine hieratic dignity.

By the 12th century, unadorned surfaces had become normal. Good examples of the style, with its growing wealth and the ever more elaborate Christian imagery, are the huge coffers made to contain relics in several Germanic cathedrals. One of the grandest of these superb shrines, the finest jewels of their age, is in Cologne Cathedral: it is nearly 2m long, 1.5m tall (6 × 5ft), it weighs 300kg (670lb). It was made between 1190 and 1220, by Nicholas of Verdun, and it contains the remains of the bodies of the three Magi, brought to Milan from the east and, under the Emperor Frederick Barbarossa, to Cologne. It is typical of a new style, part Romanesque, part Gothic. Figures chased in high relief with beautiful "hairpin loops" (*Muldenfalten*) in their drapery, show a startling flexibility and freedom. The surface of the three "naves" or containers is dotted with stones and carved cameos, some of the latter acquired from Constantinople after the conquest of the 1204 Crusade, given to Cologne by the Emperor Otto IV to consolidate his claim to be successor of the first Christian kings. The use of these cameos shows a reviving interest in antiquity, no doubt fed by the scarcity of new carved stones—the craft was hardly practised outside Byzantium between Roman times and the renaissance. They also show a good selection of stone settings, mostly a sort of fretted bezel, the tongues of which would be easy to rub over without damaging the stones. Most important on the coffer is the enamel, typical of a new school which flourished in the north along the Meuse and by the Rhine; and in the south at Limoges, usually of coarser quality and on base metal copper alloys. Cloisonné enamels on gold were common from the 8th to the 11th centuries, champlevé on copper in the 12th. The enamel is of dusky, opaque color, not shiny, set in deep cut fields, sometimes with the simple clear outlines of the champlevé technique, sometimes with the architectural panels punctuated or divided by cloisons, again thick and of powerful rather than charming effect. The fine crown of Hungary given in 1001 by the Pope to Stephen, first Christian King of Hungary, and the crown jewels of Frederick II in Palermo Cathedral, are big examples of this type and their techniques appear on many small pendant crucifixes and talismans.

After 1300, the richest and most cultured court patronage was no longer that of Germany and its western border, but came from Paris and from Burgundy. Cloisonné enamels were revived there, artistic activity shifted somewhat away from building churches, towards the ideals of chivalry and court life. Luxury was overflowing, and often expressed in metal. In metalwork, it was the age of France. At the beginning of the 15th century, during the minority and illness of the French king, Charles VI, Burgundy became probably the most lavish court of Europe. In jewelry, the feature of the times was "encrusted" or "basse-taille" enamel—enamels covered the modeled figures. The late-14th-century inventory of 3,906 objects of precious metal owned by Charles V does not mention it, whereas it is common in those of Charles VI and the Duc de Berry of the early 15th century.

The massive compositions of the 12th and 13th centuries have become linear, surrounded by gothic pinnacles and canopies and elegant flowers; the color is now all over the figures, and the background, where visible, is plain, whereas in earlier jewels the figures were uncolored, the background glowing with enamels and stones.

During the 15th century, settings for stones tended to become simpler—plain bezel rims or what are now called rub-over settings were customary, in preference to the earlier more massive surrounds which were often wide and thick enough to have gothic leaves pierced out of them or chased into their surfaces. As the settings became lower and more delicate, facets began to appear on the stones and brighter colors and light effects were flattered by the colors of foil placed behind the stones. With stone cutting, the wonderful conceits of the renaissance were at hand.

Right. Bishops' rings from Chichester cathedral. The three gold rings with sapphires date from *c* 1250, the bloodstone ring *c* 1300 makes use of a stone engraved with a Gnostic deity *c* 600 AD. Sapphire was the favorite stone for medieval bishops but has now been superseded by the amethyst.

Below right. Transparent enamels with the gold beneath engraved and patterned, in the technique known as *basse taille*, were a feature of Parisian and Burgundian work in the late 15th century, as in this tiny pendant cross.

Above. The hands of Archbishop Philipp von Daun and of another cleric, detail from a window in Cologne cathedral. Bishops' rings were made rather large, partly to fit over gloves, partly to be easy to kiss and venerate and partly to impress.

Relics of the Savior and His Saints attracted pilgrims to the churches owning them. The devout would also wear tiny exquisite reliquaries like this 15th century Burgundian representation of Christ's baptism which measures only 65mm (2½in) high. The relic was carried in the cavity beneath the figure of Christ and the rock crystal doors, when shut, allowed the sacred object to be seen and the whole kissed and adored.

RENAISSANCE GLORIES

Left. Renaissance rings were carved in high relief. This onyx head of Perseus, mounted in gold, carries the name of Lorenzo dei Medici for whom it was made. His collection, one of the outstanding renaissance jewelry archives, is now in the Pitti Palace, Florence.

In painting and sculpture, in literature and music, even in medals, the godly sobriety of the middle ages led to a supreme classical perfection which, about 1480, and especially in Italy, was dignified but unpretentious, original but well proportioned, and charming but often great as well. Alas, scarcely any jewels survive from the early Italian renaissance, but paintings show us exactly what they were like: an Italian girl painted between 1450 and 1500 by Piero della Francesca or Benozzo Gozzoli for instance, to quote one austere painter and one who loved pageantry, usually wore just one pearl necklace, one simple finger ring (some of these can still be found today) and one forehead ornament, perhaps a star made of a cabochon ruby with a pearl at each corner. No enamel, no modeled figures, no frilly surrounds, no baroque pearls, all so discreet as to be almost insignificant. The emphasis was on gorgeous fabrics and lovely coiffures.

Soon after 1500 the scene changed dramatically. The high renaissance is famed for its jewels: there are more comprehensive royal and aristocratic inventories, better documented court treasuries and more surviving treasures, more varied myths and legends, and a bigger technical virtuosity, with more processes used, than ever before. No wonder that Shakespeare illustrates his greatest passages with rubies and pearls, no wonder some of the finest painters and sculptors of the age—Botticelli and Ghirlandaio, Ghiberti and Holbein and Nicholas Hilliard—were proud of their goldsmiths' background. Life was for living, no longer for God, and jewels were a riotous symbol of the new worldly spirit.

Below. A jeweled locket with portraits of an unknown man and woman. Painters were sometimes trained as jewelers and goldsmiths often worked closely with them during the renaissance. Nicholas Hilliard, royal 'limner' to Elizabeth I and James I of England, who made this piece *c* 1590 was himself both jeweler and painter.

Below. In Italy renaissance rulers were celebrated by medals but in southern Germany more often by magnificent suites of jewels, like this group of *c* 1550 set with precious stones, enamels and a carved cameo portrait.

Below center. A group of bronze portrait medals, Italian, *c* 1450, by Pisanello and (*right*) Matteo dei Pasti. Such medals were sometimes pierced and worn as pendants.

Bottom. A gold ring of *c* 1520 containing a natural uncut diamond crystal as used for cutting glass. The point has chipped off, showing that diamonds can be fragile, although extremely hard.

Surviving jewels from the mid-16th century are quite common in museums, they are elaborate verging on the fussy, fantastic to the point of grotesque, so ornamental as to be almost formless, above all they have become complicated showpieces of technique. Early renaissance has given birth to mannerism, the golden riches of Mexico and Peru have begun to reach the workbenches of Europe, the novelty of fine dressing has worn off, jewels are again a necessary part of the human panoply.

The general trend is clear, and it is possible to trace the change in emphasis from hair and dress to jewels, from the heavily clothed portraits by Veronese and Titian, through the jeweled women, often nude, of Bronzino and Parmigianino, to Velazquez whose women (and children) carried an unparalleled weight both of cloth and bullion. By the early 17th century, it is common to find a rich German merchant's wife portrayed as wearing as many as a dozen jewels—two rings on one hand, three on the other, one central corsage ornament, earrings, pearl necklace, gold and enamel necklace, two chains wound into the hair, and a lovely circular hair ornament. In Schloss Köpenick at East Berlin, is a picture of such a merchant's store cupboard opened to show 14 such pieces—perhaps his wife's total possessions—together with half a dozen table cups in gilt and ivory, the pride of his own table. The number of jewels worn increased steadily, and so did the number of people able to afford them. The merchant classes like the Fugger or the Welser, of Augsburg, became patrons and even leaders of taste, and their jewels soon came to rival those of the older aristocracy.

All the big cities probably had jewelers, but the grander courts provided the main lure for craftsmen. It may be that, in Italy, social glamor attached more to commissioning paintings and architecture than it did to metalwork. Only Milan developed its own metal tradition—in the form of parade armor, made by the Negroli and Miseroni families, and famous throughout Europe. Milan was also known for carved rock crystal made by the Saracchi, another northern fashion, and these Milanese fantasies were exported everywhere. Florence from the same period, the mid-16th century, became, under the patronage of the Medici grand dukes, the home of elaborate inlay work in semi-precious stones, known as *pietra dura*, and used for jewels, table decorations and furniture. Venice, influenced by its oriental trade, introduced filigree. Naples was, and still is, the center for cameo cutting, then usually in hard stone like agate, now often in shell too. All the great Italian families, such as the Gonzaga of Mantua, the Este of Ferrara, the Baglioni of Perugia, the Montefeltre of Urbino, the Malatesta of Rimini, immortalized themselves through the newly revived medium of commemorative medals, often worn as pendant jewels by the family's ladies and supporters, and given to visiting well-wishers. It is typical of Italian jewels of the early renaissance that these medals were of plain bronze, noble in their restraint and discipline: enthusiasm for the finest metalwork seems to have come not from Italy, but from north of the Alps.

The main German centers were the Wittelsbach court at Munich, where the Electors, later Kings, of Bavaria, assembled the treasure now shown in their Residenz palace museum there. Dresden was home of the Wettin, Electors of Saxony, then Kings of Poland, then Kings of Saxony. Their special asset was the semi-precious stones of the nearby mountains, the Erzgebirge, and the iron and quartz mineral wealth from there, from Silesia, and from Poland. The Green Vault in Dresden, perhaps the first public treasury in Europe, opened by Augustus the Strong in his castle in the early 18th century, still displays today the astonishing variety and the international quality of patronage given by this art-loving dynasty.

The culmination of northern court metalwork patronage, came about 1600 in Prague where the Emperor Rudolf II set up what was probably the biggest nest of goldsmiths that the world has ever seen. They produced a distinctive style of arabesques picked out in champlevé enamel in gold.

Three great merchant cities, with self-governing middle class constitutions, contrasted with these royal centers and sometimes worked for them. They were Protestant Nuremberg, noted for its guilds, for watches and clocks, for tall table cups and for the Jamnitzer family of goldsmiths; and partly Roman Catholic Augsburg which came to prominence a little later, in the mid-16th century. Antwerp had been leader in all the arts but lost its ascendancy because of religious strife in the 1570s. Munich, bribed to Roman Catholicism by the Pope, used craftsmen from all three cities, but never developed a powerful craft nucleus of its own.

Opposite. An enameled pendant of the late 16th century, mounted in gold set with rubies, emeralds and diamonds. After 1600 enamels declined in favor of big stones.

Below. Engraved design by Hans Collaert, Antwerp, later half 16th century. Such engravings by leading designers were sold and circulated widely and used as sources, sometimes for a complete jewel, more often for individual parts. This is one reason why renaissance jewelry styles are so international.

Above. Design for a gold pectoral made by Benvenuto Cellini for the Medici pope Clement VII.

Below. Designs for pendants by Gilles Légaré, French, *c* 1640.

Right. Elizabeth of England, painted by Marcus Gheeraerts the younger in 1592 in connection with a spectacular entertainment at Ditchley. Not only does she wear necklaces, belt, earrings, headpieces and a ring but her gown, ruff and even her fan, are sewn with gems and pearls of great size. Such pieces sometimes recur in different portraits, thus suggesting that they did actually exist and were not imagined by the artist.

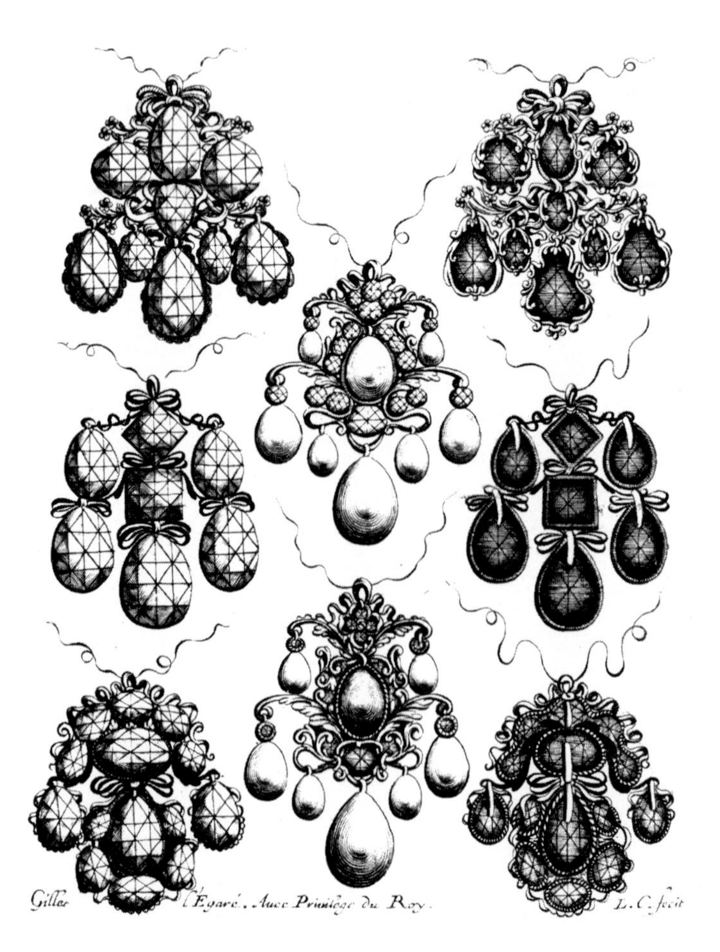

We know from records and from survivals that South Germany was a huge source of renaissance jewels in the 16th and 17th centuries. Printing had made possible the circulation of books of designs, on the one hand, and, on the other, peaceful times had just inaugurated the age of travel. Jewelry designers seem for the first time to have made their living not only from their creations but almost more from publishing and selling books of engraved illustrations which could be distributed amongst the provincial craftsmen, enabling them to copy the snob court style. The top designers were themselves continually on the move, especially in and around Germany.

With such copying of designs, such mobile creators, and finished jewels also being sent far and wide, it is almost impossible to pinpoint geographical characteristics.

Since patronage no longer depended only on the church, centers of production became international. Showing off to men by wearing jewels had become as important as wooing God with talismans.

The craft background of the time is sketched with lurid color by Benvenuto Cellini in his autobiography. Craft processes, as opposed to the life of a craftsman, are also described better in the renaissance than at any other time. Cellini in his 1568 *Treatise* discusses techniques, the choice of stones, the balance between the value of bullion and of craftsmanship, the contrast between fashionable innovation and pleasing an existing conservative market. He describes the casting of his figure of Perseus, when he had to throw into the mold, to make enough pressure for the metal to flow, "all my pewter platters porringers and dishes, to the number of some 200 pieces." This seems to be a true account, because the lead content in the upper part of Perseus is three times as high as in the Medusa beneath. Such were the risks of early technology.

The essence of renaissance jewelry is the scroll: sometimes like a tapering C, sometimes rendered double like an S. This scroll replaces the filigree wires and solid frames of the middle ages. It remained the basis of jewel design, both in section and in plan, until the advent of the machine in the 18th century made scrolls of diminishing depth or width a luxury too expensive to be common and wire of uniform width replaced these lovely comma- or tadpole-shaped conceits. At the beginning of the 16th century, jewels were in high relief. Often they featured tiny modeled groups enameled "en ronde bosse," with complicated compositions including a story in their design—the adoration of the Magi, for instance, the coat of arms of the wearer, or a portrait of the local ruler or saint. Later, stones began to stifle craftsmanship: Portuguese explorations round Africa and India, and the Spanish conquests of Mexico and Peru, led to an intoxication of Europe with imported precious stones, emeralds and gold from the Americas, rubies, sapphires and diamonds from India. The high-relief pictures of the 16th century gave place to the low-relief geometrical patterns of the 17th. The lower the relief, the later the jewel. The lapidary and stone setter slowly but steadily eroded the ascendancy of the goldsmith until, by about 1650, jewels had almost ceased to be pictorial, becoming instead a sort of miniature apparatus for exhibiting mineral wonders.

Sometimes, in France after 1500, enamels were inlaid into crevices carved into glass "émaille en résille sur verre" (enamel in webs on glass). By 1600 Limoges, in France, had a second period of greatness with flat or slightly convex plaques of copper, usually oval, oblong or square, used as the base for painted enamel pictures. The colors were distinctive—mauve, grisaille or black or purple—the scenes were classical mythology as well as Christian; the style was elongated and mannered, something like El Greco paintings. These simple

EXPECTAT
POTEST NEC

Above. The fantasy of high renaissance and mannerist jewelry yielded first, *c* 1600, to high relief geometrical enamels with a few stones (*top* : south German, *c* 1620), then to low relief patterns of big stones *c* 1700 (*above* : Spanish gold and emeralds).

Left. Pendant of St George and the Dragon in enameled gold with rubies, pearls, an emerald and a diamond, *c* 1600. Showing more stones and more exquisite metalwork than medieval jewels, this piece can also be dated by the rough cut of the stones, (which became more precise after the mid 17th century), the high relief and its comparatively large size 83mm × 51mm (3¼ × 2in). The range of color in the stones used was already sounding the death knell of enamel.

metal silhouettes, often worn as pendants, often used as decorative parts on tableware, were sometimes signed: the Penicaud, Limousin and de Court families of Limoges were pre-eminent for several generations. This was the twilight of the enamelist as a jeweler: henceforth enamel was a subsidiary and diminishing component of jewels. Color came from stones, no longer from powdered and painted glass.

Stones gradually became more numerous, but another easily recognized distinction between the earlier and later jewels is the method of cutting the individual stones. Mediaeval stones, probably because there was no revolving or power-driven equipment, were usually rubbed not pointed or faceted. The rose cut may have originated in Amsterdam in the mid-16th century, and it remained popular until displaced by the brilliant cut invented, probably in Venice, *c* 1640. The rose is formed more or less symmetrically, its essence being that it has no plateau on top and very little reflective power from the bottom. Rose cut stones are not seen before 1500, and seldom in prominent positions after 1750, except in Dutch and Turkish work, though they continued to provide decorative fringes as late as 1800. The brilliant has a plateau or table on top and, in its fully developed later form, 58 facets, all of which yield brilliant light effects.

By the 18th century the patterns were made of stones, not of shaped gold: the metal became almost invisible. One can view this evolution over three centuries simply as the decline of the goldsmiths' craft, or it may be seen as the division of goldsmiths' activities into the specialized channels of silversmiths for table plate, lapidaries and enamelers for jewelry, sculptors and modelers for small bronzes and furniture trimmings. Jewels evolved from small heavy high-relief sculptures, into geometrical displays of glitter; they became flatter and less colorful, flashing points of stone replacing the gentle curves of the renaissance.

ELEGANCE AND ARISTOCRACY

An 18th-century gold brooch in the style named after Madame de Sévigné, who made it popular, with a pendant, both set with emeralds. Note the irregular shapes of some of the stones.

Throughout Europe the upper classes began to share in the prosperity which had been limited to the noblemen, and new types of jewel were created to satisfy the huge new markets. But it was not only a question of new markets. There were new stones from the newly discovered territories; new production methods resulting from Dutch and Italian stone-cutting innovations in the 17th century and British machine technology in the 18th century; new jewelry requirements because there was more light, houses instead of castles, bigger windows and more candles and chandeliers, more entertainments and parties; an opening up of social attitudes which naturally accompanied the technical and geographical expansion.

The fashions of first one and then another country tended to lead the rest of Europe. In the 17th and for most of the 18th century, that country was France. The centralized power and the long reign of Louis XIV (1661–1715), enabled him to establish a huge system of state patronage of the arts—at his Louvre palace workshop, at his Gobelins factory and elsewhere—which became the envy of Europe. The power and splendor of the king, "Le Roi Soleil," caused the rest of his court to feel that they must emulate him and, as they lived close by him at Versailles, observation was easy. He loved jewels, but his wife Marie Thérèse was less enthusiastic. Thus the ancient custom of men playing at peacocks continued surprisingly late in European history. Louis wore the great state diamonds, he carried a pendant watch at his waist instead of the customary cross. In 1677 at Fontainebleau, for the fêtes, he wore a gold tissue coat with a great chain of jewels like a baldrick. The Duke of Orleans was decorated with one of the first recorded Brandenbourgs, or frogs in diamonds, which soon turned up in one of the queen's portraits. The published designs of Gilles Legaré (1663) showed another new shape: the drooping bow brooch called the Sévigné, named after the

Left. Susannah Hope, painted by Joseph Wright *c* 1760. Miniatures, like the one worn at this lady's hip, remained fashionable through the century. It was unusual to wear no necklace or earrings, two favorite types of jewel of the epoch.

Right. A necklace of diamonds arranged in a stylized flower and leaf motif, *c* 1760. The simple and direct charm of the design contrasts with the more elaborate and pretentious ideas of the next century. Claw settings were not yet normal so only a little light could penetrate the side of the stone.

Bottom, far left. A cameo brooch, carved in agate *c* 1740 shows surface luster and high relief. Shell carving became popular later in the century giving greater delicacy of cut but lower relief because of the softness of the material.

Bottom left. A ribbon brooch set with diamonds and with a pendant pearl, *c* 1760. Rose-cut diamonds, like the center stone, were used often throughout the 18th and early 19th centuries, though brilliant cut stones, as in the bow, became increasingly common. The popularity of the bow in jewels coincided with bows and froggings on dress and became less common as dress became heavier and more elaborate after 1840.

Right. A suite of tiara, necklace, bracelet, earrings, brooch and ring of gold and aquamarine *c* 1820. The gold suggests an early date, the ancient Greek character of the tracery shows the interest in antiquity which arose after about 1790, the regular rhythms of the chain and mounts mean some form of machine—thus one can deduce a 19th- rather than an 18th-century date.

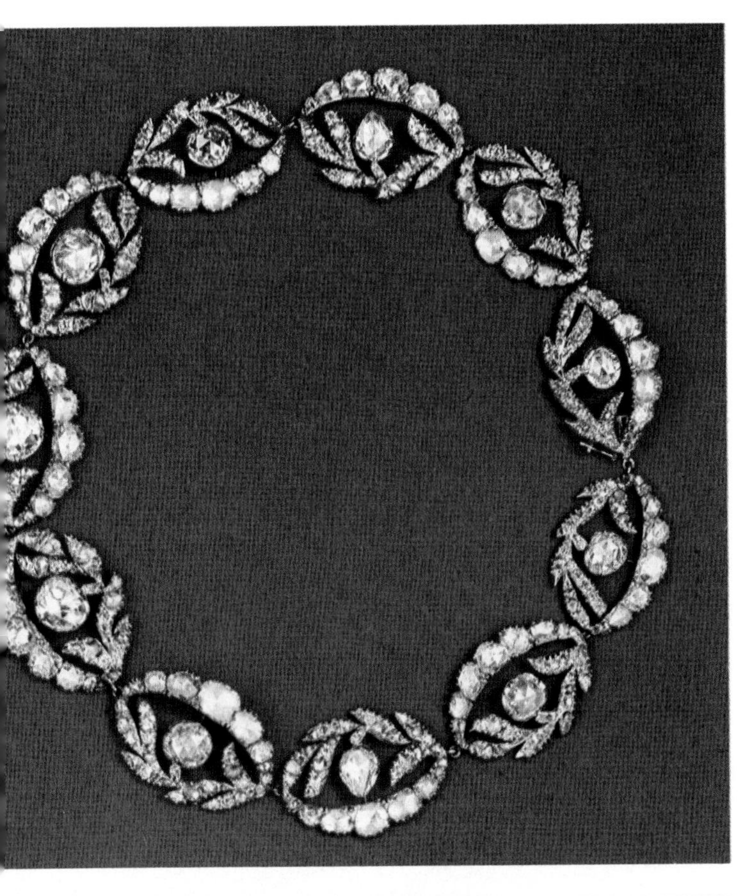

famous littérateuse Madame de Sévigné. Also featured were galleried, flexible girandole and pendeloque earrings. Up till the French revolution of 1789 French jewels tended to be identified with men, with fame and glory. Such famous women wearers as Madame de Pompadour, who may have had the biggest collection of all, and Marie Antoinette, whose unfortunate diamond necklace swindle caused a national scandal, were exceptional. Men still ruled the gallic roost. The many French names of the time show how fashionable France was in matters of jewelry and fashion: décolleté, corsage, bombe-shaped (the type of box most popular in Berlin), coiffe, aigrette, suite, châtelaine, parure, couture, bibelot, nécessaire, étui.

In the Louvre today, there is the Hortense 20 carat diamond bought by Louis XIV, and his imperial eagle of jacinth and ruby; the 136 carat Regent diamond sent from Madras in 1702 by Thomas Pitt, and bought by the Duke of Orleans in 1717 for the crown of France; and Louis XV's crown of 1722, with ancient paste instead of the original precious stones. A similar crown is under the dome of the Charlottenburg Museum at Berlin, used in 1701 at the Königsberg coronation; the leather case and metal skeleton are eloquent witness to the size of the stones, which were removed in 1741, an official state currency reserve. A nearby portrait shows the king's daughter wearing big diamonds sewn to a sort of felt forage cap; it adorns her head charmingly, but one wonders whether the stones belonged really to her or to the state! A similar skeleton crown, of Mary of Modena, is in the Museum of London. So are skeleton crowns for the British 18th- and 19th-century sovereigns. They all used hired stones until the coronation of Edward VII in 1903. Westminster Abbey Treasury has several fully-dressed funeral effigies of fashionable women about 1700, wearing paste replicas of their jewels. So there is evidence of this splendid age from surviving historic pieces as well as from documents and pictures.

In England, France's chief adversary, jewels were smaller, to judge from portraits, and were perhaps worn less by men than they were in France. The inventory of Sarah, Duchess of Marlborough, one of the leaders of early-18th-century life, lists several diamond earrings, six loops of rose diamonds, diamond buttons, diamond stay buckles and a ruby cross.

When George III's Queen Charlotte died in 1819, some of her jewels were sold. The Duchess of Northumberland was amazed at the prodigious size, color and number of pearls, and was particularly impressed by the diamonds. Amongst these was a stomacher valued at £60,000, and three drop earrings each with a center stone of £12,000. Fanny Burney records the queen's delight in her jewels, compromised by "the fatigue and trouble of putting them on, and the care they required, and the fear of losing them"—worries which still plague lesser mortals today.

Court jewels must look their best; their effect was considered so important that professional artists sometimes helped. On the king's birthday, 4th June 1787, Fanny found Benjamin West in attendance on the queen in her dressing room at St James's Palace "in order to give his opinion of the disposition of her jewels." The king disliked show, but he gave generously to his queen: in 1769, for instance, pieces which had belonged to a Bengal nabob (an English merchant who had made a fortune in India). In 1769, a friend noticed "twenty five watches, all highly adorned with jewels," in an elegant case standing beside the queen's bed.

One of the most extraordinary of German patrons was Augustus the Strong, Elector of Saxony from 1694 and King of Poland 1697–1733. Unlike many contemporary aristocrats, he preferred applied art to painting, music and literature. His principal jeweler, Johann Melchior Dinglinger, with his relations and his colleagues like Kohler, may have hit on the true

Left. A pendant cross set with diamonds and turquoises, English, *c* 1780. Gold is often a sign of early date, as later settings tended to be silver. Religious pieces for personal wear are rare by the 18th century and by then are usually very simple, without elaborate symbols or figures of saints.

Right. Seals, primarily a useful way of sealing letters, sometimes achieved a luxury of their own: this set is engraved with each day of the week, each in a different stone. English *c* 1770.

vocabulary of rococo ornament in the 1700s, even before its supposed inventors, the Bérain family of Paris. Augustus commissioned nine fabulous suites of jewelry—each centered around one type of stone, one mainly of diamonds, one of rubies, one of sapphires, one of carnelian, swords and walking sticks, not to speak of two dozen superb centerpieces which are so fantastic, so far removed from function, that they can only be called table jewels.

Further east again was Russia, with perhaps the biggest-ever gulf between rich and poor. The toughest of the Tsarinas was Catherine the Great (1729–96, reigned from 1762) whose taste for diamonds can still be assessed today. Her crown jewels were preserved, and are now in the Diamond Fund exhibition in the Moscow Kremlin. It is hardly surprising that they show little original taste, for her aim was to imitate Europe, not to create Russian styles, and she used among others a Genevan jeweler, rather than trying to encourage local talent. Her jewels, like her architecture, were fine examples of rather unenterprising cosmopolitan work.

Royal example remained the inspiration for precious jewels until late in the 19th century. Napoleon marrying Josephine in 1796, revived the wearing of magnificent tiaras, hair combs and all sorts of head wear. Queen Victoria's love of Balmoral Castle in Scotland (given her by Prince Albert in 1852) made Scottish cairngorms and pebble stones fashionable as they had never been before. Royal death brought out the black: in 1820, the assassination of the Duc de Berry put Paris into mourning and Vever in his standard history records, in 1827, several Paris firms working in black jet from Whitby in England. The Duke of Clarence's death in England had a similar effect. Darkest of all was the mourning of Queen Victoria for Prince Albert: it lasted for nearly all that remained of the century after his death in 1861, with only a partial cheer after her golden jubilee in 1887. Royal misfortune caused a boom in this black soft stone work, first found *c* 1500 BC, which now mostly came from Whitby, sometimes (although softer) from Bohemia and Silesia. Black was for mourning but, as men by then were dressed in black formal clothes throughout Europe, it must also have been considered a suitable color to flatter the conventions.

There is one type of pendant which became popular among the central European principalities. Since the renaissance, rulers had commissioned small portraits of themselves, sometimes carved in hardstone at Milan or Prague or Freiburg in Breisgau, sometimes as a bronze medal by an itinerant sculptor like Pisanello or Sperandio. By the 18th century, portrait miniature pendants, often surrounded by stones or engraved gold, came to play a critical part in political negotiations. Sometimes, like photographs in a later age, they introduced distant people to each other, sometimes they served as a sort of passport to show to whom the wearer owed allegiance, often they were magnificent bribes or tips, a so-called "Gnade Pfennig" or blessed penny. There are examples in Munich's Bavarian National Museum and in Dresden. Most telling is a full-size portrait by Joachim Falbe (1709–82) of General-Field-Marshal (Generalfeldmarschall) von Lehwald, proudly displaying just such an oval miniature beside the bigger sash and orders on his military chest in West Berlin's Charlottenburg Palace.

Outside these royal circles, tiaras were worn to complement the ladies' aristocratic coiffes, corsage ornaments were evolved to cover the laced bosom, refined successor to the décolleté of the previous decades, and the idea was born that a woman without jewels was simply not adequately dressed.

Men in the later 18th century had started the progress towards sensible clothes which has continued ever since. Men's wigs, for instance, became lighter and rarer, and the old flappy coats and high boots gave way to neater more incisive lines. So it was natural that men should give up wearing big

gold hat badges, finger rings with seals, and formal necklaces denoting orders of chivalry. Gold snuff boxes were the new craze among aristocrats in the mid-18th century, extended to the upper and even the squire classes in the early 19th century. Though not strictly jewels, they were often a man's principal ornamental sign of wealth and aristocracy, his golden passport to his class.

Jewels from the 17th century to the early 19th century can be placed by their overall design, the way in which the stones are cut and the way in which they are set according to a few basic rules:

High relief means early: low relief late.
Elaborate enamels mean early: flat, fine quality, sparse settings for stones mean late.
Solid gold backs as well as fronts suggest pre-1660.
Silver fronts and backs suggest 1660–1780.
Silver fronts with solid gold backs suggest 1750–1800.
Silver fronts with open gold backs suggest after 1780.
Claw-settings in white gold, instead of silver, imply after 1840.

Exceptions abound, especially in peasant regions such as Flanders or Normandy, but jewelry styles at court probably reflected successive fashions almost as quickly as clothes.

Top and above center. Front and back views of typical early settings. The pieces, which appear in both pictures, consist of a paste button, made in Birmingham 1790, with a solid silver back showing a hallmark with the sovereign's head, a gold ring of 1767 with silver bezel and silver back with a shell design, a diamond ring of *c* 1740 and a flower brooch, *c* 1820. Wearable jewels were not usually hallmarked in Britain until 1950 when the "works" exempted in the statute was at last deemed to mean only parts not, as formerly, whole jewels. The 1740 ring (*left*) has silver on the front and solid gold on the back. Its stones are rose- and emerald-cut. The flower brooch set with diamonds has an open silverwork front and an open gold back.

Above. A detail of a pair of earrings made in gold, silver and diamonds. The setting is silver in front, openwork gold behind, so avoiding the silver marking the skin, a method of setting used from *c* 1780 when fashions became very refined, until *c* 1850, when white gold began to displace yellow.

Below. The back of a ruby brooch made in England in 1799. The big central stones still have solid metal behind them, no doubt for safety, but the outer lines are already perforated to let in more light.

VICTORIAN SPLENDOUR

A woman without jewels before 1830 was unworthy of a grand occasion. After 1830 she simply was not properly dressed. Tiaras were the glittering descendant of the ancient Phrygian cap, which became the crown of Darius' Persian empire, then the official jeweled headwear of the Pope. By 1830 tiaras were for women and they complemented the elaborate coiffes of the time.

Corsage ornaments became softer in relief and more flowing in line as the 19th century progressed, successors to the formal flat triangle of the preceding centuries. Victorian precious jewels became larger, more florid, more fantastic, often with flowers in enamel as well as colored stones. The later the date the greater the vulgarity until the Edwardian overflow of wealth and the artists' reaction against it in the new artistic

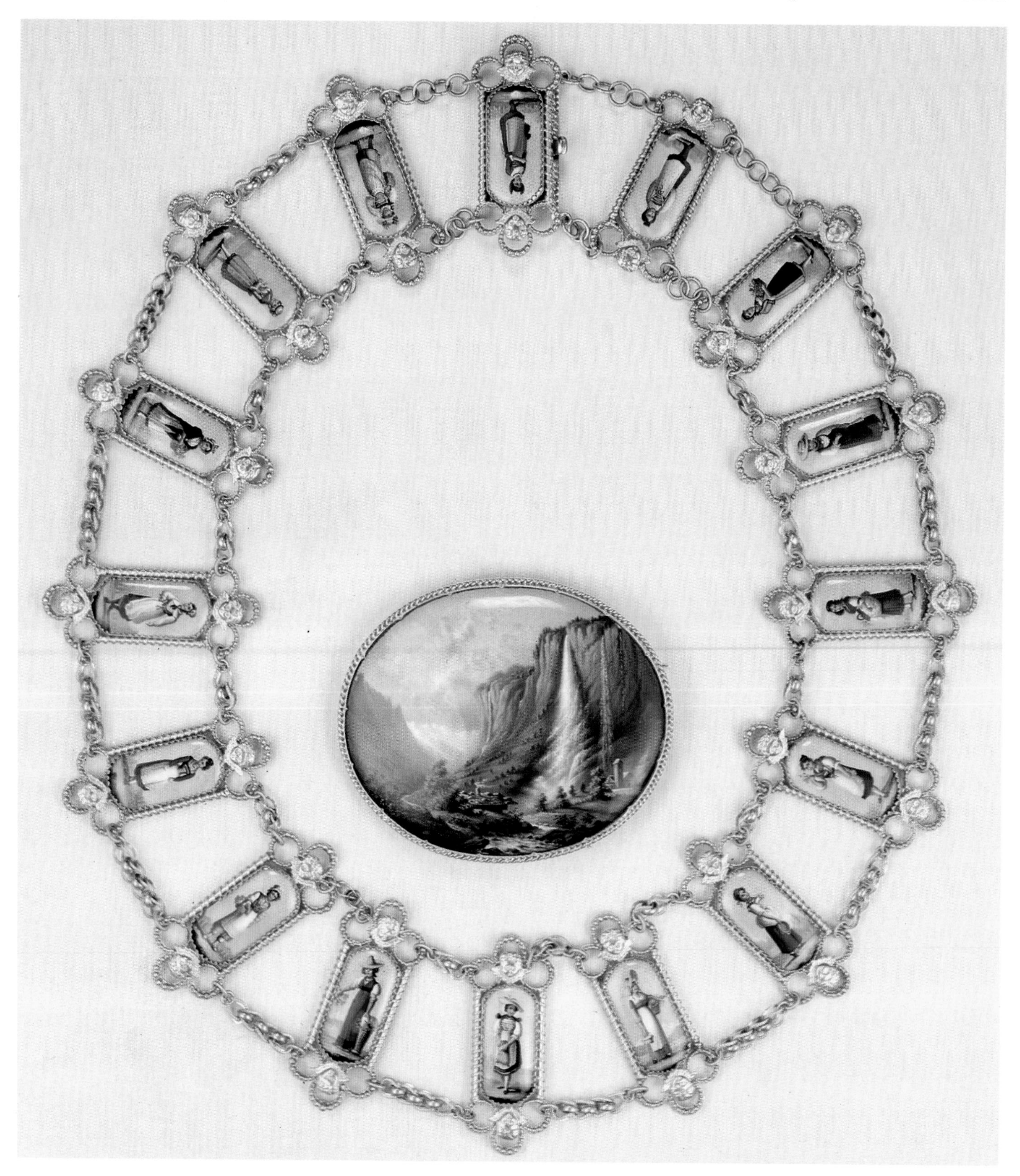

styles which flowered in art nouveau and the craft revival.

Before the mid-19th century with its full-blooded imitations and its flood of cheap cast and stamped work, there were various national fashions. The Egyptian style followed Napoleon's Egyptian expedition of 1798, and set a new trend, by which great events in national affairs influenced jewelry design immediately and obviously. Leafy diadems for ladies derived from Napoleon's own pseudo-Roman forehead wreath of glory. A later French fashion was tassels of all sorts, resulting from the Algerian campaigns of 1840 and 1860. In England Sir Henry Layard's ancient Assyrian discoveries, about 1850, intoxicated jewelers temporarily with winged beasts and rams' heads. When Queen Victoria was declared Empress of India in 1878, a vogue started for Indian motifs like the Moghul arch or, more directly, tiger and leopard claws sometimes incorporating a gun, recalling early jewels made in the old capital cities of Ceylon. The first performance of Bizet's Spanish opera, Carmen, in 1875, introduced to France a new interest in tortoiseshell, especially for combs, which were thought to be typical of high society in Seville. Much the most solid of these overseas frissons was caused by Commodore Perry's gaining access to Japanese markets after 1864. Japanese fashions became steadily more popular first with the aristocratic leaders of taste, then, in a more extreme form, with the Bohemian artistic groups who patronized art nouveau towards the end of the century.

The knot was popular in Hellenistic and Celtic times, but vanished from jewels for a thousand years or more. Knots abound in renaissance architecture and gardens and painting, but they reappeared in jewels only in the later 19th century. Perhaps they were then part of the almost mawkish symbolism inspired by Queen Victoria trying to revive the supposedly medieval standards of love, and chivalry. Bracelets formed of garters or straps owed their popularity to Queen Victoria's own Order of the Garter, which she found it improper to wear on the leg. Flowers and snakes (a snake was chosen by Queen Victoria for her engagement ring), hands and initials, hearts and birds of paradise, such was the repertory. But the treatment of these models became ever more photographic: it was not these replicas of nature but the entwined tube, the simple bar or the circle which expressed a new vision, sometimes bold enough to be worthy of the spirit of the great functional engineers like Brunel.

In England, the copying of all designs became an obsession in jewels as in architecture. Augustus Welby Pugin (1812–52) was the pioneer of gothic revival jewels. At only 15 years old he was already designing silver for the British court jewelers Rundell and Bridge, and metal bulked large in his interests. In 1835–6, he worked with Barry on the Houses of Parliament, the metalwork detailing being his province.

Left. An enamel necklace and brooch. The design is here painted on the surface of the enamel, rather than being formed by different colors inside the enamel. The necklace dates from 1840, the brooch from 1880–90. The peasant costumes and the cascade are typical of the romantic revival of the 1840s. The heavy dresses of the time restricted rapid movement, making it possible to wear such fragile jewelry.

Top right. A necklace with pendant, two rings and a pair of drop earrings in diamonds and emeralds and a diamond and ruby brooch and pendant, probably English, *c* 1840. Sumptuous early Victorian pieces using fine quality stones with mass and color, were succeeded by the harder lines and more definitely imitative styles of the later part of the century.

Right. A collection of jewels exhibited at the Great Exhibition, 1851, from a contemporary print. Designed by Pugin, they were executed by Hardman of Birmingham. The thinness of the pieces and the flatness of the surfaces are typical of insensitive Victorian craftsmanship; and the medieval gothic character of the lettering and general designs show the backward-looking nature of Victorian art.

After his conversion to Catholicism in 1835, ecclesiastical decoration became his special delight, so that cusps and finials and crosses blossomed out all over his jewels. He designed Nicholas Wiseman's Westminster Cathedral miter in 1848 and, in the same year, a set of wedding jewels for his third wife, which was often exhibited. Nearly all his designs were made up for him by John Hardman & Co. of Birmingham, associated with Jeremiah Iliffe and Hammond Turner, button makers, and G. R. Elkington, founder of Elkington & Co., who patented electroplating in 1836. Hardman were big producers: their jewels had to be cheap to reach their huge market, so they showed the light weight resulting from thinly rolled metal, the sharp edges which could have been softened only by expensive and imaginative hand hammering, and the mechanical, monotonous surface finish characteristic of the time. Machine tooling with its almost inevitable regularity, could not simulate the medieval style for which Pugin yearned. Indeed, he wrote in 1851 (a fair comment not only on his own achievement, but on his whole epoch): "I have passed my life in thinking of fine things, studying fine things, designing fine things and realizing very poor ones."

Two other rising British stars came from Italy. Fortunato Pio Castellani (1793–1865) had opened his shop in Rome in 1814, producing jewels which seemed at the time to copy the fashionable styles of London and Paris. Gradually he became interested in the Etruscan antiquities which were

being unearthed in central Italy and founded a personal Etruscan revival style, often with granulation and with filigree, a ribbon of ribbed wire surrounds. He assembled a team of peasant workers from Sant' Angelo in Vado (in the Marche) who claimed still to be using the ancient, mysterious techniques, achieving a traditional appearance which was reinforced by the use of genuine old stones, intaglios or scarabs. But Castellani never approached the technical delicacy of the ancients, the character of which was so often due to filigree and granulation, the modern key to which—colloidal hard solder—was discovered in England 80 years later. His taste for the genuine must have been stimulated by his presence at the opening of the Regulini Galassi tomb, containing the greatest of all Etruscan jewels, now in Rome's Vatican Museum. He soldered to the back of his main pieces a lozenge-shaped block of metal with his mark impressed on it, two capital letters C back to back. In 1851, he left his business to his sons Alessandro (1822–83) and Augusto (1829–1914), who became Curator of the Capitoline Museum and who eventually sold some of the family collection of genuine antique jewels to the British Museum and elsewhere. From 1848 to 1858, the Rome workshop was closed, and the family worked in Paris and London helping to spread a new respect for the idea that jewelry is not just trinket making, but serious design.

Another revivalist was Carlo Giuliano (1831–95) who specialized in precise black and white and bright-colored enamels, sometimes in renaissance style, sometimes of original design, always exquisite. His firm's marks were the initials CG and C and AG, either punched into the metal, or stamped on an oval panel soldered on to the back of a jewel. Carlo left his native Naples and by 1860 had opened a workshop in London, soon supplying Hunt and Roskell, British court jewelers. In 1875, he was strong enough to open a retail shop using the name "art jewelry." Both Giuliano and Castellani used the craftsman and designer Pasquale Novissimo, which may explain the occasional similarity of their work.

A fourth famous name of the period is Carl Fabergé who, unlike Castellani and Giuliano, concentrated more on small table objects than on wearable jewels. The Russian aristocracy, after becoming wealthy in the 18th century, employed mostly foreign artists. In the early 19th century, the leading Russian jewelers were Swedish—the Bolin family—and Finnish—Tillander. It was Peter Carl Fabergé (1846–1920) who gave Russia a national style. His father, Gustav Fabergé (1814–81) was a St Petersburg jeweler; Carl took over the family firm in 1870, having studied in Frankfurt and Dresden, at the latter of which he perhaps acquired his sophisticated taste for colored stone work. In 1881, he received the Imperial

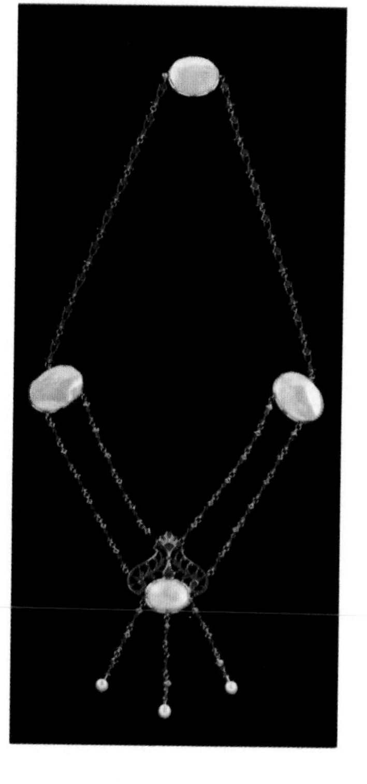

Above. Back and front of a necklace, gold and enamel set with rubies, peridots, by Carlo Giuliano, *c* 1890, showing the sensitive colors he used both for stones and enamels, in contrast with some of the more garish, big commercial houses. Open backs, to let light through stones from behind, became common after *c* 1780.

Left. Necklace by Carlo Giuliano, London, *c* 1870. Guiliano and Castellani revived ancient craft techniques, making more or less accurate reproductions of ancient jewels. They usually signed their work with their initials, one explanation of its popularity today. Giuliano was famous for his enamels, Castellani for his granulation. Their craftsmanship was meticulous and the heavy weight of their pieces pleasing, whereas much 19th-century work is light, made from thin machine-rolled metal, and insensitively executed, partly by machine.

Above left. Three diamond brooches *c* 1840, probably English. The use of yellow gold and enamels to set diamonds in the early 18th century has been succeeded by white gold, which was usually preferred from the mid 19th century, and by the clustering of stones so close together that the metal is hardly visible. Flowers were perhaps the prettiest and commonest inspiration for 19th-century jewels, especially in England where gardening was, and is, so popular.

Centre top. A selection of jewelry from a Tiffany catalogue of *c* 1870. The Tiffany firm started near Santa Fe early in the century, shared in the new industrial wealth of the US, and became New York's leading jewelry company, supplying this kind of sumptuous, but stylistically nondescript, color to customers who liked to wear their wealth and to show exotic stones from far away.

Above. An opal and gold bracelet, English, *c* 1880. Queen Victoria made the opal popular. It is a fragile stone and the possibility of its shattering has earned it an unfair reputation for bad luck. The claw setting allows light to penetrate behind the stone. Claw settings were common after *c* 1840; repeated stones appealed to the Victorian love of order.

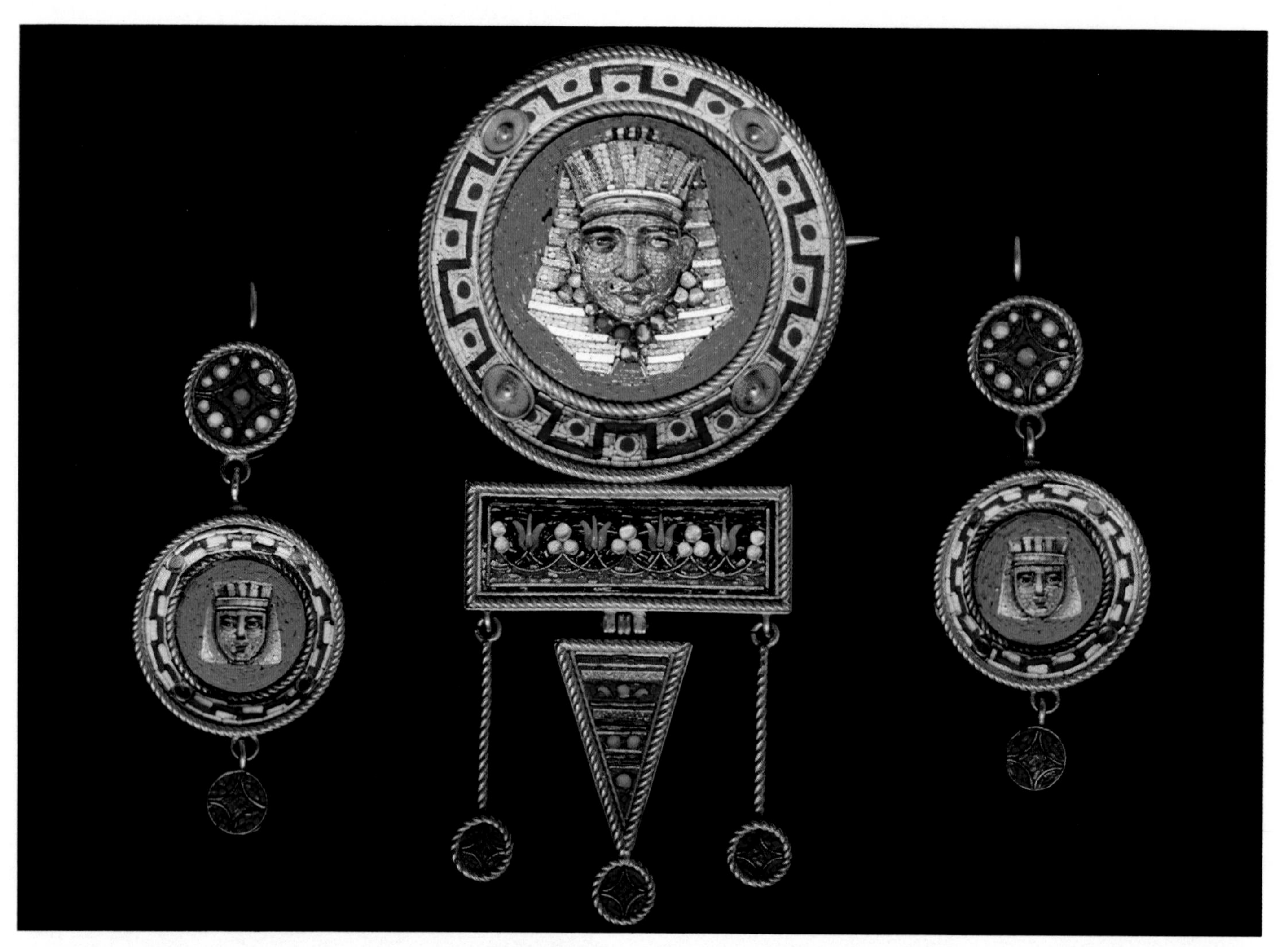

Warrant from Tsar Alexander and in the following year made the first of the jeweled Easter eggs for Alexander and for his son, Nicholas II, which became annual gifts to the Tsarinas, and set a fashion throughout the nobility. In 1887, Fabergé opened in Moscow and subsequently in Odessa, Kiev and in 1906, London. Fabergé's four chief workmasters—Holmstrom and Thielemann in St Petersburg, Piehl and Wigström in Moscow—ran their workshops with considerable independence and had their own marks.

Fabergé won a gold medal in the 1882 Pan Russia Exhibition and again in 1885 at Nuremberg, showing some copies of Scythian and Hellenistic gold from the Crimea (Faberge style was always strongly flavored by the past, usually French, Louis XVI). More medals followed and the French Legion of Honor. In 1918, the Bolsheviks seized Fabergé's stock, Fabergé himself escaped to Switzerland and died in Lausanne in 1920.

Good Fabergé eggs, miniature carved enamels or figures such as soldiers or monks or tiny vases full of flowers, may fetch great sums today. But his personal fobs like spectacles, may be found for a few hundred, and his jewels, often in silver or platinum, for comparatively modest figures. They are usually marked in Cyrillic script with his name and the initials of the workmaster concerned. Always exquisitely made, with a rather large proportion of crisp, fine carving both in metal and in stone, their craftsmanship is an inspiration at just the time when 19th-century machine work was beginning to sap the vitality of jewels. His mind was ingenious more than creative, and it was not him, but the art nouveau designers of western Europe who initiated the revival of jewelry as creative art.

It is tempting to describe an epoch in terms of its leading designers: individual people are more interesting than anonymous trends and it is the people that often cause the trends. But from the late 18th century until the outburst of art nouveau in about 1885, these more or less creative artists were a drop in the ocean of big scale production, both hand work and machine work. Jewelry design was really very unenterprising.

The jewels of the 19th century, like its women and like 19th-century life as a whole, were dominated by the wish to conform. After 1850 inspirations from the past were used as prototypes rather than as spurs to the imagination. The exquisite original styles of 1770 to 1830, married to the huge wealth created by modern industry, might have caused an exciting explosion. In fact, there was almost no artistic cross fertilization. The marriage proved sterile. It proved to be a century of copies, not creation: its significance was quantity, not quality.

Left. Throughout the 19th century, successive waves of exotic foreign fashion freshened the jewelry scene, public imagination often being carried away by the new additions to the overseas empires of the European powers. This brooch and earrings on an Egyptian theme *c* 1860 were probably made near Naples, where many workshops still practice the crafts of mosaic and cameo cutting.

Bottom left. A necklace in gold, enamelled in various colors and textures, by Carl Fabergé, St Petersburg, *c* 1900. Fabergé was famous for his meticulous craftsmanship and his rather unenterprising designs earned almost universal acceptance. Perhaps his most original idea was the jeweled table Easter egg, often given by the tsar and tsarina, from which he derived this type of more domestic necklace. Several comparable necklaces have survived.

Above. Detail of the central pendant of a large gold and enamel necklace using old rose cut diamonds set against foil with a silver back. Made by Tiffany of New York *c* 1890 it echoes the renaissance style of the materials it reuses, but at the same time the beginnings of art nouveau may be sensed in the curvy outlines, and in the use of the relatively non-reflective stones. An earlier piece would probably have used brilliant cut stones and a brighter color scheme to achieve a more obvious show of wealth.

Right. "The Young Bride" by Alcide Robaudi, painted in 1883. With her somewhat romantically classical wedding gown the bride wears large drop earrings, a snake bracelet and a necklace of huge pearls. As so often with late-Victorian jewels the designs are not original but copied from earlier styles.

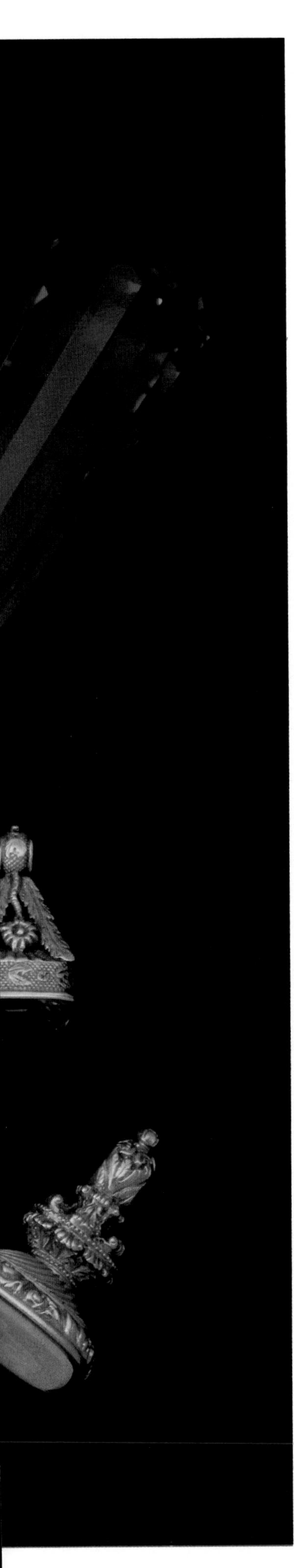

MASS MARKETS

From the mid-18th century, the meaning of the word jewelry changed: it came to include all sorts of beautiful accessories or "toys:" buckles for shoes, hats, belts and stays; buttons and clasps for coats, cloaks, and boots; as well as étuis (boxes for patches and cosmetics, sometimes hung from the belt), aigrettes (hair ornaments), vinaigrettes, like the old pomander, to carry scent, dangling from the waist, spectacles and quizzing glasses, fobs of all sorts, seals and signet rings. For women there were châtelaines, dangling from their tiny waists: delicate belts and clasps, to which were fixed by chain all the household necessaries, or nécessaires as they were called, such as needle cases, spectacles, smelling salts, pencils, pincushions, note pads, scissors, magnifying glasses, keys and

Above. Seals of *c* 1810 show charming scenes of cupid fishing or hearts entwined in gold or pinchbeck mounts. French inscriptions, as here, suggest a date before Napoleon made France unpopular in England. In the 18th and early 19th centuries English people tended to think French jewelry was supreme and English workshops emulated the French. French jewels of the time are rare, few have survived the wars and revolutions which devastated France. Seals like these were carried on one end of a man's watch chain, in his waistcoat pocket, or, less often, hanging from a lady's chatelaine.

Left. A group of mid 19th-century seals and fobs, English except for top left. Especially popular in the age of the dandy after 1815, when used to decorate men's elegant waists, seals became rarer after 1850 as men's dress became black and boring, and adhesive envelopes displaced sealing wax.

seals. The châtelaine was originally used for keys, the nécessaire for sewing equipment, but the words soon became imprecise.

A man's small pendant dress seal often went with his quizzing glass and the drop or fob watch; and if he had these he would have jeweled buckles on his shoes. This was the age of the dandy—Beau Brummel most famous of them—before Victorian pomposity killed male jewelry.

Pinchbeck became as popular as gold though it was never so lustrous. Christopher Pinchbeck was a Fleet Street, London, watchmaker, who died in 1732 and he invented the copper and zinc alloy, some 96% copper and 4% zinc, named after him, which is today often confused with gold. It is, in fact, lighter in weight and harder in function than most gold, and therefore, apart from its appeal on the ground of economy, it was especially popular for guard chains—those exotic festoons which went from one pocket to another across the front of a portly 18th-century gentleman, usually with a watch at one end, a seal at the other.

Seals were, of course, used to seal letters and envelopes with sealing wax, but until perhaps 1830 they normally were engraved with some classical scene with a woman's figure representing, for instance, one of the graces, hope, or virtue. The Napoleonic wars slowly killed England's love of France and the French language, but English seals often bore a French inscription, for instance cupid fishing and the words "*Je meurs sans toi*" ("I die without you"). After 1830, the poetry of these seals was lost, and they seldom showed scenes, only the owner's initials cut in florid, copperplate script. Later crests or coats of arms became normal. The ponderous orthodoxy of 19th-century materialism was at hand.

Engraved stones showing classical myths, were popular in both Britain and France; usually they were set, as in ancient Rome, in simple gold rims. The glyptic art—low relief sculpture—became more popular than it had been since classical times, to which it was indeed a direct reference. The building of "Glyptothek" museums in the early 19th century in Copenhagen, Munich and elsewhere, was a symptom of this revived enthusiasm. The many-colored carved stones were set in necklaces and rings and fob seals. Some of the best artists signed their names or initials in tiny letters cut into the stone, among them Johan Nater of Paris (whose signature was a snake and who left a valuable chronicle of his craft), the Pichler family of Vienna, Antonio Berini of Milan and, in London, James Brown, Edward Burch and Nathaniel Merchant. Berini is said to have carved a portrait of Napoleon in 1802, revealing by chance a red flaw in the agate round the emperor's neck. Berini was assumed to have symbolized the assassination of the emperor, so was himself imprisoned! Miniature painted portraits, cameos and medals were often more esteemed as a permanent record than the large-scale ceremonial oil portraits: hence the reaction of the authorities to Berini's ring of "blood." Everything on a large cameo was assumed to be true, just as portraits on coins and medals in the renaissance were often more reliable likenesses than the pompous political pictures.

Towards 1800, dress became plainer with the impact of revolution and neo-classicism. At the same time, the long-standing passion for classical antiquity became increasingly accurate, as ruins were excavated and finds published with academic precision: Herculaneum and Pompeii were yielding up their treasure. All sorts of Roman urns, fountains, obelisks, flower garlands, weeping women and glimpses of arcadia were pictured in painted enamel, often on small brooches or pendants. Seals were especially popular among the expanding middle class of Britain and Ireland.

To date a seal stone bearing a classical group is difficult especially if in carnelian, because this dark red stone was favored throughout the ages for this purpose. If the carving is deep and spirited, and shows off only a few strokes of the graver, rather than many shadings, then it may be Hellenistic, *c* 300 BC. If the carving is still in high relief, but clearer cut, it may be late renaissance Milan *c* 1550. If the effect is of delicacy in low relief, then it may be classical revival, *c* 1800, by which time tools included hardened metal instead of the ancient technique of grinding with soft metal and powdered hard stone.

The settings were seldom hallmarked—the hallmark laws were in those days applied in England only to larger pieces, such as spectacles or table plate, though in France many gold boxes have been fully marked: hence some of their appeal to collectors. The earlier settings tended to be simple rims or collets, as in ancient Rome, and were often gold; after about 1820, seals took on a flowery, decorative aspect, but they lost their early superb lines.

The most delightful 19th-century jewels are the smallest; like the mourning rings made in England, from about 1770–1830. These rings often contained the hair of a dead

Right. Three cameo brooches, 1800–40. In the renaissance and in ancient times carving was in hardstone, in the later 18th century shell, which allowed more detail although less vivid color, also became popular. Shortly after, molded glass imitations, which were much cheaper but less precise, tended to debase the art. *Left to right:* Wedgwood *c* 1800, ceramic; glass, *c* 1830; composition *c* 1840; all three mounted in gold.

Below right. Three English mourning rings, all engraved in memory of the deceased. Made of gold and incorporating hair, with pearls and paste. They record deaths in 1817 (*left*) 1783 and 1767 (*center*) and *c*1820.

Below center. Four men's shoe buckles in silver, gold and paste made in England between 1760 and 1820. The round "stones" tend to be a sign of later date and the rectangular and lozenge shapes indicate earlier in the period, as in the garnet and hair mourning brooch, *c* 1760, included to show the large size of the buckles.

Far right. The Biedermeier style, the ideal of the continental bourgeois, inspired by the English Regency and French Napoleonic. From *c* 1820 to *c* 1840 such full-blooded pieces were common throughout central Europe and are very popular there today. They are surprisingly light in weight—made from machine-rolled thin gold sheet, but their skillful design makes them look heavy. Made first in Breslau, Silesia, then in Berlin, Vienna and other centers. The four brooches here are set with turquoise and pearls (*top left*), ornamented with niello (*top right*), enameled (*bottom right*) and enameled with a diamond, with a matching pair of earrings.

person, or were engraved with his or her initials, or painted with an exquisite legend in dark colored enamels, often including a date so that they can now be accurately documented. They represent true sentiment with a real personal message, as opposed to the pompous sentimentality of the century's later decades.

Rings were, for women, in this respect like seals for men; charming, intimate symbols. Buckles were rather larger and less personal. Worn by men and women alike, they were decorated with borders of diamonds, paste, cut steel or marcasite. Marcasite (or iron pyrites) is a natural iron-bearing rock and slowly displaced steel, probably because its natural crystal shapes did not need polishing, and it was therefore cheaper. Furthermore, it had a color and luster which steel, with its cold precision, lacked. To our eyes, steel, like so much 18th-century design, showed superb delicacy and structural efficiency and the steel springs and pins on the backs of shoe buckles are pure joy. The rich colors and textures of marcasite by contrast suited the florid 19th-century taste when fussy detail often obscured the over-all conception of the jewel.

Buckles show a steady evolution which can be a guide to other jewels, too. Samuel Pepys records that on 4th January, 1659, he began to wear shoe buckles, a custom which lasted thereafter for over one and a half centuries. During that time, buckles were a sort of social barometer: a glance at the buckles of both men and women would tell their class and wealth. Their importance may be suggested by the action of a footpad who robbed George II in Kensington Palace Gardens with "much deference" taking not only his purse and watch, but his buckles too.

Buckles began the 18th century rather small and simple, with a big double-spiked tongue looking like a hay fork, and hinged to the metal bar which supported the moveable chape or inside link. For the first half of the century, they often had square or flat, rather lack-luster, stones like the dark red garnet.

Later buckles got bigger to cater for the need for elegant dress, so that they would curve round the side of the shoe. The stones became bigger too, but were still usually square. Round stones tended to be a little later. By the 1780s, spring clips were being tried (unsuccessfully) and the growing skill of paste-makers led to long rectangular stones which complemented the fine engineering of the hinge work and spindles beneath.

Belt buckles, being flatter and smaller, have rather less style than their bigger brothers on the shoe, usually with a simple bar behind instead of an elaborate moving steel pin, and are therefore rather less sought after today. But, whereas shoe laces entirely replaced the buckle in the early 19th century, despite petitions from the buckle makers who rightly felt their living was threatened, belt buckles remained, and still remain, in use, being particularly prominent in Edwardian times: the

smaller the waist, the bigger the buckle, to draw attention to it.

Another fashion resulted not from the growing tenderness and grace of life, but from the deepening décolletage of women, laying bare a truly wonderful temptation for jewelers—the neck. As the neck got longer so did earrings to dangle against it. From the 1850s, they were often semi-hand made in silver or base metal engraved with quite personal arabesques. The forms beneath derived from geometry—pyramid on cube, cone on sphere for instance, and were usually carved from solid blocks of metal, giving them a pleasing heavy feel.

The industrial revolution began in England in the 1760s; the immense repetitive power of steam engines and factories began the decline of personal responsibility and the decay of personal taste from which we are still suffering today. Production moved into the new industrial centers, which were often far distant from the customers, fashionable society.

The engraved book of patterns had facilitated production far away from the workshop of the originating designer and the 18th-century trade card published by small workshops had invited the public to call in. Both gave way to the illustrated list, or catalog, intended to bring orders from the expanding world markets to a large, specialized, central factory. Each design was numbered, it could not be copied for the right price without the right machinery, and orders were invited by the factory—which had the tools. This early advertising was addressed not so much to the local public as to remote markets, and in particular to a new group of middlemen, the retailers.

Mail-order catalogs started in England in about 1760. The first Midlands industry to issue them was the Birmingham brass foundries in 1766. Chippendale had led the way with his

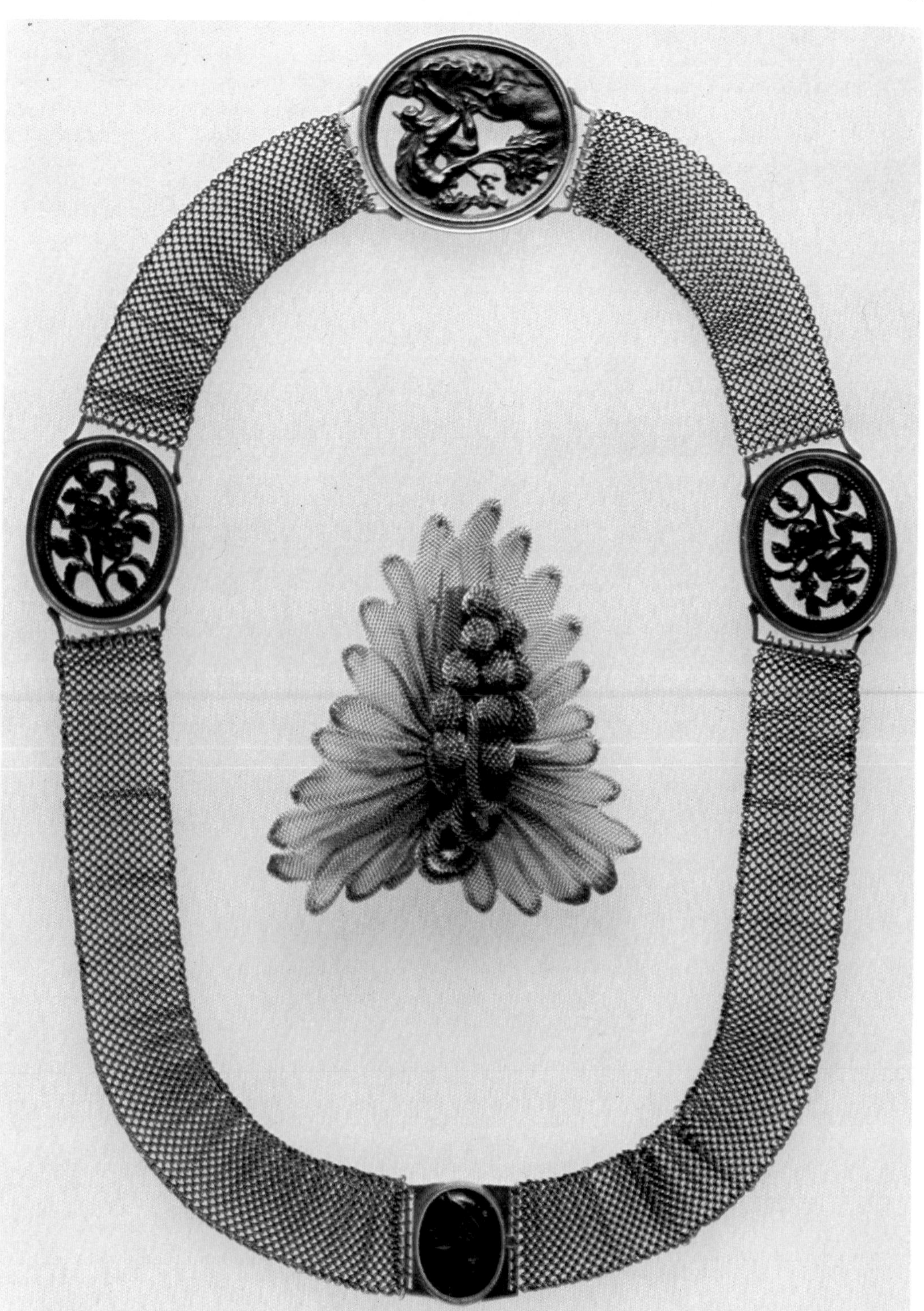

Left. A necklace and brooch of silver mesh inset with Berlin ironwork, *c*1850. The fineness of casting and the novel black color on the newly revealed bare flesh with open light clothing made this delicate ironwork popular throughout the German countries. It was associated originally with the Prussian fight against Napoleon, to finance which the Prussian government collected gold and gave iron in exchange with a certificate of thanks from the king. Throughout the 19th century chain became more common, and more varied in design, as chain-making machines were invented and refined.

Right. Gold bangle bracelets, one with pearls, one with turquoise, one enameled, all on the theme of straps and buckles, English, *c*1850. Like the brooches from central Europe they are made of thin gold sheet. The edges, turned over to conceal the thinness, are usually rather sharp and uncomfortable to the touch. By 1900 jewelry was often of heavier metal.

Far right, top. Bracelets in garnet and gilt metal, *c*1860, probably silver fire-gilt. Garnets came from northern Bohemia where the supplies are now almost exhausted. In the 18th century the mineral wealth of central Europe and the easy communications between the German principalities made garnets a popular substitute for rubies, not only on the continent but in England too. Garnet is darker and less translucent than ruby. These jewels were assembled in cottages over a large area of Bohemia and Silesia, not by virtuoso craftsmen, so their construction and character is very solid. They have survived well, have not dated, and are much collected and worn today.

Bottom right. Mid-Victorian mourning jewels. The gold borders are stamped, not hand chased. *Top, left :* Large brooch in gold, black enamel and banded agate with initials, 1848; *right :* gold brooch with black enamel and hair, 1844; *center :* circular star brooch, jet *c* 1880; *bottom right :* Wreath brooch in black bog oak, *c* 1870; *bottom left :* gold brooch with black enamel and banded agate *c* 1850.

successful pattern book *Gentlemen and Cabinet Maker's Directory* of 1754 which ran to a third edition with a French text in 1763. Josiah Wedgwood's catalogs of 1773–88 were produced in English, French, German and Dutch, and they built outlets for him in Leningrad, Genoa, Amsterdam and Germany. In 1765, he wrote "for the islands of North America we cannot make anything too rich or costly." By 1780 30 Birmingham foundries were producing 1,000 tons (over 1 million kg) of brass annually. A typical small family business was that of Archibald Kenrick, son of a plater, who by 1791 had added an iron foundry to his plating business in St Paul's Square, the center of Birmingham's jewelry area; now it is a big factory. By 1821, even the catalogs were produced in quantity: Wrightson's Birmingham Directory of 1821 advertised "Pattern cards suitable for button makers, jewelers, gilt and steel toy makers"—an early facility for commercial publicity. The age of mass-production was at hand.

Throughout the century and a half till 1850, hand-made jewelry and small craft workshops ruled the scene. But machines were already busy stamping and casting in Birmingham, in Pforzheim, Germany, in Jablonec, Czechoslovakia, in Providence, Rhode Island, USA. The surge of work of uncertain quality threatened to swamp the personal ideals of the hand craftsman.

Whitby employed 1,500 jet jewelry workers about 1870 compared with 2 in 1832, and Birmingham's work force rose from 7,500 in 1866 to 14,000 in 1886, but the initiative was passing from the workshop to the factory, from the hand to the machine.

One of the last, possibly the last, of the "toy" makers to specialize in the old craft industry was George Unite who was apprenticed to Joseph Willmore and took over his own workshop in 1864. Soon after that, these decorative trivia, founded on craft batch production, succumbed to the uniformity of true mass production, until, in the 20th century, plain function for the common man succeeded the 18th- and 19th-century decorative delights for the aristocrats and the middle classes. For the first time, the taste of poor people began to influence the rich.

Birmingham became important because of its position in the center of England and its accessibility to the capital city, then the world's metropolis; Sheffield specialized in tableware, whereas Birmingham developed a big light industry for jewels. In 1772 both cities established their own assay offices because their factories objected to the long journey to the nearest assay offices at Chester or at Goldsmiths' Hall in London.

In the United States local production steadily increased, nourished by an import duty on European jewels imposed in 1850. In 1810, there were about 100 jewelry workmen in Providence, Rhode Island; in 1876 nearly 2,000. In 1880 in Newark, New Jersey, 2,200. The Philadelphia 1876 World Exhibition showed both a rather coarse standard of craftsmanship for local products and the straight lines and regular intervals between ornamental units, such as flowers or dots, which betray the use of machined parts. This was to be the future for "hand-made" jewels, which became increasingly a matter of assembly rather than of construction. Not until the arrival of sophisticated casting methods in the 1960s, did ordinary jewels regain some of their old hand-made look, the result of one man's thought rather than of a production line.

Dominant among Birmingham's industrialists was Matthew Boulton (1728–1809). He inherited a small factory from his father in 1759 and from his Soho Manufactory all manner of silver and small wares poured forth to destinations all over the world. Some were designed by his friend Robert Adam, the architect, who concentrated on table ornaments, such as candlesticks and urns made from local stones, especially Blue John from Derbyshire, decorated with cast and forged brass flowers, wreaths, garlands and bands of Greek key pattern. Boulton was exceptional in every way: friendly with the aristocracy and with the royal family, it was largely his influence which overcame London's opposition to the founding of Birmingham's assay office. When it eventually opened, he and his salesman partner John Fothergill submitted 840 ounces of silver for marking with the makers' initials—MB and JF. In the Birmingham Museum for

Science and Industry today, can be seen evidence of his greatness: with James Watt, he developed the steam engine, he pioneered workers' insurance and old age pension schemes; he always insisted on good working conditions, in contrast to those of most of the neighboring factories. Boulton used, and enjoyed the company of, the leading artists of the day, including Flaxman and Chambers, and scientists such as Joseph Priestley and Benjamin Franklin, and, most important, he scrapped a large proportion of his production because it did not satisfy his own high standards. But there remains an element of mystery about Boulton: what exactly did he make? We can identify his silver by his maker's mark—MB—and it is usually heavy, well made and of distinguished design. But there is no recognizable group today of Boulton's jewelry: we can only imagine that some of the best work of this time—and it is very common—came from his sophisticated machines.

Two other pioneers are, perhaps in contrast, better known for their products than for their lives. James Tassie (1735–99), an amateur gemologist, developed about 1763, perhaps with Henry Quin, Regius Professor of Physics at Dublin, a sort of glass into which an image could be impressed, similar enough to a carved stone seal, to sell very widely. He settled in London about 1766 and started his business, making sulfur and wax casts from engravings. From these casts, cameos and intaglios could be made in glass: he quoted a price of 1s 6d and 2s 6d for an intaglio, whilst cameos cost more. By 1791, a catalogue of his casts listed about 15,000 designs. He had a great success: the Empress of Russia ordered from him a complete set of several thousand casts. Today, Tassie glass is popular with collectors because it is sufficiently common to be found, it is of sophisticated, classical design—often in the form of a classical head with wreath or diadem. The color is usually dark red, dark blue or dark green, the substance is semi-translucent, more so than a stone would be, the surface is, as one would expect, usually chipped, and the modeling, having been impressed, not cut, is soft and smudgy round the edge.

Josiah Wedgwood (1730–95) was a member with Boulton and Darwin of Birmingham's "Lunar Society" which used to meet in its members' homes. Gladstone called him "the greatest man who ever in any age or in any country applied himself to the important work of uniting art with industry." He opened his business in 1759, mainly to produce tableware, for which he sometimes collaborated with Matthew Boulton. But their joint expertise was probably more often used in the pendants and plaques which soon became world-famous. Wedgwood's 1773 catalog lists his ring and bracelet cameos, with his larger wall and furniture decorations. Small unset cameos were 1s each, larger 3s 6d or 5s and set in gilt metal. The texture, not being shiny, was different from that of stone or of Tassie glass (though the Tassie brothers designed for him, with others more famous, including Flaxman and Reynolds), and the production technique, being generally in high relief, allowed a crisper outline. Tassie's colors were usually dark, whereas Wedgwood's tended to be black with his basalts, or, with his jasper and creamware, light green, light blue or buff with the subject raised in white. Like Tassie's pendant seals, Wedgwood medallions were usually mounted in pinchbeck or cut steel borders.

In the later 19th century jewels were usually made from machine-prepared sheet and are surprisingly light in weight compared with 18th century and earlier pieces. Hat and hair pins were used to cope with the vogue for enormous hats and elaborate coiffures, cuff links and men's buttons to fasten the now austere and colorless male clothing, lockets to hold the new photographic portraits or hair (a popular Victorian sentimental souvenir). There was a fashion for amber, jet, coral (*right*), shell cameos, and non-precious stones such as turquoise and onyx, black enamel and elaborate painted enamels (*left*), and handsome, heavy chains usually-machine-made from strip, which is easier to solder than circular wire (*center right*, the watch chain is probably 20th century). Photographically realistic painted enamels and Italian mosaics (*left*) contrast with the stylization of earlier work. A new type of geometrically patterned ornament is in evidence and the influence of engineering is apparent in the bold economy of means with repeated large circles or squares contrasted with the irregular scrolls of earlier periods.

When a piece seems to be completely, or mostly, hand-made it is often highly ornamented and there is a general tendency to overall pattern which is often fussy. Sharp and geometrically precise edges contrast with earlier free shapes. Revivals of earlier styles, especially rococo (background to coral brooch) are usually much more precisely executed than the original design on which they are based.

Other typical points which indicate late 19th century date include the (*far left*) shells around the inlaid brooch, wires and balls on the brooch above it and the mechanical rhythm of the other brooches the upper of which is ivory mounted in pinchbeck; pendant forms (*left*), ball decorations and balls around the pin (*center right*) and knot-like wires.

Bottom right. Europe became obsessed by Japanese work after Japan was opened to European trade *c*1870. Japanese style jewels like this fan-shaped brooch in silver and gold eventually led to art nouveau. Although the design is inspired by Japan, Japanese women never wore this type of jewel—at this time their jewelry was confined to hair ornaments and rich gold thread embroidery. In England such jewels were often cut and stamped by machine, then engraved by hand.

Britain was the most stable and wealthy imperial power throughout the 19th century, but mass markets and marketing methods everywhere followed the British example. In 1767 the Margrave Karl Friedrich of Baden, whose castle was at Karlsruhe, set up the Pforzheim jewelry industry which was to become the world's biggest (in 1976 employing some 25,000 people). He hired skilled jewelers from Switzerland and France, most of whom were disenchanted by their local religious troubles, and installed them in an orphanage, where they trained the local orphans. The special strength of Pforzheim, then as now, was its efficient use of machine tools: it was a machine, not a hand-craft center from its very beginning. But there are no Pforzheim jewels before 1840 in the local Reuchlinhaus Museum: the rarity of early German pieces is partly due to subsequent wars and revolutions, partly to the small size of the market before Bismarck unified the country in the 1870s and gave it an empire, partly because the German industry started perhaps half a century after the British.

The older centers of jewelry production in central Europe, were not in the small principalities, but in the huge old empire of Austria–Hungary: Vienna for fine hand-made pieces, Jablonec in North Bohemia for the popular cheap garnet jewels mounted in silver, often fire-gilt, or in the white metal (nickel and zinc), known as "German silver." This was cottage work spread over dozens of square miles, and it was—and is—organized into co-operatives with only the simplest mechanical devices like fly-presses. But it was fed, just like Birmingham, from the late 18th century, with teams of commercial travellers who carried samples and sample books, throughout the continent. Some early hand-written

books, with sample metal rings and bracelets not yet set with stones, are in the Jablonec museum today. The actual stones were mined from nearby Mount Kozakov and cut into brilliant, flat, facetted or cabochon shapes by farmers during the long winter months, then set into silver fire-gilt mounts, usually simple and pleasing bracelets, or star brooches. Garnet jewel production spread to Brno and Breslau, then to Kattowitz in Silesia. It was dispersed through thousands of country cottages as is the modern glass costume jewelry industry, which provided one of the staple exports of Czechoslovakia after the exhaustion of the garnet supplies.

Berlin ironwork, the earliest example of large-scale repetition castings in jewelry, is supposed to be the result of Napoleon's 1804 siege of Berlin. It was indeed in 1804 that the Royal Berlin Foundry started production, but whether its only motive was to replace diamond and gold handed in by rich people to support the Prussian war effort, is questionable. The Prussians hated Napoleon almost as much as the British did, and the Prussian government's certificates (*Urkunde*), given in exchange for gold jewels, with the cast iron (often appropriately inscribed) were a popular patriotic token. Some are now at Schloss Köpenick in East Berlin. But the basic appeal of the iron was probably simply its beauty and the novelty of its technique—the frilly, perforated designs were always cast with amazing fineness. The unpolished matt surface had strong fashionable appeal on the new bare skin and muslin dresses: black and white have always been complementary. "Berlin" ironwork was made in bigger quantities near the coal and iron mines of Silesia near Breslau than it ever was in Berlin. More likely it was the product not of patriotism but of the new capitalist strength of Prussia, fortified as it had been by Frederick the Great's recent snatching of valuable mining country from neighboring Saxony. Black and heavy, Berlin ironwork answered the century's yearning for solemnity and gloom.

From Vienna, then capital of half Europe, came the Biedermeier style, first probably in furniture, then in jewelry and applied art generally; a fat and pleasing bourgeois relaxation of the precision of true classical revival. It started about 1820, and lasted till about 1848 when the political upheaval everywhere, returned Europe towards feudalism. Once despised, this unshowy work is now back in favor with collectors, although the jewelry is nameless.

Paste

George Ravenscroft, the English 17th-century glass technologist, proprietor of the Savoy Glasshouse, developed on a commercial scale, about 1676, "glass of lead," a heavy glass, transparent and with good light dispersion. By adding oxide of lead to flint glass, he has as strong a claim as anyone, to be the inventor of paste jewelry. Perhaps the earliest innovator elsewhere was George Frederick Strass who, until 1719, was in Strasburg as a jeweler's apprentice, and appeared five years later on the Quai des Orfèvres in Paris, where he seems to have practised from about 1730 until his death in 1773. In 1732, he was appointed jeweler to the King of France, and he died very wealthy. Strass' interest extended from the finest diamonds, to their subtlest imitations. But his importance to history was his paste jewelry: his name is still used today all over the continent to describe paste. Strass' 1735 trade card announced paste as the "latest perfect secret." Paste was especially admired in France where it had, and still has, the name Pierre du Rhin (or rhinestone); probably a case of false identity, artificial 18th-century paste being confused with the earlier natural rock crystal which in the 16th and 17th centuries came from the banks of the Rhine in Alsace.

Paste designs were perhaps more enterprising than those of real diamonds. Paste, being soft, could be cut to any shape, whereas diamond, being hard, could not. So the density of paste in an old jewel is very high, with the glass cut to a fascinating variety of shapes, with few gaps between and with very little silver visible. Consequently paste jewels often satisfied the 18th-century jewelers' ideal of an almost invisible setting, better than diamonds could do. The mounts were nearly always of silver with closed backs to protect the foil. Gold backs, to avoid marking clothes and skin, were introduced in the early 19th century, but claws and coronets were never used with paste which was too soft and therefore vulnerable to such sharp points of metal. Until about 1840, the foil behind the paste was not fixed to it; afterwards the same technique was used as for mirrors, giving a shallower, less lustrous effect.

The spread of paste was due partly to the new accessibility of diamonds from India, and later from Brazil. Before the 18th century, jewels had generally been for color; afterwards, the emphasis was on glitter. Colored pastes were sometimes opaline, sometimes all uniform tone, much of the color coming from the foil behind: but as the 18th century progressed, and diamonds became commoner, so white paste, with silver foil behind to increase its brilliance, slowly drove out the color.

Watches

There was one area where the machine brought blessings: uniformity made jewels seem cheap and impersonal, but it made watches more accurate and more delightful. Watches at last began to work almost as well as the older long-case or grandfather clocks so famous in Britain's late 17th and 18th century, and the chronometers of the early 19th. Watches are the glory of the later 19th century.

The main center was Switzerland, which for the first time made a unique contribution to jewelry. The first goldsmiths were recorded in Geneva in the 13th century. By the 16th, there were enough of them for Calvin to object that they were frivolous, and at that time many of them had to turn to watchmaking, which was more acceptable to the puritanical reformers. Watches were a loop-hole through which jewelers could squeeze a continuous livelihood. By the 18th century, Geneva watchmakers had started making fun with their time, and were famous for their lovely enamels, perhaps more clear in style, more inventive and playful in subject matter, than the equally famous French enamels to be seen on snuff boxes and elsewhere. The difference was one of function: most French enamels were made to place on the table in a grand home or salon, most Geneva enamels were made to carry, applied to pendant watches, because grand homes simply did not exist.

The spiral spring, which made small watches possible, was first developed at the end of the 17th century; by the end of the 18th, porcelain and enamel decorations were common; by the end of the 19th portable watches moved away from the waist line to the wrist. The precision in watch and clock dials which may be traced back to Abraham Breguet and his family in

Paris about 1810, reached Geneva with its new wrist watch industry about 1910.

Finer watches were in fact made in England than in Switzerland, until Swiss patience and thoroughness triumphed over English impatience and greed for the big profits of big stone jewels after 1815. Many leading modern Swiss firms began at this time, and the biggest of them all, Ebauches SA, makes in quantity the tiny cogs and levers and spindles, the accurate standardization of which made possible the miracle of Geneva. There may be—as the locals claim—a special purity in Swiss water, which made possible their elaborate and large-scale enamel fantasies. In Norway, with similarly pure water and an equally long mountain winter when agriculture is impossible, enamel work has recently become a national pastime. The true cause in Switzerland was probably simple prosperity—Geneva, recently an independent republic, was a haven from the troubles of Europe for all sorts of enlightened and wealthy patrons like Voltaire and Gibbon. They provided fertile soil to bring to flower the tradition of miniature ingenuity which was Geneva. Children's toys and jokes with working metal parts of dazzling complexity delight the visitor today to Geneva's new Musée de l'Horlogerie. What a contrast to the cold, masculine precision of the 18th-century Harrison chronometers in Britain's Greenwich Museum!

Geneva box- and toy-work at the end of the 18th century was different, for instance, from the perhaps more solid pieces from Paris or Dresden of 50 years before, because Geneva catered for an international middle class market, and used standard parts and light machinery, as it has done ever since—whereas Paris and Dresden concentrated on the very rich. The intrinsic value of Geneva pocket or "fob" watches was seldom more than the weight of the gold, and this was usually quite thin. Paris and Dresden used bigger stones suited to their more aristocratic clients. Whilst London, with its watchmaking area round Clerkenwell Road, slowly faded from the watch scene, Liverpool (to be precise, its suburb Prescot) produced a dramatic advance in watch skill in the first four decades of the 19th century, coinciding with the city's domination of the trans-Atlantic shipping route. These craftsmen made heavy flat "hunter" (with a hinged gold shield in front, to protect the glass), and "half-hunter" fobs (with a partly glass front) with dials of sometimes as many as four colors. A miracle of early 19th-century engineering was extensively used: incised geometric engraving or "engine-turning"—a criss-cross diaper pattern cut on a predetermined framework grid by a sharp steel blade. The Liverpool watches bear the hallmark of Chester, the nearest assay office to Liverpool, and were loved by English country squires (hence the name hunter) and gentry alike. But the future for the watch towards the turn of the century lay on the wrist, not in the pocket, and it was the Swiss "toy" industry, whose output in the 18th century was the lightest and slightest in Europe, which invented it.

Machines and findings

Mass-produced settings are recorded in 1852 by Vever who was writing of his own friends and contemporaries. A jeweler called Beltête evolved a device for cutting out and stamping the metal settings for gemstones, which is probably the basis

Left. A Victorian paste tiara. Paste, although intended as a cheap substitute for diamonds, could be set in a more free manner, and is therefore now valued in its own right for its often spontaneous and charming designs. Paste was seldom set in solid gold, silver or silver gilt being preferred. Here the gilding has worn to reveal the metal underneath.

Right. Portable watches were invented in the 17th century and became increasingly delicate until the arrival of the inventive fantasy of the Geneva enamellers *c* 1770. This openwork case is still the size of an English 17th-century fob, but with a new continental grace.

A selection of 19th-century jewels showing the increasingly shallow and trinkety nature of design as the century progressed. The diamond buckle (*bottom right*) compares with the much more common but visually more amusing paste buckles of the period. The blue enamel ring set with diamonds is the earliest piece, 1799; the rose diamond cluster ring next to it and the rose diamond pendant earrings are all *c* 1800; the buckle brooch, 1825; the pair of bracelets, which can be fitted together to form a necklace are made in pinchbeck and set with red paste, *c* 1830; the pearl and ruby cluster ring is inscribed 1834; the garnet and diamond ring and the gold and black enamel brooch (*top right*) set with pearls, turquoise and diamonds are both *c* 1850; the blue enamel and diamond ring inscribed 1858; the locket with colored enamels, rubies, diamonds and a pendant pearl, and the diamond cross are both *c* 1860; the enamel pansy brooch with a single diamond, and the enamel brooch (*bottom row*) set with chrysoberyl, pearls, sapphires and diamonds are both *c* 1880; the necklace of pink and green tourmalines is also late Victorian.

of much modern work today. In England, the baleful effects of the machine may be detected a few decades earlier than in France. But all over Europe, and in America, the ordinary jeweler was becoming more of an assembler than a creator: he would buy "findings," that is pins for the backs, cup-shaped bits of metal often with rather feeble claws ready for use, into which stones could be dropped, minute flowers and leaves and all sort of wire and mesh.

To distinguish machine-made jewels from hand-made, is mostly a question of the instinct for quality. This ancient human sense may itself be coarsening under the pressure of American-style marketing and planned obsolescence—nothing must last too long, or the factories will produce more of everything than society can consume, and there will be unemployment. Old-fashioned people can often judge and enjoy inherent quality better than the modern jet-set. It is partly a question of weight—jewels were made heavy until the materialism of industry reversed the old equation. If you make 100 identical brooches, a pennyweight difference on each will make a gramme on the group. So machine-made jewels tended to be lighter, until the age of casting after 1960.

A hand-made piece will often not only be thicker, and therefore heavier: the thickness may vary. Instead of being stamped as thin as practical for strength, and made from sheet which is bought, precision-gauged from a big rolling-mill, it will be built lovingly by its maker who will forge the metal thick where strength is needed, thin for elegance. Machines produce straight lines and regularity.

The impact of machines until the middle of the 19th century was indirect. They rolled the metal, stamped the clips and mounts, cut the edges, polished the surfaces, plated or gilded the base metal with a precious, deceiving layer of gold or silver, all of which details added up to a hard mechanical finish. A visit to the big 19th-century production centers, the "jewelry quarter" round Vyse Street, Birmingham, or in the rolling hill country near Jablonec in North Bohemia, will reveal that there are still no big factories even today. Jewelry was mostly the product of small people in small workshops, assembling machine-made parts.

Machine-made jewels were beautiful as long as the first generation of innovators lasted in the factories. After their death the manufacturers did not design to exploit the techniques of the machine, they wanted only the profits of bulk production. Instead of speaking a new mechanical language they began to imitate hand work. Jewelry designs from the factories lost their character, and from the 1850s, became poor derivations of earlier styles. True mass-production, the stamping of thousands of identical jewels, did not arrive until late in the century, and then only on a small scale, but machines had a generally deadening influence.

ART NOUVEAU

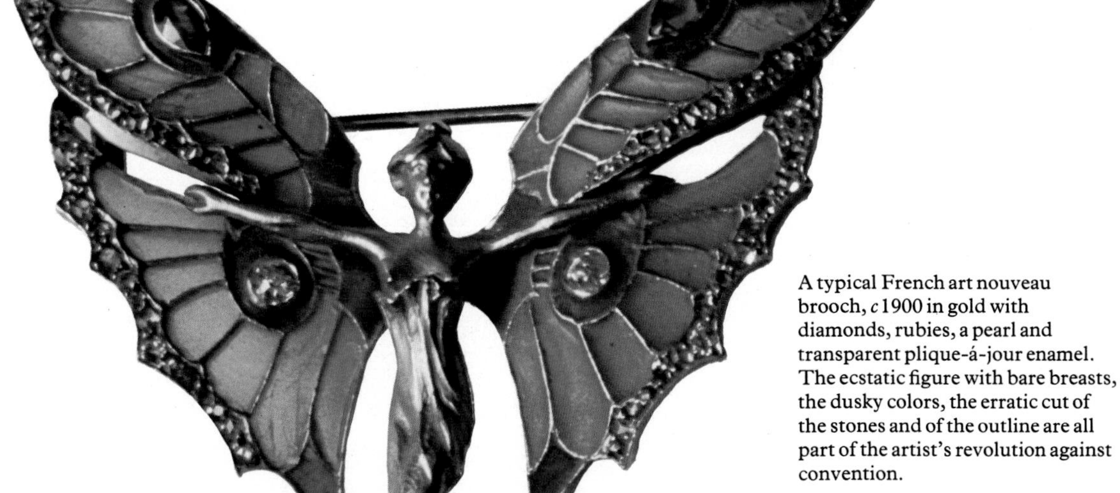

A typical French art nouveau brooch, *c* 1900 in gold with diamonds, rubies, a pearl and transparent plique-á-jour enamel. The ecstatic figure with bare breasts, the dusky colors, the erratic cut of the stones and of the outline are all part of the artist's revolution against convention.

Art nouveau was probably less important at the time, and more recorded subsequently, than any other art movement. Queen Alexandra of England, for example, who led jewelry fashions, and whose husband King Edward VII, invited Cartier to open in London and build their frontage in 1903, never wore it. Cartier held 18 royal appointments, they made 27 tiaras for Edward's coronation but none in art-nouveau style.

Art-nouveau jewelry was made for 25 years from about 1885 to 1910, but never achieved the patronage of high society. At the time it was the product of a small fringe movement, less significant to its contemporaries than Impressionist painting, which at least caused some fury, less noticed than the corresponding literary breakaway of Rimbaud, Mallarmé, Baudelaire, Maeterlinck and the Symbolists. These jewels seem to have been bought by less rich people who had the initiative to want to react against wealthy fashion, rather than apeing it, to value individuality instead of convention.

Actresses like Sarah Bernhardt may have liked art nouveau (Alphonse Mucha, one of its leading exponents designed her posters) but they would hardly have helped it to aristocratic acceptance, for the stage was still considered disreputable. Then there were a few bankers and industrialists like Stoclet of Brussels whose smallish home, the "Palais Stoclet" is still Europe's best art nouveau treasure house. Paris Metro stations and many British pub interiors are examples of special patronage, but the main buyers of this dreamy, imaginative, sometimes nightmarish style, were the big exhibitions.

Paris 1878 saw some gropings, for instance by Britain's Minton china. But the tiaras went on and so did conventional society life, almost undisturbed. By the Paris Exposition Universelle of 1889, the style had arrived. Chicago 1893, Vienna 1898, Paris 1900, St Louis 1904 each gave prizes for art nouveau and led to government commissions. Many of the jewels in the Musée des Arts Décoratifs in Paris today were bought from the Paris shows, and the French government made gifts from them for instance to the Tsar of Russia.

But today art nouveau, because of its imaginative beauty, has become an obsession. There is a philosophical reason, too: it was the product of artists' rebellion against the machine on the one hand, and against convention on the other, both of which stifled creativity, both of which somehow seemed to have betrayed society. We are experiencing the same feeling of betrayal today: no wonder we look to art nouveau both as an example and an escape.

The British arts and crafts movement, inspired by William Morris, did more thinking than making: the small hand workshops he favored and helped to create could not bring their prices down to achieve the mass people's market for which he fought. But the Guild of Handicraft, started by C. R. Ashbee the architect, produced good jewels, easily recognized because they were often hallmarked and their style was distinctive, consisting of coarse entwined wires with silver flat-chased flowers or birds, and embellishments of mother-of-pearl, ivory, turquoise and other pale colors, a reaction against conventional court magnificence and its dark, rich colors.

The other main British jewelry producers at the time worked for Liberty's, Arthur Lasenby Liberty's London store, founded in 1875, which employed many designers but did not advertise their names so that their work is difficult to identify today. Some of the foremost were Archibald Knox, A. H. Jones, and Reginald (Rex) Silver. In 1899 Liberty's launched their "Cymric" silver and jewelry range, usually marked with that word; in 1901, their "Tudric" pewter, mostly made in Birmingham. The form was fleshy and coarse, not too extreme, so that it remained saleable until the 1930s.

At home, British production was low and most British jewels timid and restrained: overseas by contrast, the British reputation for ideas was enormous. About the time the Vienna Sezession movement of radical reforming artists started in 1897, the architect Otto Wagner, one of its chiefs, said, "something impractical can never be beautiful" and Adolf Loos, another famous architect, "ornament is crime," both distinctly un-art-nouveau views. But the creative element in the Sezession triumphed over the rational, and it was to Britain that the creators turned for leadership. The eighth

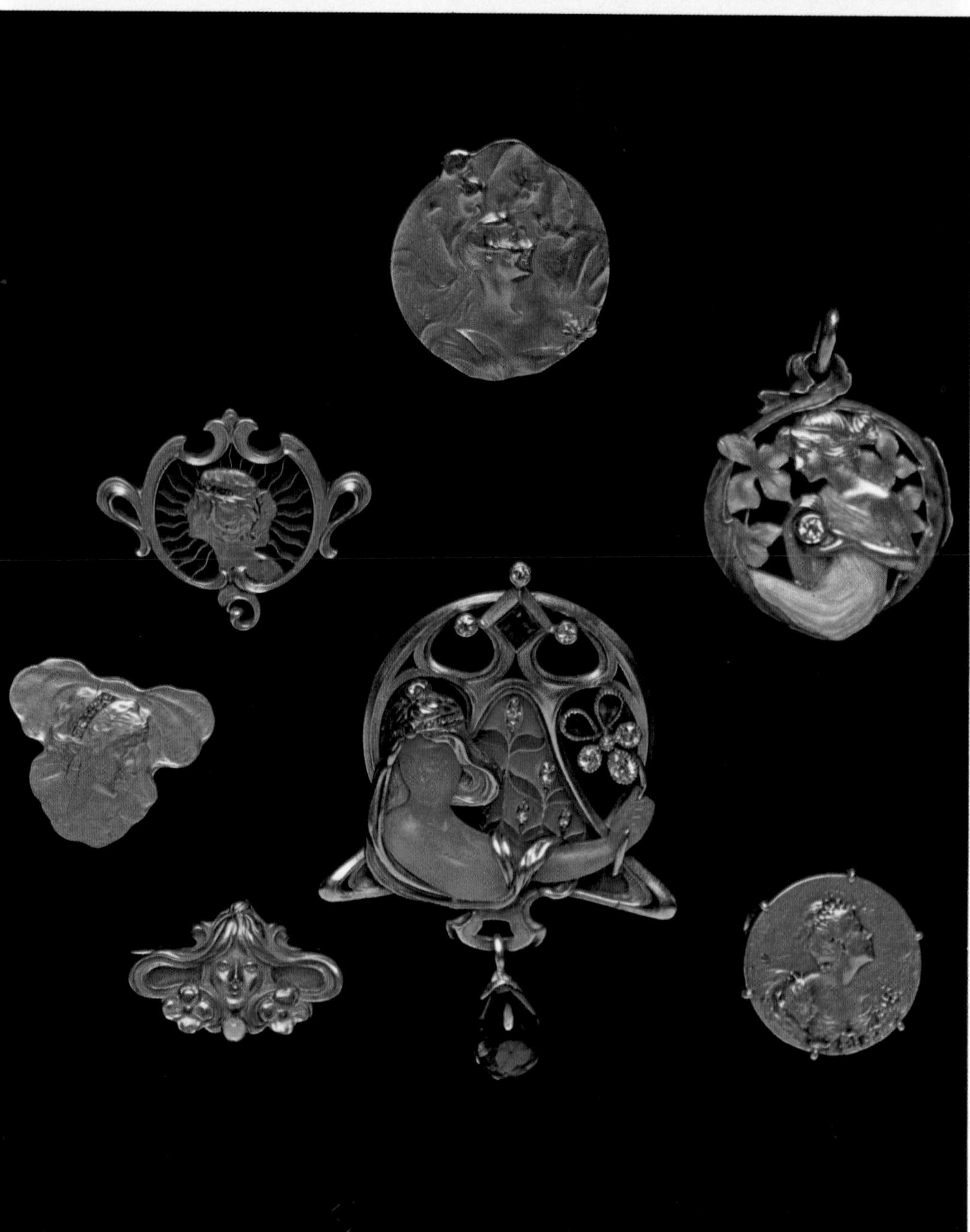

Left. Dragonfly brooches with articulated wings, one in gold with plique-à-jour red enamel wings and diamonds forming the body, the other gold with Montana sapphires of distinctive color and diamond tipped wings. Art nouveau in mood rather than style, because the lines are not entirely continuous and sinuous, but the dusky color of these French brooches of *c* 1900 and the transparent enamel are typical of the turn of the century.

Bottom left. Dreamy ladies, usually shown in profile or half-profile are especially characteristic of the style in France and Belgium. The jewelers represented include Jules Cherat (*top*), Vever (*center*), Masriera (*right*, with diamond), and Compt Epinay de Briot (*bottom right*). Materials include gold, enamels, amethysts, turquoise, diamonds and pearls.

Right. Two postcards and an etching displaying contemporary beauties in art nouveau jewelry shapes capture the spirit of art nouveau style.

Far right. A brooch in silver and glass by René Lalique, Paris, *c* 1900. Molded glass was probably making its first regular appearance in jewels since Egyptian times, but now used as sculpted forms. A mixture of semi-precious and non-precious materials such as horn, glass, bone and iron are all typical of art nouveau.

Sezession exhibition in 1901 featured and honored work by two of the most original British art nouveau designers, C. R. Ashbee and Charles Rennie Mackintosh, the Glasgow genius who, with his wife Mary MacDonald, led the Glasgow School. In 1903, the young banker Waendorfer was persuaded by members of the Sezession to finance and found (on the model of Ashbee's already ailing Guild of Handicraft) Austria's craft co-operative, the Wiener Werkstätten. One hundred masters and artisans made many small masterpieces including jewels, but Joseph Hoffmann and Koloman Moser, the two main figures, were unable to find enough commercial or industrial outlets, although the guild managed just to survive until 1931.

Joseph Olbrich in 1900 settled in Darmstadt at the invitation of Archduke Ernst Ludwig of Hesse, creating there a whole artists' colony where British work was again shown and admired. The Turin international exhibition of 1902 was Mackintosh's last great overseas art nouveau triumph. The "Jugendstil" in Germany, the "Stile Liberty" in Italy, were both well integrated into the jewelry factories as opposed to the craft workshops, with the result that their jewels were undistinguished. Elsewhere the "Modern Style," as it was called, showed echoes of the endless undulating line which we now find so intoxicating. But the farther away one looks from the fashionable axis of Brussels, Paris and Vienna, the fatter the shapes and the less attenuated the lines become. The fine-featured, sleepy women who decorated so many French brooches, were superseded in Denmark by the fruits and berries of Georg Jensen, and in Germany by the Teutonic angles and squares of the Pforzheim silver jewelry industry.

Emile Gallé of Nancy (1846–1904) and his floral style inspired his generation and it was he, as much as anyone, who changed the taste of Europe, although he made no jewels, only glass. The Paris Universal Exhibitions of 1889 and 1900 were his moments of glory. In the US, Louis Comfort Tiffany (1848–1933) was the giant. His primary interests were glass and interior decorating, but he also designed jewels which are rare and sought after today, not perhaps so much for their quality—they are much less distinguished than his glass—as for their name: they usually have TIFFANY stamped on the back, a strong lure for collectors.

The great designers in France were René Lalique, Georges Fouquet, Alphonse Mucha, Feuillâtre, Gaillard and Grasset, whose names were often carved on their pieces. In Belgium, Philippe Wolfers of the crown jewelers' firm, led the field. In Spain it was Luis Masriera. In Russia, Carl Fabergé, more revivalist than pioneer, whetted the aristocrats' appetite for local frivolities, but his style was always closer to the 18th century than to Parisian art nouveau. In those few countries where art nouveau and Jugendstil became more than a minority freak, the style died of its fantasy when it became too impractical and too expensive.

Art nouveau may have failed to conquer industry and high society but its rediscovery generated real excitement. The thrill of art nouveau came from the brilliance of a few creators. They emerged on to a tired artistic scene, and exploded a series of fireworks whose effect was smaller at the time, but much bigger today, than anyone could have anticipated.

ART DECO

Left. A large necklet with pendant in gold, silver and aquamarine by Jean Fouquet of Paris. The essence of art deco was big squares, triangles and geometric forms which reached its extreme in France. Generally jewels of the 1920s used smaller stones and less bold patterns than those of the 1930s.

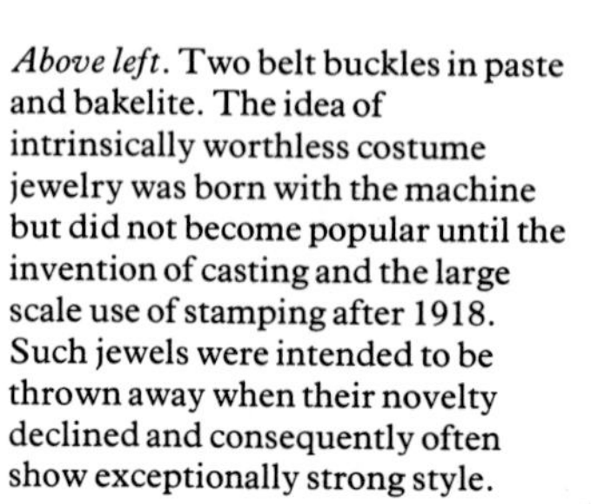

Above left. Two belt buckles in paste and bakelite. The idea of intrinsically worthless costume jewelry was born with the machine but did not become popular until the invention of casting and the large scale use of stamping after 1918. Such jewels were intended to be thrown away when their novelty declined and consequently often show exceptionally strong style.

French art deco brooch in platinum, rubies, diamonds and wood by Mauboussin of Paris. Fluctuations in fashion affect investment value: the money risked in small stones is small, so the buyer often felt better able to be playful. At this time the wealthy Paris retailers led the fashion scene.

Art deco after World War I was a conscious expression of a wish to get away from the horrors of war. It finished before 1939, when forebodings of the forthcoming doom of the next war submerged the sources of cheer.

The name was probably first used as part of the sub-title of an exhibition in Paris in 1966 but has now become firmly attached to the systematic use of squares and triangles in the decoration of the 1930s, derived from cubism in the painting of a generation earlier.

Its characteristics are easily recognized in the architecture of the Chrysler, Chanin, Empire State or RCA Buildings in New York, all of 1929–30, the BBC or the Hoover factory in London, the Marine Building in Vancouver and innumerable "picture palaces" of the era. Interior design, wallpapers, fabrics, the fretted fronts of radio and gramophone cabinets—clothes and fashion too—all reflect the style. Chromium plate, plastics and bakelite were new materials, new pleasures, which brought lightness and fun to jewels.

Magazines were fascinated: *The Studio*, in May 1930, wrote "The novelty for 1929 lies in the completely white note. But how new is this white stone jewelry and how much it differs from the old! Progress has been made in working on the diamond—pieces are composed and carried out which consist of a mixture of brilliants and brilliants cut in the form of wands, triangles, or any other form, allowing the artist to obtain from diamonds whatever effect he chooses."

The 1966 exhibition proved a surprisingly close connection between art nouveau and art deco. Indeed, some famous designers grew out of the first idiom into the second, like Daum, Majorelle and Lalique. The "modern style" show of 1900, had led to the formation of the Société des Artistes Décorateurs, a group of artists whose aim was to break down public hostility to their fundamental new vision. After successful exhibitions in Ghent, Turin, Liége and elsewhere, they planned to bring their triumph home to Paris in 1916. Postponed by war, this fruition of art nouveau did not eventually materialize until 1925 in the Pavillon de Marsan, now the Musée des Arts Décoratifs. In 1928, a breakaway group of artists including Jean Puiforcat and the jeweler-silversmith Raymond Templier formed the "Union des Artistes Modernes" (UAM) devoted to "Le Beau Dans l'Utile." Their work was shown in 1930 in the same Musée des Arts Décoratifs.

In jewels, Paris was still pre-eminent. Following Paul Poiret, her jewelers all signed their pieces and those bearing names like Jean Desprez, Georges and Jean Fouquet, Gustav Miklos, Gérard Sandoz and Raymond Templier are now much sought after. Their concoctions looked blank, geometrical and inhuman at the time: huge squares, triangles and circles, using unfamiliar shiny precious stones more or less like lacquer; fishbone and rock crystal with ivory, aquamarine, citrine and onyx.

These years were the twilight of the ancient aristocracy, but there were still dominant and, in Paris at least, intelligent patrons. Nubar Gulbenkian records how Paris Cartier often stayed open specially in the evening, right up until 1939, because one of their well-known customers was in town. Henry "Chips" Channon, the American young man about town, already middle-aged, eloquently records in his diary, a rather old-fashioned London dinner party of 1936: "The King will never precede the ladies, and dislikes being asked to do so. There was an awkward pause at first as Princess Olga had not yet arrived, and soup was served before she finally appeared, in a vast tiara and wearing two ropes of diamonds. She greeted Honor, and curtsied to the King and then dinner proceeded, and well . . . Honor got on famously with the King who ate a lot, drank claret and laughed much . . . Tiaras nodded, diamonds sparkled, the service was excellent."

Right. Fashion prints provide a good idea of the style of a period. Here huge plastic jewels steal the limelight from clothing.

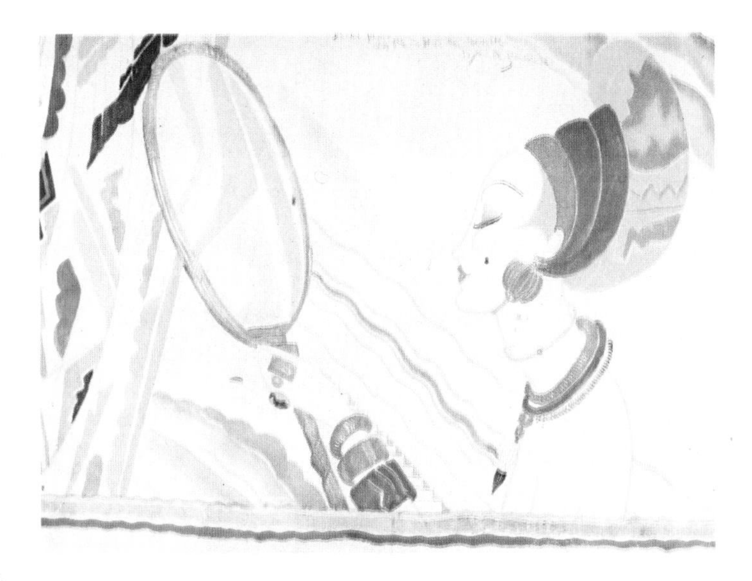

For once, commercial companies were leaders of design, not followers a generation or so after the creative artists. The big shops intoxicated and led high society. Three Paris firms especially admired for their art deco jewels, on the back of which the firm's name was usually carved, were Cartier, founded in Paris in 1859, and later with branches in New York, Palm Beach, Caracas, Cannes, Monte Carlo and London. La Cloche, established in 1897, who specialized in jewelry enriched with enamels and carved stones in the oriental manner; and Boucheron, founded in 1858, with branches also in London and Biarritz, who were noted for their lavish diamond jewelry. Each firm usually signed its products.

Artists and jewels were not so prominent after 1918 as before 1914; the modern collection of Martin Battersby (one of Britain's leading interior decorators at the time) now on show at Brighton Art Gallery, is a fair representation. Many of the best pieces are the anonymous products of big factories. One can date them fairly accurately: in 1920, it was tiny stones with very narrow channels of color between, all in symmetrical, angular groups; by 1930 the stones and shapes were bigger, the groups often unsymmetrical, for instance with a huge loop or swag of "fabric" made of diamonds, bulging from its restraining girdle.

The honors really go to America; it was the age of prohibition and jazz, later of the jazz big band and swing, and of the Charleston and of huge wealth. The most engaging account is from the best-seller *Gentlemen Prefer Blondes*, by Anita Loos, published in 1925 and translated into 13 languages: "So I told Dorothy I thought I would put the real diamond tiara in the safe at the Ritz and then I would buy an imitation of a diamond tiara at the jewelry store that has the imitations that are called paste.

"Lady Francis Beekman has never seen the real diamond tiara and the imitation of a diamond tiara would really deceive her . . . I mean the imitation of a diamond tiara would only cost about 65 dollars . . . So Dorothy and I have some quite cute models of evening gowns that are all covered with imitations of diamonds, only they do not call them 'paste' when they are on a dress but they call them 'diamonteys' and I really think a girl looks cute when she is covered all over with 'diamonteys.'"

These paragraphs are fun but they are more than that. We can sense the pleasure in shopping, the new materialism. The age represents big money, quickly acquired and quickly spent. Small wonder if the dominant characteristic was big stones. Before 1914, very rich people were mostly accustomed to their wealth. They assumed that it would last forever, and therefore did not need an ostentatious show. After 1918, a kind of desperate temporary joy becomes apparent in jewelry: the effect must be big, even if it was false: most people would not know the difference anyway, and wanted effect rather than integrity. For the first time, imitation jewelry was able to fake the real thing successfully. Unemployment and poverty were increasing on the one hand, wealth and exclusivity and determination to seize pleasure while it lasted, on the other. We learn from Anita Loos that paste was worth perhaps 1/20th the amount of real diamonds (they must have been bad diamonds) and that if nobody knew the difference, paste was perfectly adequate. We learn too, that people still wore tiaras at the Folies Bergère, that stealing had become a real problem.

Designers were little known. The period is often consequently portrayed as soulless. Perhaps it would be more accurate to claim that art deco is the true culmination of art nouveau. In the first period, we had artists who failed to achieve production, wonderful dreams without reality; in the second, the artists were overshadowed by commercial success. Art nouveau was a vision, art deco a fact.

MODERN JEWELRY

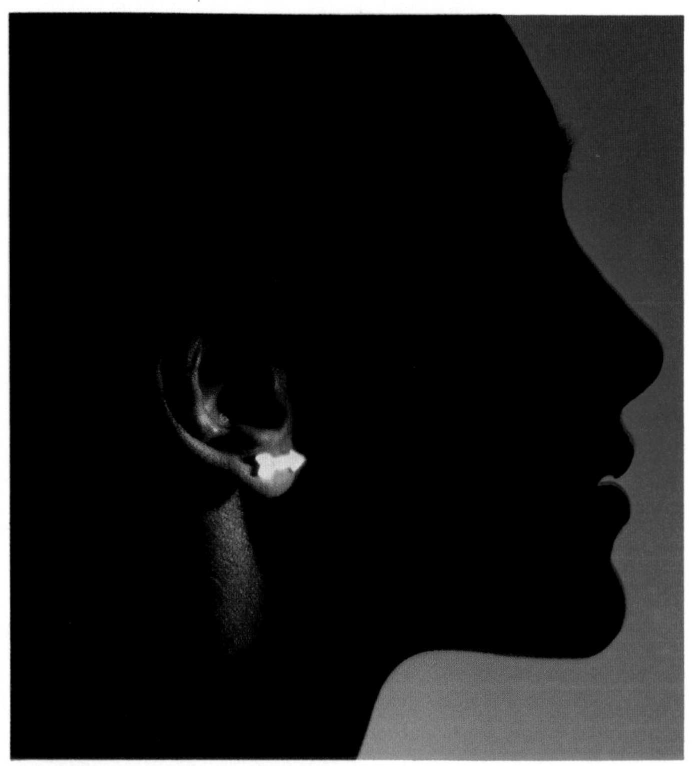

Modern jewels are being up-graded, gaining a place in galleries and museums all over the wealthier world; artist jewelers are springing up, not in the ones and twos of a century ago, but by the dozen. Their work is original, personal, fashionable and shows endless variety of texture and form.

Meanwhile the steady trade of the old crown jewelers has dwindled with the number of crowns. But ordinary people are richer than ever before in large areas of the West and, despite current economic problems, have more leisure and more money to spend on luxuries. Hence the tremendous increase in turnover and prosperity of the chainstore jewelers who have small branches scattered throughout their countries. Hence also the birth of the "do it yourself" hobbyists—millions of people now make jewelry in their leisure time, sometimes they sell it, always they gain a more intelligent appreciation of other people's jewels.

At the mass end of the modern market there is the huge production made possible by modern technology: casting, pressing, stamping, vacuum evaporation, spark eroding, argon welding—and indeed the airplane—have all made possible quicker production and marketing. Gori and Zucchi, of Arezzo in Italy, one of the world's biggest and most efficient factories, used more gold in 1975 than the whole of Great Britain: an indication of the size and scope now possible for industry. In 1977 in Britain, where jewelry factories are all small, the Assay Office at Goldsmiths' Hall, London, marked about 15 million pieces, and the number is steadily increasing. These pieces, having little intrinsic value, are sometimes more fun, more vulgar—like the popular charm bracelets and

Left. Silver bangle by Pol Bury, Paris and USA, 1972. A successful artist, especially with mobile and light effects, he has designed limited editions for Gem Monte Bello, the Milan producers of artists' jewels.
Above. Much modern jewelry has a striking but effective simplicity.

souvenirs for vacation centers—and more varied, than the hand-made investment pieces, but their design is limited by mass-production processes and by the caution of bulk buyers.

With increased affluence has come greater educational opportunity: free schooling, often including free art classes, is available to more people than ever before and, in some countries, such as Britain and Germany, art schools have expanded rapidly. As a result there is much more popular interest than ever before in cultural affairs, including jewelry: millions of people will queue for hours to see a great jewelry exhibition.

Against these excitements must be set the alarming decline in security which makes people reluctant to wear jewels. A woman is less likely to wear gold and precious gems which may attract the attention of a mugger, and husbands become reluctant for valuable trinkets to be kept at home. High taxation is making expensive jewels beyond the reach of many who once would have bought them and, even among the very wealthy, modern good taste suggests that a display of ostentation in the face of the poverty of so much of the world is no longer to be praised. For all these reasons the trend is towards small jewels for ordinary people.

More significant than these social developments is the increasing number of successful designer craftsmen. More significant because designers are the one section of the craft which aims to lead, not to follow public demand. In many Western countries small designers' workshops have appeared and multiplied amazingly during the past decades. Most of them have no connection with industry, making a few pieces each week rather than several hundred. Sometimes an artist will become a full-time factory employee, but more often, designer craftsmen (who are almost always expert with their hands) will set up in their own small workshops, the proliferation of which is closely related to the expansion of state art education. In England, for instance, silver and some other crafts had been taught at art schools for over a century, but the schools neglected jewels except in 1900–14, perhaps because, like fashion (another underprivileged subject), they were considered essentially feminine and frivolous. In the British art school revival of the 1950s industrial design became the magnet around which all applied art revolved and jewelry, which had been included in technical courses at a few schools, lost still more ground. By 1960 training for making precious jewelry was confined to technical classes at Birmingham and at London's Sir John Cass School. The Royal College of Art directed their vision to mass-produced base-metal costume jewelry which, being industrial rather than craft-based, seemed the way of the future. There was in England almost no hand-made jewelry of modern design.

The first modern British designer-craftsman was perhaps Gerda Flockinger, who opened her Hampstead studio in 1956, and started the country's first jewelry art classes in 1962 at Hornsey College of Art in north London. Another turning point was the world's first exhibition of modern art jewelry at Goldsmith's Hall in 1961, with 1,300 jewels from 30 different countries, a revelation to the trade in general, and especially to designers. The growth since has been stupendous. There are now 19 art schools in Britain with serious

Far left. Three rings by Louis Osman, Canons Ashby, England: wreath in white gold and pale emeralds, 1970; shield with diamonds, 1973; font-shape carved in gold, 1973.

Left. Opal parure by Louis Osman, 1973, opals in 22 carat gold with claw settings to allow light behind. Osman's work shows outstanding originality and strength.

Below. Earrings by Gerda Flockinger, London, 1970, in gold and tourmaline show her sensitive control over metal relief surfaces.

Left. Brooch in gold, diamonds and citrine commissioned by HM the Queen from Andrew Grima, London, for presentation to the wife of the President of France in 1973. Note the ingenious placing of the royal monogram to be seen through the stone.

Far left. Gold can offer a unique range of textures. (*Left to right*) Paperweight by Yasuki Hiramatsu, Tokyo, 1977, with wrinkles from casting and carving. Pendant watch by Gilbert Albert, Geneva, 1961, with rough cast matt texture. Earring by Gerda Flockinger, London, 1975, showing her techniques of fusing one kind of gold upon another by careful heat control and reticulation, or partial melting, of the surface.

Above. A brooch in the form of spectacles by Ulrike Bahrs, Munich, 1972. Such visual puns—spectacles in both form and function, and the reflection in the lens, are becoming more common in modern jewels. Jewelry is thus coming to resemble sculpture and painting in miniature. The use of a wide range of stones hitherto hardly accessible to jewelers also brings modern art jewels closer to painting by allowing a more subtle chromatic balance.

Right. Necklace, earrings and bracelet in silver and resin by Susanna Heron, London, 1977. Two new artist's materials are acrylic, which is bought solid and can be bent and carved but not colored, and resin, applied in treacly form with colors mixed in by the artist while still liquid. This jeweler has pioneered resin, not as an enamel substitute, but in its own right, for its color and varied translucency.

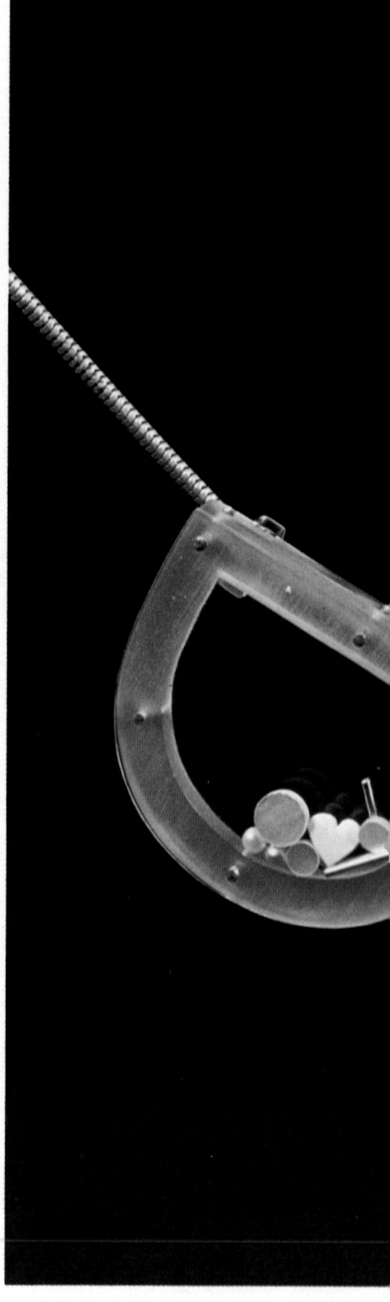

modern jewelry departments, together producing 60–80 designer craftsmen every year.

The situation is changing fast. Many of the big factories which used to supply the shop-windows have vanished in the past decade, collapsing in the face of what are euphemistically called "rising overheads." It is arguable whether that mellifluous phrase covers too many workers producing too little work, or, more important perhaps, a lack of sensitivity to buyers' taste. One can even suggest that modern industrial technology does not work because it does not give sufficient satisfaction to its operators.

A radical disillusionment with factory methods has added to the attraction of the individual artist and craftsman. Many people hate the boredom and inhumanity of factory work, small workshops are found to give more satisfaction, even if the monetary rewards are smaller.

Whatever the reasons there has been a splendid outburst of talent from the small jewelry workshops. Meanwhile the old jewelry centers, London and Birmingham in England, Valenza Po in Italy, Pforzheim and Hanau in Germany—are all in depression. Their production has sometimes halved in only ten years.

In their place are hundreds of small workshops, often housed in romantic converted warehouses or old industrial buildings, often in humble back sheds. Some of them are in the traditional jewelry centers, such as Hatton Garden in London and 47th Street in New York City, more often they are out in the countryside where overheads are low and life is clean. In London the Assay Office at Goldsmiths' Hall registers about six new makers of jewelry and silver every day, perhaps 1,500 each year, and every one represents a brain and a pair of hands. Add to this human talent the rise of modern casting potential, which enables one person to cast hundreds of jewels every day, and one can see the birth of a huge new cottage industry throughout the world.

Parallel with the rise of the country-based individual and the decline of the factory is the arrival of the boutique gallery. A few American cities have their modern jewel galleries and every English city has them, as do the European capitals. These are all small outlets devoted to art and artists: the crucial difference between them and retail shops is that they advertise the names of their designers.

The old-established retailers may feel that these new workshops and galleries, who count their turnover in

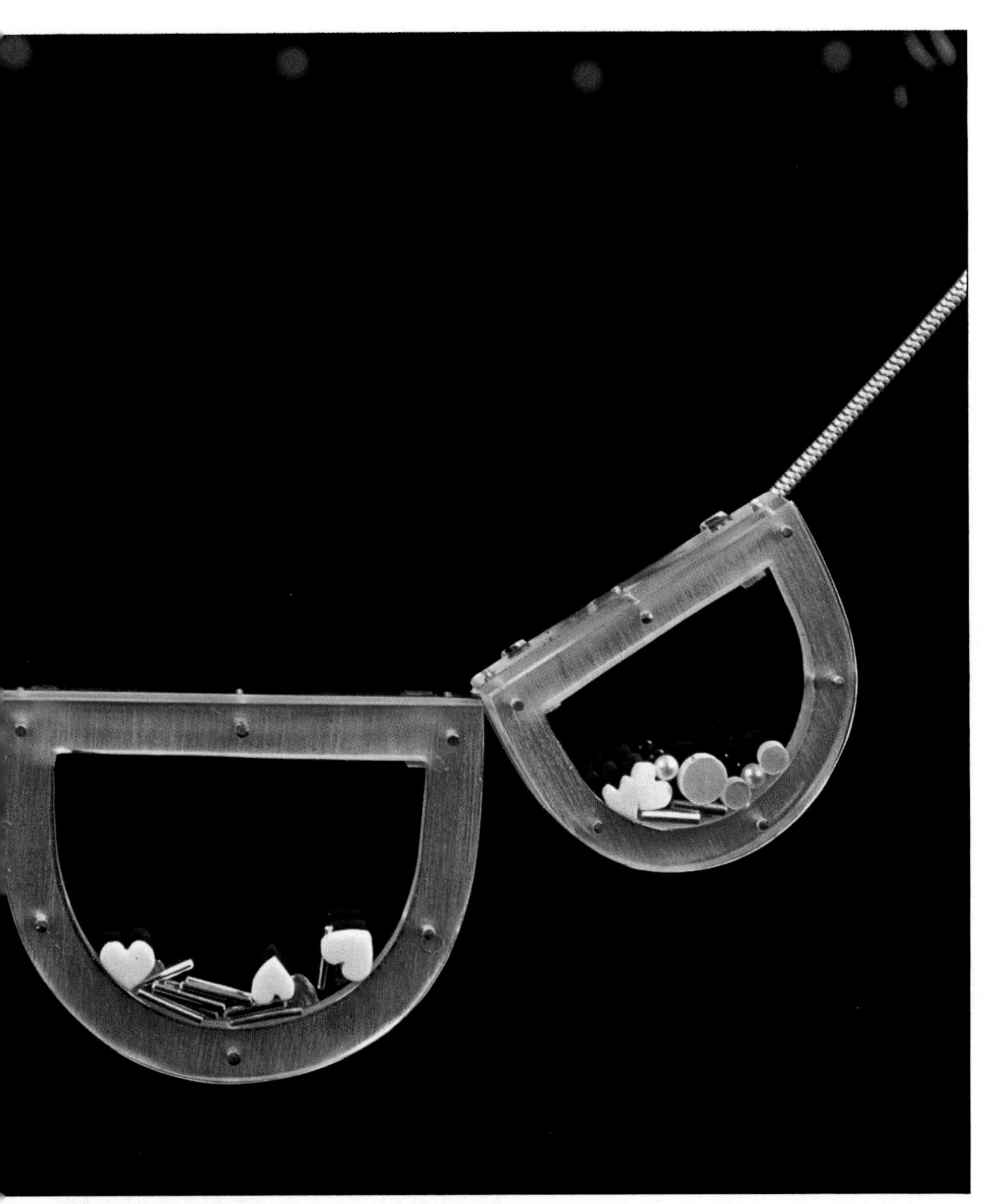

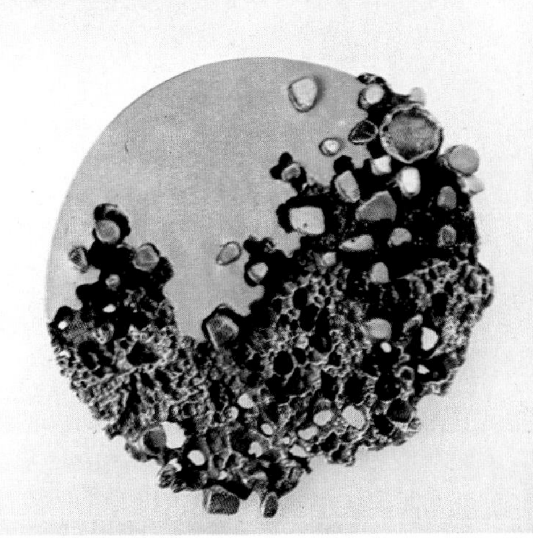

Above. A brooch in gold and diamonds by Elizabeth Kodre and her husband, Helfried Defner, of Vienna, 1977. They have evolved an impressive personal style of contrasted low relief ornament with polished surfaces and sometimes craggy edges, with 'drips' of metal down the crevices.

Left. Necklace in plastic with gold links by Gunilla Treen, London 1975. Plastics were invented between the two World Wars and sometimes used then for cheap costume jewelry but they were easily scratched and only in the last decade have harder plastics such as perspex, plexiglass and acrylics been used by the best artist-jewelers, attracted by the exotic colors, soft textures and luminous, transparent, effects possible. Gunilla Treen was among the first to use such materials and, as development fellow of the Worshipful Company of Goldsmiths, introduced modern plastics and photoetching techniques to the British jewelry industry.

thousands of dollars rather than hundreds of thousands, are more of a stimulant to trade than a threat. The fact is that together they represent a new vision of modern jewelry as an art, created by artists and craftsmen whose aim is beauty rather than money.

Let one example show the speed and scale of the transformation. A leading artist-jeweler in the art nouveau period was Paul Cooper. Never a great stylist, he was little known. Between 1899 and 1910 his account books suggest that he made 225 objects, about two dozen pieces annually, and in England there were no more than a dozen independent artists like him, each with a similar tiny output. Today there are hundreds, if not thousands, of comparable producers; one, whose status is comparable to Paul Cooper's, is John Donald. He makes about 1,000 pieces every year—and has his own outlet in the Middle East, with a shop at Bahrain as well as at Richmond and in London's old city.

The new jewelry scene has become so rapidly established that it is easy to forget how much it has changed. Jewels have come to express not so much a wearer's wealth in the form of a huge stone, nor stability in the form of classical flower brooches or three-stone rings, nor class. In the past the aristocracy may have worn big diamonds, the upper class small diamonds, the upper middle classes sapphires, rubies and perhaps aquamarines, the rest nothing at all. Our new society has become ashamed of class, and people wear what they like, no longer what their social equals expect them to wear. Jewels, like clothes have become part of the wearer's personality, to show personal taste, no longer a badge of office indicating which pigeon hole one fits for money class and age but an expression of oneself.

The use of inexpensive materials and simple techniques have enabled jewelry to follow fashionable trends at the low-price end of the market for ephemeral fun jewelry which may prove a vogue for thonged leather one season, tiny colored beads the next, becoming a uniform especially among the young, as ubiquitous as faded denim. Yet even in more lasting work materials have often not been those used by the traditional jeweler. Plastics and new metals such as titanium have offered challenging opportunities to use entirely new techniques and to produce startling new and beautiful effects.

International competitions and exhibitions have been a stimulating new development and sometimes they can be a vital help in the difficult process of a jeweler becoming recognized and established. The organizers are not usually philanthropists—what they want is publicity. By far the largest commercial firm in modern jewelry is De Beers, the company who dominate the diamond scene with some 85% of the world's total diamond sales. Their Diamonds-International Awards scheme started as an American venture in 1954, partly because De Beers, being almost a monopoly, is not allowed to advertise or trade under its own name in the USA. By 1975 the contest had become truly international with four or six judges, at least two of them from overseas, and about 2,000 drawings entered by designers from all over the world. The competitors get no cash prize and, if they win are obliged to translate their design into solid jewels—but the power of publicity is overwhelming and there is never a shortage of competitors.

At the opposite end of the scale the British Goldsmiths', Silversmiths', and Jewellers' Art Council of London have since 1908 offered modest prizes in distinct categories for excellence in craft techniques. It is certainly easier to judge the relative merit of two pieces of low relief chased decoration as in one category of this competition than to choose a "best" jewel out of all those of every kind entered for De Beers' Award.

In West Germany, each year since 1970, the Deutsche Schmuck und Edelsteinpreis has been held at Idar Oberstein. Then there are the Juwel des Jahres organized by the GDE, associated with the Jewelen-Institut of Hamburg, the Goldene Lupe (Golden Magnifying Glass) awarded at the annual gathering of jewelers—the Deutsche Edelsteintag, held in Munich, and the Golden Rose of Baden-Baden, staged at the Black Forest spa by the Jewelen-Institut.

In terms of art patronage the most interesting of the competitions are those of the Deutsche Gesellschaft für Goldschmiedekunst in Hamburg, a small voluntary society devoted to artistic improvement, rather than commercial expansion. Most of the entries are from freelance artist jewelers and the subjects imaginative—such as "king and queen" (chessmen) in 1973 or "ten grammes of gold" in 1977 (to show what can be done with such a small amount of the expensive yellow metal). Ideas in such an esoteric area provide a good basis for comparison. The society's competition entries are usually shown in the museums of Hamburg, Hanau and Pforzheim. Companies and factories have celebrated anniversaries with competitions, serving the double purpose of encouraging artists and publicising the company.

Since 1959 the city of Geneva has staged an annual competition, the "Prix de la Ville de Genève," with categories for clocks and watches, jewels, small works (bijoux) and enamels. In 1975, 55 pieces were selected to be made up and the Montres et Bijoux exhibition now alternates annually between Geneva's Musée Rath and a foreign center such as London, New York or Tokyo.

There are also regular trade fairs in Basle, Birmingham, Blackpool, Milan, Munich, Valencia, New York, Paris, Vicenza and Copenhagen while at the Pforzheim museum there is staged a biennial or triennial exhibition "Tendenzen" presenting Europe's most advanced artist jewelers, an inspiring contrast with the Pforzheim manufacturers' plodding permanent trade show in the basement.

In London a recent development has been "Loot" an annual selling exhibition staged at Goldsmiths' Hall catering largely for small producers and showing work of modest price. Good modern work need not be inexpensive and, contrary to the view of so many conservative trade firms, it can be popular.

Below. Brooches by Edward De-Large, London, 1977 in silver and titanium. He has pioneered the use of titanium in jewels.

Right. "Ice bird" pendant of ivory, titanium, gold and silk designed by Karen Lawrence, London, 1976. Picture jewels, which were so popular in the sixteenth century are now returning to fashion. Titanium, a rare, tough metal which has only recently been available to jewelers, changes color when heated to give exotic mauves and purples.

Above. A silver bracelet, set with a carnelian, by Jacqueline Stieger, Welton, England, 1977, executed with Jacqueline's skilful casting using tar, to keep down the cost.

Right. Necklace of white gold and lapis lazuli and enamels by Wendy Ramshaw, 1975. The big choice of stones available today makes exciting chromatic contrasts possible.

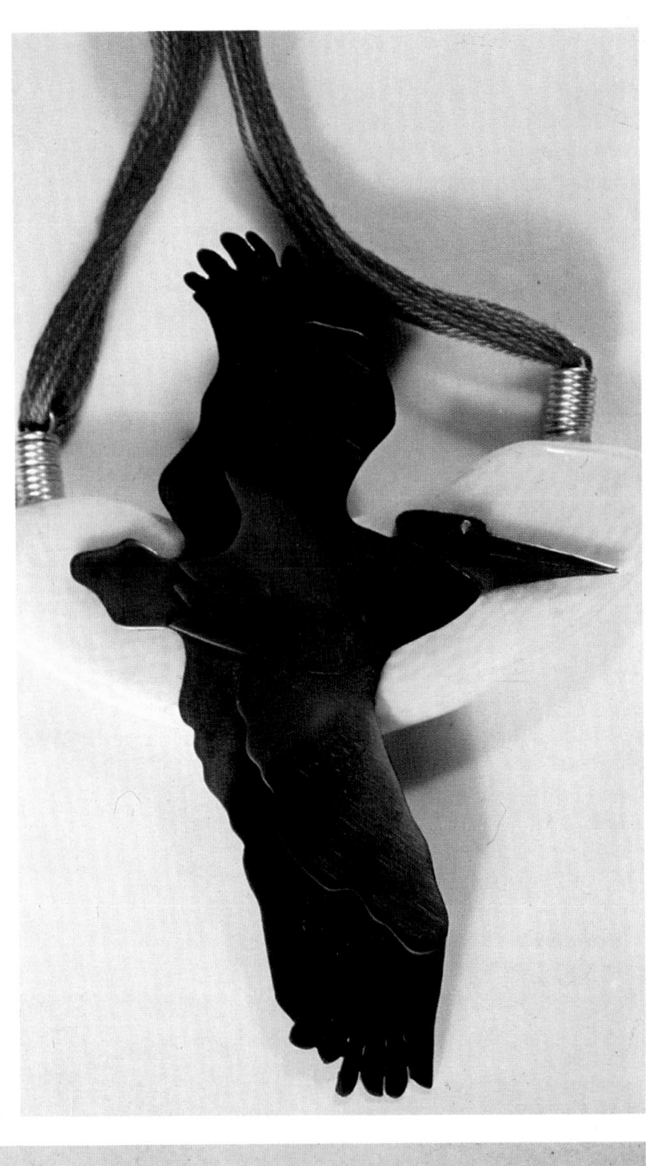

Below. "Hand," a gold enamel brooch by Herman Jünger, Pöring, Germany. The random lines make an abstract composition within the frame of the hand, and the smooth edges make the brooch easily wearable. Many enamelers, like Jünger, evolve their own surface textures.

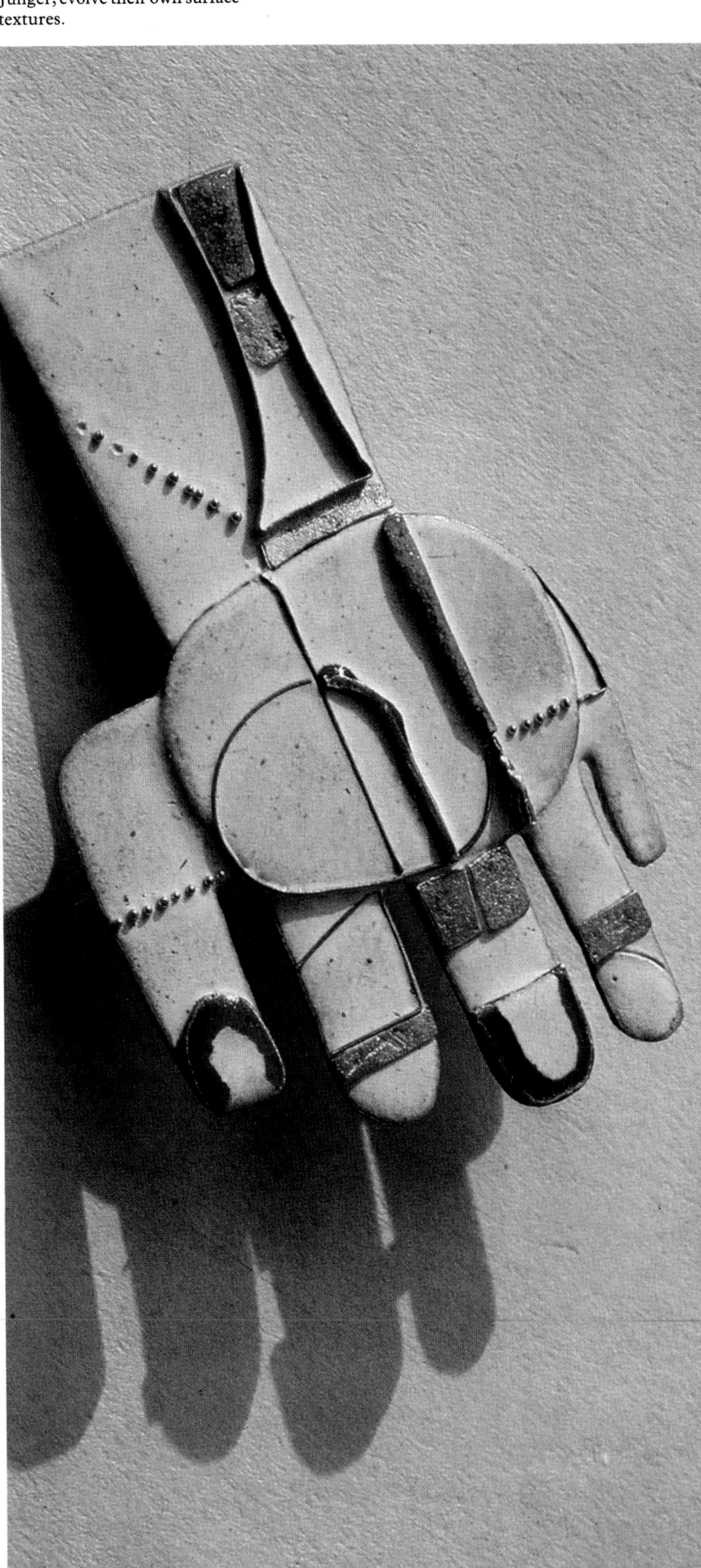

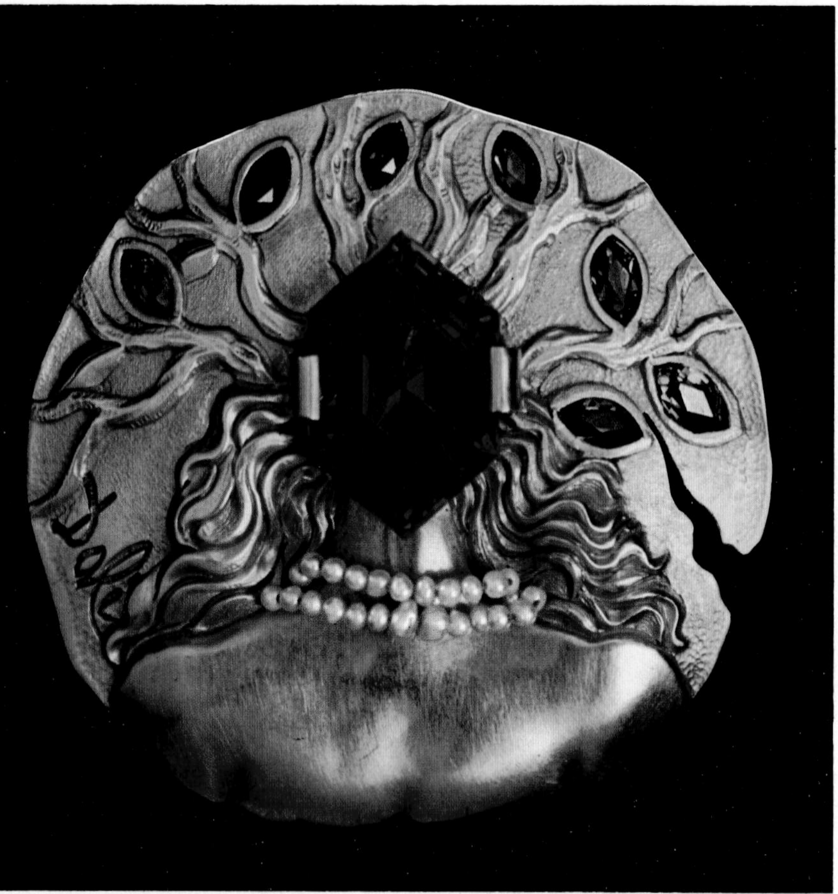

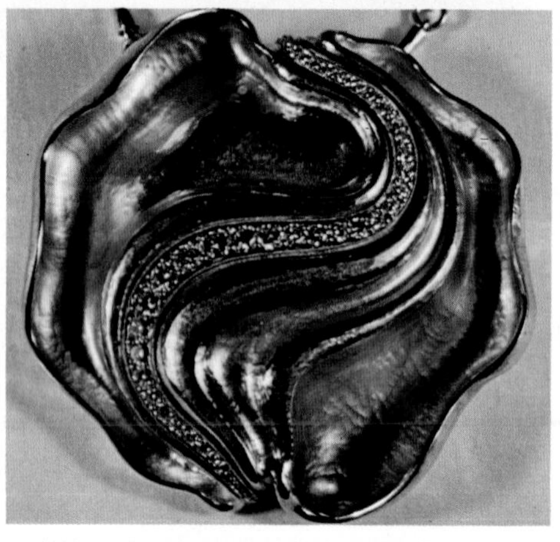

Top. A gold brooch inset with ruby, pearls and tourmaline, designed by Salvador Dali and made in 1960 by Carlos Alemany, New York, who makes most of Dali's jewels. It was commissioned by the Cheatham Foundation and exhibited in aid of charity. An effective medium for surrealism, large enough to be clear, small enough to intrigue, bright enough to be fun.

Above left. Gold brooch by Miko Matsue, Yokohama, 1973. This piece was an entry in the triennial Tendenzen exhibition at Reuchlinhaus Museum in the German jewelry center of Pforzheim, one of the main international surveys of jewelry as an art. Modern jewelers are fascinated by surface treatment, here worked on to a beautiful cast sculptured form.

Above right. Gold and diamond pendant by Leo de Vroomen, London, 1976. The relief design is embossed from the front by hammer and punch, a process known as chasing. The diamonds are brilliant cut with 58 facets, a style evolved in Venice in the mid-17th century. The best jewels are still made by hand, often, as here, using processes unchanged for thousands of years.

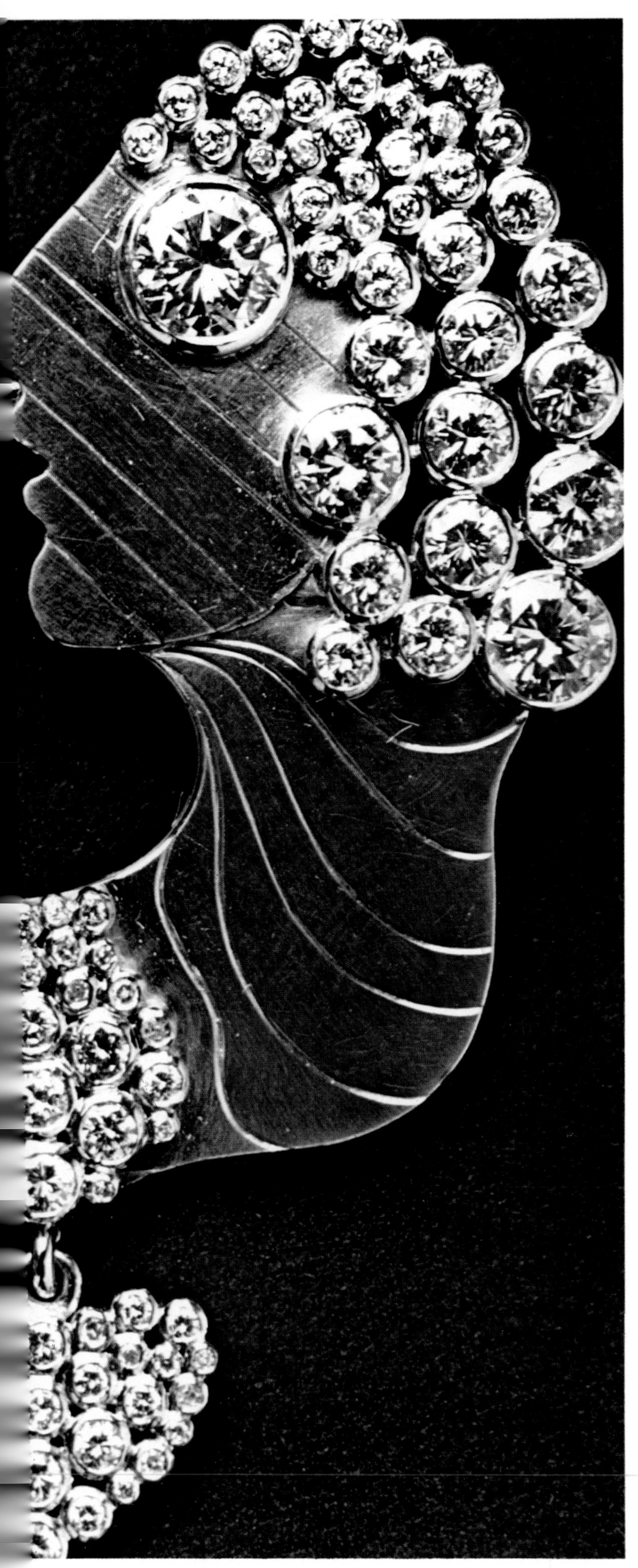

Above. Silver brooch with garnet and pearl by Eli Gera, Jaffa, Israel, 1975. Often working to a large scale—this piece is 11 cm ($4\frac{1}{2}$in) long—he treats cast metal in an original and free style.

Left. White gold and diamond brooch by Gisela Flugge, Lauheim, Germany. De Beers Diamonds—International Award, 1975. Striking and practical, it is unusual to find precious diamonds set with such wit today.

Below. A brooch cast in silver and set with lapis lazuli by Hidero Yamahara, Tokyo, 1974. The parallels are cast from one slab of wax composed of many wax strips a technique reminiscent of early Mexican work. Many designers and craft workshops evolve their own specialized production techniques to suit their personal design vision.

Top left. Five sets of multiple rings mounted on nickel and colored acrylic stands by Wendy Ramshaw, London, 1970. Both rings and stands show her gift for creating beautiful baluster forms on a simple lathe.

Left. Bracelet and brooch in yellow and white gold by Ros Conway, Kendal, England, 1977.

Center left. Fan-shaped brooch in boxwood, ebony, briar, rosewood, silver, ivory and amber; bangle in boxwood, ivory, silver and awabi shell by David Hensel, East Grinstead, England, 1977. He has revived the idea of figurative carving in jewels.

Right. A gold and moonstone tiara by Andrew Grima, worn as a neck ornament. Since Edwardian times, tiaras have often been convertible into necklaces.

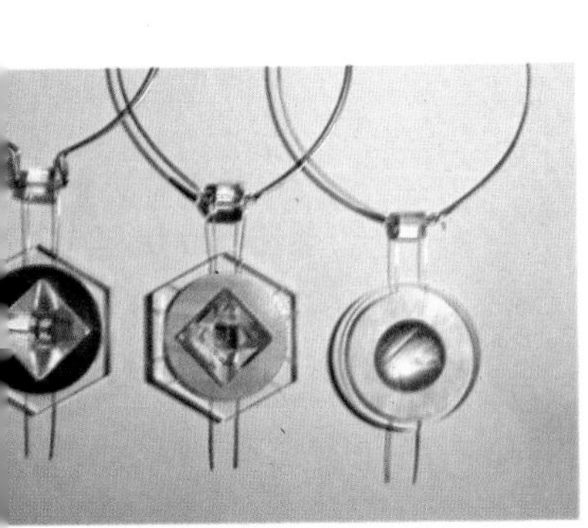

Above. Three pendants in silver and perspex/plexiglass by Pietro Gentili, Florence and Milan, 1969. A painter and sculptor self-trained as a jeweler, he avoids too precious materials so that poorer people can afford his work.

Left. Finger rings in silver and ivory by Michael Burton, Martock, England. With typical English fantasy, Burton engraves and carves houses near his home.

Below. The work of American innovators. A belt made of silver and feathers by Arlene Fisch, San Diego, California, who, like many artists, is inspired by the idea of the feather jewelry used in ancient Mexico, of which almost none survives. A brooch pin by Stanley Lechtzin of Philadelphia made in silver gilt with agate by an electroforming technique which he pioneered. American art jewels tend to be very large. The finger ring of gold, set with diamonds and natural emerald crystal by Arthur King, New York, gives an idea of scale. All three pieces 1975–7.

Above. Two necklaces by David Courts and Bill Hackett, London, 1974. Unusually for artist jewelers these two make rather valuable pieces like this necklace of gold pods with freshwater pearls and the exotic tie-up cord of silk (crochet by Sally Gidal) using mother of pearl, ivory, seed pearls and gold.

Right. Gold pin set with diamonds by Henry Shawah, Cambridge, Mass. He specializes in hammering gold to a fine tension, often leaving the marks as decoration. This piece is mounted on an 18th-century snuff box lid for display when not being worn and Shawah also makes small sculptured figures for wall decoration.

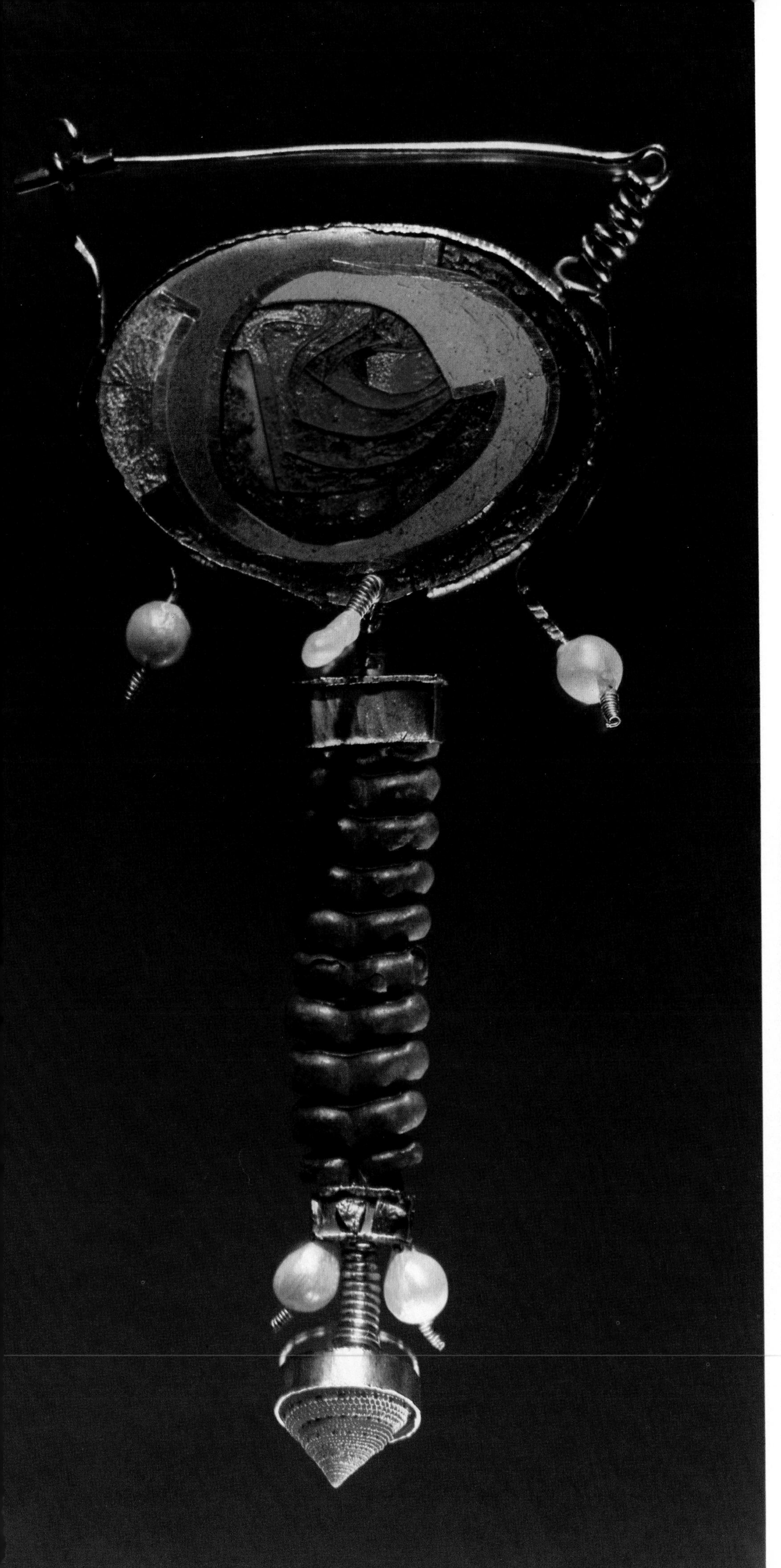

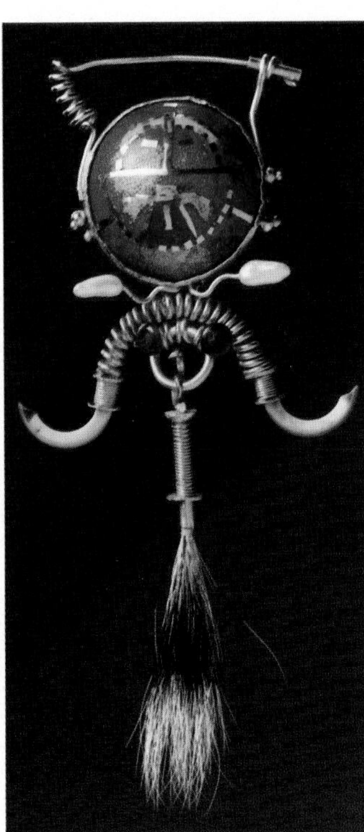

Above and left. Gold pins by Bill Harper, Tallahassee, Florida, 1977. Harper, who teaches at Florida State University, has invented a colorful style of cloisonné enamel and incorporates such found objects in his work as beetle shells, rattlesnake rattles, chipmunk teeth and hair as well as gems and freshwater pearls.

Left. Costume jewelry is intrinsically worthless but often of very vigorous design. Usually made of light, inexpensive metal such as dyed or anodized aluminum, it is shiny and unsatisfying to the touch, has not enough weight to feel good when worn and is not made to last. Although its impermanence allows design to follow contemporary fads the requirements of mass production limit the designer's scope.

Below. Popular low-priced boutique jewelry in silver and silver wire with a gray agate pendant and non-precious stones.

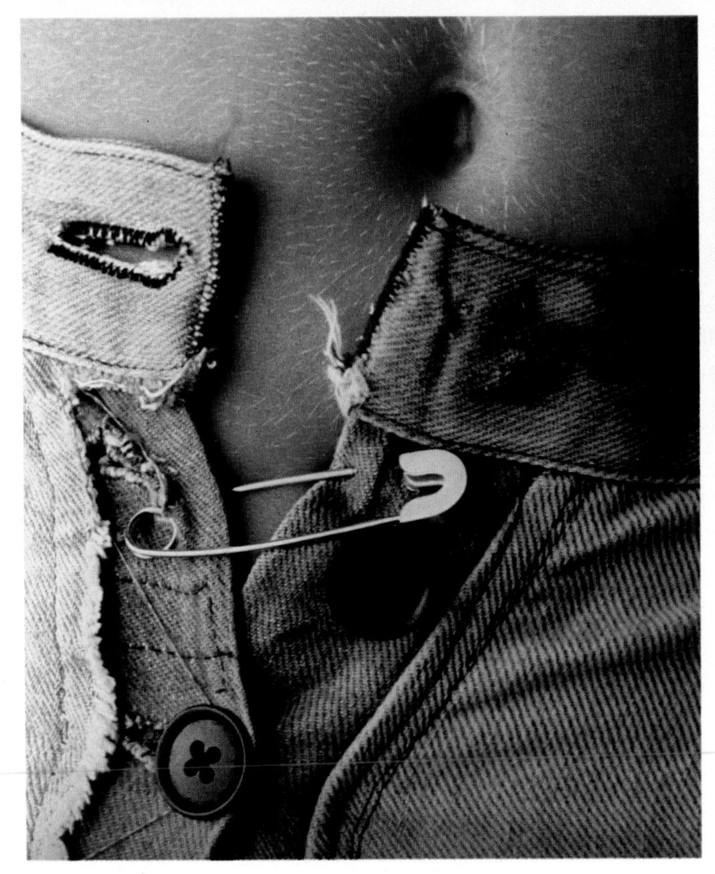

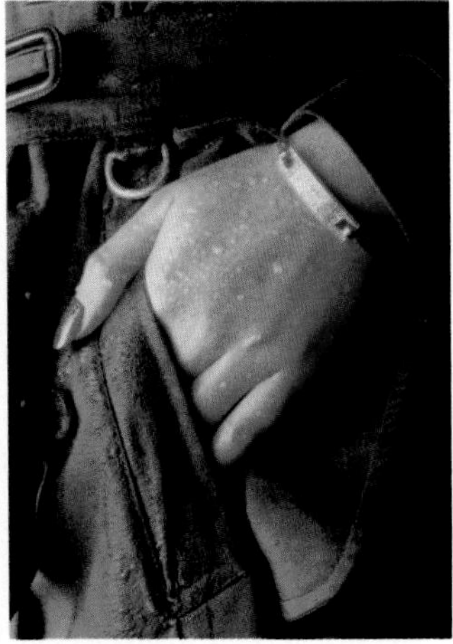

Above. Despite its high cost the appeal of gold is so strong, both intrinsically and as an investment, that quite simple pieces such as gold-hallmarked tags, identity bracelets and simple wrist ornaments like this are very popular.

Left. The simple shape of a safety-pin balances the display of wealth in a way that appeals to the fashion-conscious chic.

FOLK TRADITIONS

Folk jewels are easy to know, difficult to define. They are part of the continuous anonymous stream of life that we call ethnic. They represent races and tribes, not individuals. Because most of the world's population is poor, they are usually made from inexpensive local materials like shell, bone, leather or bronze. They are traditional, unselfconscious, not specially designed by or for a particular client, and they are usually limited to one area of people for whom they sometimes serve as a sort of badge. They often have a local geographical limitation and they usually have a strong character. They are the opposite of modern design and modern industry because they are timeless, and hand-made. But they seem fresh and distinguished to many people today in industrial societies who are tired of the meretricious ways of modern industry with its constant striving for change and lack of personal conviction.

As peasant and tribal communities grow weaker under modern commercial pressures, so we value their products more. The Paris left-bank art galleries commonly feature not only African masks, but beads and carved wood jewels too from the old French colonies of North and West Africa. London's boutiques, and there are more of them than in any other city, include specialists in Bedouin, Berber, Bali, Nigeria, Australian aboriginal, American Indian, and Eskimo and jewelry from many other areas. La Cienega Boulevard in Los Angeles, where only a century ago the "forty-niner" white men were trying to extinguish the Indians who got in the way of the gold rush, now features Indian jewels in a dozen of the smartest galleries.

Some of these jewels were used for money, as tokens of exchange. They often formed part or the whole of the Bride Price—what a husband had to pay to his new wife's family. As

Above. A Xingu Indian of Brazil wears an earring of mother of pearl made from river shells and suspended by rotan, a jungle vine. The Upper Xingu trade them with the Lower. Local jewels are made from anything found in the river or forest but are highly prized.

Right. The forging of metal gives tribal jewels a strong similarity although their origins are different. These bracelets and bangles come from (*left to right*) Somali, Ethiopia, Nigeria, Thailand and India. The Nigerian piece is in brass and made by the Hausa people, the others are alloys containing varying amounts of silver. Such ethnic pieces are becoming extremely popular in the West and increasing in value among collectors.

the owners were often nomadic, jewels made convenient trade tokens to pay not only for brides but for all the other commodities too—bows and arrows, spears, rolls of tobacco, guns and Western beads. Jewels were sometimes specially made to look valuable, like the heavy bronze bangles from Nigeria and West Africa called manillas, the bronze crosses of Icatanga, or the beautiful dragon's head silver bracelets from Thailand's old capital Ayudha, which are too massive for easy wearing, and sometimes too small in radius to fit over the wrist. More often jewels were simply whatever was most colorful, rare and therefore precious, like the round discs of ostrich egg shell broken and rubbed to shape by the bushmen of southwestern Africa, the feather fishing baits and ornaments of the South Pacific, or skins, teeth and bears claws for the Eskimos, or, most interesting, wampum. Wampum consists of strings of blue discs made from the centers of Atlantic coast clam shells, and it was so popular that the word wampum has come to mean all objects used by the American Indians for money.

The Indians of North America make a good starting point. They are typical of the decline of races, the growth of materialism which is happening everywhere—more than most, they have been persecuted and betrayed by the white men who conquered them. They were first massacred, then exiled from their territories, then confined to their reserves, then tamed and cultivated as tourist attractions. Now, the ancient connection with the natural world which gave the people their strength and dignity, is lost, and with it their indifference to "art" and to possession, their preference for useful objects and a good pure life. Instead, museums try to buy and categorize Indian jewels which were intended for gift and use, not for purchase and hoarding; and tourists want to

Above. Women from the Santo Domingo reserves sell jewels made by their menfolk.

Top left. Necklaces from the Indian tribes of Venezuela who live on the upper Orinoco river, in the foothills of the Andes. Seeds are used all over the world in ethnic jewelry and especially in India; they often have drug or sex attributes. The gray seeds, toasted from the original green color of the natural *cox lacryma jobi*, were made by the Hoti tribe; the white trade beads with melon-shaped seeds from the Cucurbita plant are from the Yekuana, as is the leather tassel, worn only by males and taboo for women; the deep red seed strung with wild boar's teeth was made by Piaroa Indians. These seeds have been drilled with palm spines, old fishooks and the teeth of the picure rodent.

Above right. Turquoise and silver, both being common in the South West, are favored materials, especially with the Navajo who made this so-called naga pendant. It is strong and simple, like all Indian work, and forms one of their basic design elements. Its origin is probably the round sun: most Indian art was closely related to the great mystic and sympathetic power of nature.

Opposite, top. New jewels made on Indian reservations in southwestern USA. The style of different tribes is still fairly distinct: the simple rhythm of the silver necklace with squash blossom and old Mexican coins is typical Navajo, as is the belt, strongly influenced by Mexican leatherwork. The turquoise and silver necklace and one of colorful hashi, thin shells, are Zuni work from near Santa Fé. Hopi work often uses decoration pierced through the outer layer of silver, of semi-abstract animal design, showing the silhouette on the darkened surface beneath. The round pendant is a funeral jewel with turquoise, coral and resin inlaid in silver; the headband in beads, originally bought from the white man, is typical of the work of many tribes.

Opposite, bottom. A group of new jewels made in British Columbia, where Indian culture is the strongest in North America. Silver buckle engraved with beaver by Russel Smith, Kwakiutl tribe, Vancouver; brooches in argillite, a local stone now reserved exclusively for Indian use, by Pat Dixon of Haida tribe, Queen Charlotte Is., symbolizing killer whale and raven; bangle by Earl Muldoe, one of the best known and most versatile artists of the Indian craft village at Ksan, Hazelton; ivory and abalone head by Ron Sebastian of Ksan. Animal and bird themes predominate in Canadian Indian jewels; abstract patterns are popular in the US.

have and wear what was to the Indians not a decoration but a sort of incarnation of the great spirit of nature.

The Indian languages have no word for art: Indian products were all functional, often with a view to enhancing the people's feeling of relationship with, and dependence upon, nature. In so far as Indians decorated themselves, they usually wanted to define their rank, ferocity, agility: there was more to their appearance than simply looking beautiful.

American Indians hardly had access to metalwork and stone until the white man arrived about 100 years ago. Metal was important for jewelry, because it facilitated cutting, filing and chasing; stone (which was often mined and polished with the help of metal apparatus) provided the bright colors which Indians have always loved. But to speak of traditional American Indian jewels is to smooth over a central question: is folk art a continuation of what was old, or is it that made by the masses for the masses, regardless of its resemblance to antiquity?

The main production of Indian jewelry was in the south west, where silver became available from Mexico after 1853, and where turquoise shells and other stones were easily found in the ground as soon as the tribes stopped being nomadic hunters, and settled, usually unwillingly, into a home territory of their own.

The jewelry pioneers seem to have been the Navajo. During their brutal exile by the US government at Basque Redondo by Fort Sumner, they lost a way of life but found a new craft. They discovered metal at the same time as their textiles ceased to have a central spiritual significance. They stopped making the blankets which are now world famous and started making silver jewelry, possibly as a result of having to fake their metal ration tickets, whose official supply was insufficient to avoid starvation. Silver, after the Navajo exile finished in 1868, soon became for them, and for the Pueblo, a symbol for tribal pride. Ever since then, the Navajo and Pueblo, have been the chief metal workers. The Pueblo, being village-based, were influenced by, and sometimes converted to, Roman Catholicism, so that, unlike the Navajo, they often used the cross as an ornament.

At first, professional traders used to be the only people buying jewelry in the Indian reservations but slowly the public appetite increased, on the one hand causing some of the Indians themselves to make special tourist pieces for their visitors, and on the other, the creation of commercial producers. After 1899, for example, the Fred Harvey company was set up, associated with Hermann Schweizer and the Santa Fé railroad; railroad passengers were offered jewelry which was Indian in varying degrees. As the years passed, the Indian content diminished, until some producers used few, if any Indian craftsmen.

The vintage period was 1880 to 1900, when the Indians used first US, then Mexican coins, to melt into jewelry, before this was forbidden in 1899. By 1976, the trickle of "Indian" jewelry had become a cataract, much of it originating in Hong Kong and the Philippine Islands. Only nine states in USA have established any legislation to enforce accurate trade descriptions: elsewhere, shops easily can, and many do, misrepresent any simple silver jewelry as Indian. The booming public demand is now so undiscriminating, that few Indians benefit from it, most of the profit going into non-Indian pockets.

The best place to find the jewels is of course in the reservations. The Navajo are in the corner formed by the states of Utah, Colorado, New Mexico and Arizona where the main towns are Ganado, Crystal and Gallup. The Zuni, one of the Pueblo tribes taught by the Navajo, are in western New Mexico between Santa Fé, Gallup and Albuquerque. For them, silver is a stage for stone and shell: they love mosaic, inlay, channel and row work—for which they arrange more or less similar bits of turquoise in a rhythmical order with a charming irregularity. Another Zuni distinguishing feature is their animal fetishes, which they carve in abalone, clam shell, coral, jet, mother-of-pearl, turquoise, serpentine, tortoise-shell, pipestone and soapstone.

The Hopi were taught by the Zuni: their reservation is inside that of the Navajo in south-east Arizona, north-east of Flagstaff, by Phoenix and Winslow. They evolved a distinctive technique of overlay by which a pattern is pierced through a sheet of silver which is then soldered to a flat base beneath, somewhat like cut-card ornament on British antique silver. The Hopi have formed their own silver craft guild, an encouraging sign for the future. The Santo Domingo reservation is between Albuquerque and Santa Fé. They share with the Zuni a preference for turquoise and shell, especially the heshi from which they make substantial and satisfying beads. Santo Domingo jewels make a fine market show under the colonnade of the old Governor's Palace in Santa Fé.

Stones were first used about 1900; solder was also rare till then. Till 1932 (when it became illegal), coins were often soldered to a loop and used as buttons, then reused as coins when needed. In the 1920s and after, pawning became possible through the new white man's banks. Heavy silver heirloom pieces were often pawned until the harvest came in or the sheep were sheared, and then redeemed; often, if not redeemed, they reached the market, or were melted for bullion at the Denver Mint. Until quite recently, the main influence on Indian silver jewelry, was the traveling Mexican smiths or plateros, although stylistically Navajo work is perhaps closer to Mexican leather.

The concha or shell was the standard ornament for belts—an oval pierced with two triangles through which the belt passed. Squash blossom is the name (perhaps derived from the squash flower, probably in fact showing a pomegranate), the form is a sphere with a sort of tripod through it, the basis of many necklace designs. The naja is the crescent, again prominent in many necklaces. The jacla is the turquoise bead necklace which was originally tied through a hole in the ear lobe with a thong, and yanked off if the bride was unfaithful. Small wonder that in recent times they are seldom seen worn as earrings.

Beads, which are so popular in the north-west of America and in Canada, replacing the old porcupine quills, were made available by white men only after the true open air life of the natives was limited by the hunters and the railroads less than a century ago. The arrival of hard cutting metal in the shape of knives, and of aniline dies replacing the softer vegetable colors, had little direct effect on jewels but helped to change a way of life. Nostalgia and history explain some of the appeal of these crudely made, but powerful statements.

Round Cape Alaska in the North, the Chilkat sub-tribe invented a type of blanket with a bear, so to speak, spread out flat all over it; the Tlingit tribe nearby, decorate their similar dance aprons with dangling thongs bearing puffin beaks and deer hooves alternatively, to make a rattling noise as well as a jewel-like dangling fringe. These are supposed to be the spirits of mythological beings who could help the shamans or doctors to cure an ill patient. The Hurons, of Quebec province, used dyed moose hair sewn on to black-dyed deerskin, to decorate bags and pouches until they became as colorful as any enamel neckpieces. Jewels were mostly made by women—the men of the tribe concentrated on the arts of war and religion.

The Cherokee are typical of these unfortunate people; in

1838–9 the "Trail of Tears" led them from their Carolina home, to what was then inhospitable Oklahoma. There may be as many as 50,000 of them settled there today, the second largest tribe in USA; they have almost no artistic identity, they have lost their aboriginal culture, adapted to the whites and preserved only their versatility and simple vision of fitness for purpose, together with a love of pattern to counteract the vastness of nature. The same can be said of the Mohawks, with their trading stations scattered along the Mohawk Trail into the Berkshire Mountains of Northern Massachusetts. There is an enormous and splendid heritage from the great open spaces but it is questionable whether the jewels can still honestly be called "folk."

At the turn of the century, the more an Indian paid for his jewelry, the more prestige he could claim it gave to him; today, the tourist mind works in precisely the opposite direction: boasts are made about the cheapness of purchases from often unsuspecting native producers. One can only hope that the US government which has so nearly extinguished the fascinating natural culture of the American Indian, will preserve some vestige of their dignified and beautiful jewelry, one of the only surviving indigenous crafts in the whole vastness of the country.

It is the same story with many other tribal jewels and people the world over: the bantu of South Africa, the aborigines of Australia, the "hairy" Ainu of Japan, that country's original inhabitants, who can today be found only as tourist attractions in small villages of rush-thatched huts like Shiraoi near Noboribetsu in the North island of Hokkaido. Native jewels, where they survived, as with the niello-inlaid silver of Thailand or the gold-inlaid iron of Toledo, the carved gourds of Equador or Bali's deep-cut gewgaws made of nuts, are often of rather recent commercial derivation, a barely recognizable travesty of some much different original.

But there are at least four huge areas where folk jewels are still made in the old style. Africa, moving fast in the face of political "advancement;" Arabia, where oil is found to be more entrancing than any peasant customs but where the old bedouin life with its tents and its wandering herds of sheep and goats remains very strong and where also the Moslem religion, with its custom of keeping women secluded in purdah, still shapes everyone's life; India and Pakistan, miraculously unchanging; and Mexico also wonderfully constant with its thin tin and silver jewels centred on the city of Taxco.

African jewels begin with the clever sophisticated cast bronze and gold "soul bearers" badges of Ghana, originated by the Ashanti and Baule tribes, some of the most creative people on the whole continent. From the 17th century, when the tribes came near to their present location, they perfected casting methods giving a wonderful delicacy of finish which is still achieved today. The gold content is usually very low by European standards—Europeans call the dark color "native gold" but the surface textures have the delicious tactile appeal of the finest silken fabric. Worn, usually by men, as badges of religious or martial office, the jewels often show local animals such as crocodiles or wolves, creeping in miniature through some finely drawn geometrical fantasy, a circular maze or spiral web. Some of the strength and ferocity of the animals was presumably imparted in this way to the wearer. Now, tourist demand for instance from the Hausa traders on the waterfront at Accra harbor, seems big enough to ensure the

survival of these superb designs based as they are more on fine technique than on ancient magic. The new cast jewels from Kumasi are almost identical to the old, a tribute to the ancestral skill of strong peasant cultures.

Inland lay the huge 14th- and 15th-century kingdom of the Manding civilization, called Mali, much larger than the modern state that has adopted that name. Here, too, local gold was and is the basis of the local taste for jewels. The style is different from Ashanti: perhaps flavored by the presence of numerous Arab traders in salt and slaves. Mali pieces are often made in a rather Arab taste with endless filigree perfections and circular bosses and they are forged, not cast. Whereas Arab jewels along the North African coast from Mogadishu, Eritrea or in Malta, tend to be light and flimsy, almost transparent, giving them an unpleasant trinkety cheapness, creations round the Sahara have an impressive size, weight and solidity. Worn mostly by women, they represent wealth and beauty in a way that Europeans can well understand. Not far away, the powerful masks of the Dogon peoples plunge us into the Africa of witch doctors and superstition, a reminder that jewels without people do not carry their full message. Masks, indeed, are the real jewels of Africa—sometimes carried before the face, sometimes placed over the head, sometimes waved almost as a flag, these rather than gold, are the African's passport to eternity.

The Masai tribes of Kenya evolved an imposing headdress of feathers ranged parallel in columns like ladders on either side of the head, with wisps of giraffe hair at the end. The lucky wearer assumes some of the grace of a bird, some of the speed of a giraffe. The Samburu, related to the Masai people, whose territory is some 220 miles North of Nairobi, until this

Above. An Ethiopian woman wears glass and shell beads, silver bracelets and earrings. The silver in locally made folk jewelry often comes from melted down Austrian thaler coins, distributed in Ethiopia in the late 19th century. Ethiopian cast metal beads, especially silver, are heavy and some of the finest in Africa.

Opposite. A group of folk jewelry, 1977. Two necklets made of brightly colored European beads assembled by Bantu tribesmen near Johannesburg. The three silver buttons were made in Karachi. The ends are pulled through the fabric like "bachelor's buttons."

Above left. More bead jewelry. A wedding necklace from Afghanistan using coral, silver plain and filigree beads and black glass, which shows extensive use of granulation (*left*); a hair ornament made of shells and cotton from Pakistan and a Tibetan necklace made of coral, turquoise and amber beads (*right*).

Top right. Older tribal jewelry, once thought of as magic, is now seen as powerful sculpture. The 19th-century cast brass fish and necklet from Senufa, Senegal, probably once represented river food in a dry country. The 15th-century carved jade eagle "axe-god" and beads from Costa Rica may have symbolized the freedom of flight and travel in a small country confined by sea. Both these pieces were assembled by a modern artist jeweler, Irena Corwin of New York, in 1976. Tribal jewels have had a strong influence on modern work, both among art jewelers and in ethnic inspired costume jewelry made from materials such as leather, cheap metals, beads and shell.

Above. A girl from Sumba Island in Indonesia wears huge, simple, ivory bracelets and large gold earrings, intricately formed in the shape of female genitalia as a fertility symbol. The local craftsmen no longer work in gold and these are heirlooms 200 years old.

century, used to terrify the East African bantu farming tribes. Just as a Masai did not, and does not feel properly himself without a spear, so a Samburu will want to be one of the warriors (Mozani) painted with red ochre, with hair plaited in small braids greased to lie down smooth and look like a cap, and carrying a white, red and black shield of buffalo hide and a long (now illegal) javelin. Cattle robbery and war, hitherto the chief pastimes, are now prohibited, so that care of their own appearance is now a chief occupation. The women have broad necklaces of beads, collars of palm bast and bright colored pearls, bangles of silver wire, and of copper which contains some gold. They carry water in large leather flasks, milk in plaited waterproof baskets, and they drink from hollowed horns. Often a garland of beads goes over the head above the forehead and another across each cheek nestling in the groove between mouth and chin, both garlands meeting above the ear. To detach this sort of jewel from the life to which it belongs is to lose its glory. Some African bracelets were as important as weapons as for adornment.

Further south, elephant hair is woven into plaited bracelets. In South Africa itself, native women, who have emigrated from many northern territories, like to thread tiny colored glass European beads into rather stiff necklets or bangles patterned into bright primary colored triangles or squares, much like the cheerful paintwork on the walls of native villages on the veldt. In Nigeria and along the north coast, large cylindrical glass beads, made of many different colors laminated, have been imported from Venice since the 17th century, and for centuries formed the basis of a tribal money system. Now, European people often think erroneously that these beads are an indigenous African creation; what they do show is the African's love of bright color and incident, which mix so well with the jungle, the opposite of restrained European good taste. A Suk girl in Kenya may wear as many as 40 necklaces and rows of beads all at once, stretching from upper neck to outer shoulder, and perhaps six round earrings in each ear too.

In the Arabic world, jewels are mostly silver, made now in the remoter part of Oman (especially in the silver city of Nizwa) and Yemen. The tradition of the desert is not as much colorful as dense: thick camel hair bedouin blankets mostly black and dark brown with patterns in white, dark red and purple rings woven by the wandering Qashqai tribes of Iran, tiny circular mirrors glittering in the red and blue encrusted wool wall hangings for the tents. Arab silver and brass jewels are more massive than delicate, perhaps symbols of the near-slavery to men of the women who wear them. Big silver bangles and anklets look surprisingly like manacles. It is appropriate that the best places to see such things, are the old prisons, once fortresses, now museums, in the new Gulf states like Qatar and Dubai. A Jewish bride in the Yemen may take 4 or 5 hours to drape herself in all her jewels, dozens of gold and silver sphere necklaces, hundreds of thin coin pendants and pearl and seed pearl necklaces. When fully dressed, she is so heavy she can hardly move, a symbol of feminine subservience to the dominant male.

In India and Pakistan, jewels are not so much ceremonial symbols as everyday dress. All women, and some men too in the remoter parts, want simply to wear their wealth: banks are not much trusted, so you just put your bank balance around your neck every day to give you a feeling of security and to impress your friends. There is no high mysticism here; this no more than a prudent wish to survive, to keep one's securities intact. Gold is the premier metal—its import into India is illegal, yet India remains the world's biggest gold importer. The gold bazaar in Karachi or New Delhi will know the latest price for gold within minutes of the London fixing—so for that matter will the primitive looking Armenian section of the Damascus bazaar. A simple ring or stud for ear or nose is the normal merchandise, a weighing machine the means by which it is priced.

With Indian silver jewels a new dimension appears. Noise, all sorts of dangling bits, shake one against the other to give an agreeable feeling of activity both to wearer and observer. India and Pakistan are full of silver jewelers, most working in their own shops in the bazaar High Street, sometimes up a few steps in a sort of public front room as in the old city of Bundi, sometimes at stalls in the street in the new silver bazaars at Karachi and New Delhi. Most Indian jewels are light and graceful, made of silver wire rather roughly soldered. They are sold throughout the continent and in Europe too, cheap, and unpretentious, decorative and rather mundane.

Folk jewels are a modern link with the past, in their way as evocative and beautiful as any modern artist's fantasy.

MUSEUMS & EXHIBITIONS

A guide to major museums and other collections open to the public.

Aachen *Cathedral Treasury :* Superb early medieval shrines and reliquary jewels.
Amsterdam *Rijksmuseum :* Fine renaissance jewels and plate in treasure room.
Andechs (Bavaria) *Benedictine Abbey :* Wonderful early medieval religious pilgrimage objects.
Ankara *National Museum :* Center for Hittite culture.
Athens *National Archaeological Museum :* Foremost Mycenean gold, including Schliemann's discoveries; ancient and Hellenistic jewels, including recently bequeathed Stathatos collection. *Benaki Museum :* Superb Hellenistic and 19th-century folk jewels.
Axum (Ethiopia) *Cathedral :* Big silver crowns and regalia.
Baghdad *National Museum :* World's foremost Sumerian, Babylonian and Assyrian gold and seals including Woolley's discoveries from Ur (others at British Museum, Pennsylvania University, Philadelphia).
Baltimore *Walters Art Gallery :* Superb renaissance carved stones and other 16th-century conceits; good dark ages and art nouveau collections. Shown in a brilliant modern installation.
Basel *City Museum :* Medieval guild treasures, shown in historic converted church.
Beirut *National Museum :* Phoenician seals and glass, ceremonial axes.
Berlin (West) *Antike Sammlung :* Among world's foremost ancient Greek collections; Roman treasure and Ptolemaic mummy portraits wearing jewels. Superb modern installation with lectures, films etc. *Charlottenburg Palace* (Kunstgewerbemuseum): Superb dark ages and medieval jewels, including Guelph treasure. *Dahlem Museums :* Among world's best general displays, especially of pre-Columbian and Byzantine work. (**East**) *Schloss Köpenick :* Empress Gisela treasure (1,000 years old) unearthed by canal digging at Mainz; good Berlin ironwork.
Berne *Historisches Museum :* Dark ages buckles, Alemmanic and Burgundian treasures, later medieval badges.
Birmingham (England) *City Museum :* Early 19th-century industrial production, including Matthew Boulton pieces.
Bogota *Museo de Oro :* Over 10,000 gold jewels and emeralds bought by government to prevent smuggling and loss of pre-Columbian history. Brilliant modern installation.
Boston (Mass.) *Fine Art Museum :* General survey dispersed through many rooms.
Brno *National Museum :* Dark ages jewels.
Brussels *Musée du Cinquantenaire :* Relics of 15th-century Burgundian empire.
Bucharest *National Museum :* Dark ages work, including superb Petrossa treasure.
Budapest *National Gallery :* Dark ages and late medieval jewels. *Royal Palace :* Crown jewels, including King Stephen's crown (1001) recently returned from USA
Cairo *Egyptian Museum :* World's foremost for Egyptology, including discoveries from Tutenkhamun's tomb.
Cambridge (England) *Fitzwilliam Museum :* Some medieval work.
Cambridge (Mass.) *Peabody Museum :* Pre-Columbian gold (seldom shown).
Cleveland (Ohio) *Art Museum :* General survey.
Cologne *Römisch-Germanisches Museum :* One of Europe's finest treasure rooms, including Roman and dark ages jewels.
Copenhagen *National Museum :* Magnificent bronze age and Viking bronze and gold. *Kuntstindustrimuseet :* General survey since renaissance, including art nouveau, Jensen and modern jewels. *Rosenborg Castle :* 16th-century orders of Christian IV, including garter given by England's Elizabeth I.
Cracow *Wawel Castle :* Polish crown jewels, especially 17th- and 18th-century orders.
Dallas *Fine Art Museum :* Pre-Columbian gold, Wise Collection.
Darmstadt *Hessisches Landes Museum :* Art nouveau and Bauhaus jewels.
Delhi *National Museum :* Moghul jewels, a few of the world's best—if on show.
Dresden *Grünes Gewölbe* (Green Vault): Crown jewels of Saxony, the world's richest treasury, 16th-19th century, including masterpieces by Dinglinger for Augustus the Strong (18th century).
Dublin *National Museum :* World's best prehistoric torcs, Celtic and early Christian.
Dumbarton Oaks (Washington D.C.) *Research Library and Collection :* World's best Byzantine collection.
Edinburgh *National Museum of Antiquities :* Early medieval and dark ages Scottish jewels, including the Traprain treasure. *Royal Scottish Museum :* General survey, including replicas.
Essen *Cathedral treasury :* World's best medieval brooches.
Flagstaff (Arizona) *Museum of Northern Arizona :* Finest Navajo and Hopi jewels.
Florence *Archaeological Museum :* Etruscan jewels. *Bargello :* Fine renaissance jewels, including 15th-century jewels and medals in contemporary setting. *Pitti Palace (Museo dell'Argenti) :* Later renaissance jewels, mainly small but including Lorenzo dei Medici 15th-century cups and ornaments in florid rooms.
Hamburg *Kunstgewerbe Museum :* General survey, including ancient Greek.
Heraklion *Archaeological Museum :* World's finest Minoan collection, including discoveries from Knossos (some also at Oxford).
Hyderabad *Salar Jung Museum :* Fine Moghul jewels.
Istanbul *Topkapi Museum :* Sultans' crown jewels 16th-19th century. *Archaeological Museum :* Discoveries from Troy and the world's best Islamic jewels.
Jerusalem *Jewish Museum :* World's finest Jewish ritual jewels, also ancient glass, shown in a superb modern installation.
Karachi *National Museum :* Beads from Mohenjo Daro, Hellenistic Taxila hoard.
Karlsruhe *Schloss :* Good general survey.
Kiev *National Museum :* Scythian and Greek jewels.
Leningrad *Hermitage :* World's best Scythian, Greek and Sassanian jewels. The gold room is not always accessible but is worth a long wait.
Liège *St Paul's Cathedral treasury :* Superb 15th-century Burgundian enamels, Charles the Bold reliquary (1471).
Lima *Mujica Gallo :* Pre-Columbian gold collection, Inca and earlier.
Lisbon *Gulbenkian Museum :* Superb Lalique and art nouveau jewels.
Liverpool *City Museum :* Napoleon's jewels.
London *British Museum :* Wonderful survey from ancient times to the renaissance, the world's richest, but dispersed through many galleries, includes Sumerian treasure from Ur, Aegina hoard (Minoan), Ziwiye (Persian), Mildenhall (Roman), Esquitine (Roman), Sutton Hoo (Anglo-Saxon). *Victoria and Albert Museum :* Superb jewelry room, the world's best general, ancient-to-modern survey, including 19th-century Cory bequest. *Tower of London :* British crown jewels. *Museum of London :* Jewelry workshops and tools, Roman to 16th century; Cheapside hoard (also represented in British Museum and Victoria and Albert). *Museum of Mankind :* World's best pre-Columbian jewels and folk jewels from everywhere. *Horniman Museum :* Good folk jewels. *Goldsmiths' Hall :* World's biggest modern collection, often on loan, appointment necessary to view.
Los Angeles *Museum of the Southwest :* Survey of Californian Indian work.
Mainz *Römisch-Germanisches Zentral (Schloss)* and *Mittelrheinishes Landesmuseum :* Both rich in dark ages work, hundreds of fibulas, including replicas.
Madrid *Museo Arqueologico :* Iberian and dark ages jewels well shown; Guarrazar and Juvea treasure. *Museo Lazaro Galdeano :* Good Byzantine and folk collections.

Mexico City *Anthropological Museum* : Stunning modern display of Aztec and pre-Aztec life, but few jewels.
Monza *Cathedral treasury* : Theodelinda's jewels, iron crown of Lombardy (*c* 800).
Moscow *Kremlin Armory* : Crowns of the tsars, Byzantine jewels, *Diamond Fund* (also in Kremlin), Catherine the Great's crown jewels, Orlov diamond. Displays open only irregularly.
Munich *Residenz Palace* : Crown jewels of the Wittelsbach electors and kings of Bavaria, medieval to 19th-century, one of Europe's richest treasuries with renaissance masterpieces. *Bavarian National Museum* : Good survey in period rooms. *Antike Sammlung* : One of Europe's most modern exhibitions, excellent Greek and Roman collection.
Naples *National Museum* : Roman jewels from Pompeii etc, Farnese renaissance cameos. Irregular opening.
New York *Metropolitan Museum* : Good general survey, especially fine Egyptian jewels. *Museum of the American Indian* : Good Indian jewels, irregularly shown.
Nuremberg *Germanisches National Museum* : Dark ages jewels in a superb modern building.
Oviedo *Cathedral treasury* : Dark ages jewels.
Oxford *Ashmolean Museum* : Ancient jewels, especially Evans' Knossos discoveries (including the best Minoan seals), 18th-century watches, survey of finger rings.
Palermo *Cathedral* : Jewels of Frederick II (*c* 1215).
Paris *Louvre* : General survey, especially ancient jewels and 18th-century gold boxes; crown jewels in Galerie d'Apollon. *Musée des Arts Décoratifs* : 18th-century paste and art nouveau jewels, irregularly shown. *Bibliothèque Nationale (Cabinet des Médailles)* : Earliest crown jewels of Childeric, renaissance medals. *Musée de Cluny* : Medieval jewels.
Philadelphia *Pennsylvania University* : Superb ancient jewels, including some from Ur and recent middle east excavations.
Pforzheim *Reuchlinhaus Museum* : International collection of modern artists' jewels in fine modern installation; superb general survey ancient to 19th century.
Prague *St Vitus Cathedral* : Crown jewels shown every ten years. *National Museum* : Dark ages jewels.
Quito *National Bank* : Pre-Columbian gold.
Rheims *Cathedral* : Charlemagne talisman and early medieval jewels.
Rome *Vatican Museum* : World's best Etruscan collection. *Villa Giulia* : Etruscan jewels. *Alto Medioevo Museo* : Medieval jewels.
St Maurice d'Agaune (Switzerland) *Abbey* : Early medieval relics.
Skokloster (Sweden) *Castle* : Gustavus Adolphus relics.
Stockholm *Royal Palace* : Crown jewels. *Nordiska Museum* : Prehistoric and folk jewels. *National Museum of Antiquities* : World's best Viking gold.
Stuttgart *LGA* (Landesgewerbeamt) *Museum* : World's best Jugendstil.
Taipeh (Taiwan) *Peking imperial treasury* : World's best ancient Chinese.
Taranto *National Museum* : World's best Hellenistic collection.
Taxila (Pakistan) *Monastery* : Early Buddhist gold.
Tehran *Bank Mehli* : Crown jewels, fabulous wealth. *National Museum of Archaeology* : Ancient gold room, including excavations from Persepolis.
Tel Aviv *Glass Museum* : Phoenician and Roman glass and jewels.
Tokyo *National Museum* : Prehistoric jewels, samurai armor.
Toledo *Cathedral treasury* : Dark ages jewels.
Vancouver *University of Columbia* : Huge Indian collection, brilliantly displayed.
Victoria (Vancouver Is.) *Provincial Museum* : Best collection of British Columbian jewels.
Vienna *Kunsthistorisches Museum* : General survey, especially dark ages, Byzantine and renaissance, including Rudolph II treasures. *Hofburg Schatzkammer* : Superb collection, including Charlemagne crown jewels and 15th-century Burgundian work. *Museum für Angewandte Kunst* : Jugendstil, Berlin ironwork.
Visby (Sweden) *Gotland Museum* : Viking jewels.
Washington, D.C. *National Gallery* : Widener collection of renaissance jewels, irregularly shown.
York *Castle Museum* : 18th- and 19th-century craft workshops.
Zürich *National Museum* : General survey, period rooms.

BIBLIOGRAPHY

Artamanov, M. I. *Treasures from Scythian Tombs*, Thames & Hudson, London, 1969
Aldred, Cyril, *Jewels of the Pharaohs*, Thames & Hudson, 1971
Cellini, Benvenuto, *Treatise on Goldsmithing* (trs. C. R. Ashbee), Essex House, London, 1898
Gallo, M. M., *The Gold of Peru*, Aurel Bongers, Recklinghausen, 1959
Gere, Charlotte, *Victorian Jewellery Design*, William Kimber, London, 1972
Hayward, J. F., *Virtuoso Goldsmiths* (late renaissance/mannerist), Sotheby-Park Bernet, London, 1976
Higgins, R. A., *Greek and Roman Jewellery*, Methuen, London, 1961
Hughes, Graham, *Modern Jewellery*, Studio Vista, London (revised ed.) 1968; *Art of Jewelry*, Studio Vista, London, 1972
Lewis, D. S., *Antique Paste Jewellery*, Faber & Faber, London, 1970.
Oman, Charles, *British Rings, 800–1914*, Batsford, London, 1974
Snowman, K., Art of Carl Fabergé, Faber & Faber, London, 1953
Siviero, Rodolfo, *Jewelry and Amber of Italy* (collection of National Museum, Naples, archaic to 19th century), McGraw-Hill, London, 1959
Twining, Lord, *A History of the Crown Jewels of Europe*, Batsford, London, 1960; *European Regalia*, Batsford, London, 1967
Tylecote, R. F., *A History of Metallurgy*, Metals Society, London, 1976

ACKNOWLEDGEMENTS

Unless otherwise stated all the illustrations on a given page are credited to the same source.
Photographs were supplied by Dr Atkins page 27*tl*, 27*tr*; Asprey page 78, 88; Cooper-Bridgeman Library page 5, 60–61, 64*t*, 68*t*, 68*br*, 69*t*, 70*l*, 73*t*, 73*b*, 74–75, 76*b*, 77*r*; Crafts Advisory Committee page 97*cr*; de Beers page 24; Editions Graphiques Gallery page 91*tl*, 91*tc*, 91*b*, 93*r*; Andre Emmerich Gallery page 48; Werner Forman Archive page 44–45, 49*bl*; Garrard page 69*b*, 72; Gold Information Bureau page 6–7, 9*l*, 95, 109*bl*, 109*br*; Andrew Grima page 24*br*, 25*tl*, 26*tr*, 26*br*, 97*bl*, 105*r*; Sonia Halliday page 47*br*, 59*tl*; Robert Harding Associates page 16, 17*tl*, 17*tr*, 24*tr*, 28*b*, 115*b*; Michael Holford page 9*r*, 12, 37*t*, 38–39, 43*l*, 47*tr*, 47*bl*, 50–51, 51*b*, 56, 61, 67, 74*l*, 82; Graham Hughes page 11, 15, 17*cr*, 19*t*, 23, 26*bl*, 29*t*, 30, 31, 32, 34, 35, 36, 37*b*, 38*b*, 41, 42, 43*r*, 44*t*, 46*l*, 46–47, 49*br*, 51*t*, 52*l*, 53, 54, 55, 57, 58, 59*tr*, 59*cr*, 59*b*, 60, 61, 66, 68*bl*, 70, 71, 75*t*, 75*cr*, 75*bl*, 77*l*, 79, 80*bl*, 80*br*, 81, 83, 85*b*, 87, 89, 90*t*, 92*l*, 92*r*, 94, 96, 97*tl*, 97*tr*, 98, 99, 100, 101, 102, 103, 104, 105*l*, 106, 107, 112, 113, 114, 115*tr*; Alan Hutchison page 8, 10, 17*cl*; Institute of Geological Sciences page 24*bl*, 25*tr*, 25*b*, 27*br*; Jones Jewellery page 14; Kutchinsky/Norman Parkinson/Slade Bluff and Bigg page 22; Andrew Lawson page 17*b*; Bill Leimbach page 110*tl*, 115*cr*; Museo Arqueologico Nacional, Madrid page 45*b*; National Portrait Gallery page 65; Picturepoint page 27*bl*; Platinum Guild page 20–21; Mauro Pucciarelli page 38*t*; Scala page 44*bl*; Sotheby's Belgravia page 91*tr*; Victoria and Albert Museum page 63, 64*b*; ZEFA (UK) Ltd page 28*t*, 29*cl*, 29*cr*, 108.
Special photography was carried out by A. C. Cooper page 75*br*; Paul Forrester jacket, page 1, 3, 13, 18, 19*b*, 52*r*, 76*t*, 80*t*, 84, 85*t*, 85*c*, 86, 90*b*, 92–93, 109*t*, 110–111, 115*l*
Jewellery was made available for photography by Best of British page 109*t*; N. Bloom and Son page 13*b*, 92–93; Cameo Corner jacket, page 3, 19*b*, 76*t*, 80*t*, 84, 85, 86; Davies Antiques page 18; Editions Graphiques Gallery page 90*b*; Jasper and Jade page 27–28; Georg Jensen page 13*t*; M. McAleer page 84, 85; Nihon Token page 52*r*; S. J. Phillips page 75*br*; Mrs Powell-Wheatley page 84, 85; Turak Gallery page 110–111, 115*t*
The publishers have attempted to observe the legal requirements with respect to the rights of the suppliers of photographic materials. Nevertheless persons who have claims are invited to apply to the publishers

INDEX